Kenneth H. Waldron Ph.D. is a psychologist who spent almost 40 years working in family and marital therapy and family law, in situations where spouses were going through or had gone through a divorce, or unmarried parents who had gone through a separation. He has provided extensive marital counselling and developed counselling approaches addressing interpersonal conflict based on science. He has studied both marriage and divorce, has done original research on co-parenting relationship conflict and published extensively. He has also presented to other professionals around the United States and international audiences.

Allan R. Koritzinsky J.D. is a family law attorney, mediator and arbitrator, who has handled thousands of divorce cases over his 50-plus year career. He has also written, taught and spoken to professionals, law students and judicial groups across the country. He is a retired partner at Foley & Lardner LLP and was the former Chair of the law firm's Family Law Team. He focused his practice on divorce and family law. He has a law degree from the University of Wisconsin. He was named a Wisconsin Super Lawyer and listed in The Best Lawyers in America. He was a Lecturer/Instructor at the University of Wisconsin Law School. He co-authored of *Tax Strategies in Divorce*, *Divorce Practice Handbook,* and *Wisconsin Family Law Case Notes & Quotes*. While in Vietnam, he taught at the Saigon Law School. He was Fellow in the American Academy of Matrimonial Lawyers and a Diplomat in the American College of Family Trial Lawyers.

This book is dedicated to parents who have orchestrated an amicable divorce and co-parenting relationship, overcoming a myriad of obstacles to do so. The book is also dedicated to the sixty percent of divorcing parents who get caught in traps of conflict and who simply lack the information on skills needed to move from divorce conflict to a strongly desired amicable co-parenting relationship between separated parents.

The authors wrote this book for divorcing and divorced parents, although lawyers and mental health professionals may find useful information to help them reach their goals of providing practical guidance to separating parents. We chose to avoid cumbersome cites and research details. However, we dedicate this book to the many authors and researchers who undergird much of the information in this book.

We also dedicate this book to separated parents who would like to end their anguished co-parenting relationship and give their children a better family life.

Finally, the authors dedicate this book to our wives (Carol and Kathy), who had the patience to support the writing relationship between the authors that took so much time away from our extraordinary marriages.

Kenneth H. Waldron Ph.D. and Allan R. Koritzinsky J.D.

PLANNING A SENSIBLE DIVORCE

AVOID THE TOXIC DANCE OF A MESSY DIVORCE

AUSTIN MACAULEY PUBLISHERS™

LONDON • CAMBRIDGE • NEW YORK • SHARJAH

A CIP catalogue record for this title is available from the British Library.

ISBN 9781035815852 (Paperback)
ISBN 9781035815869 (ePub e-book)

www.austinmacauley.com

First Published 2024
Austin Macauley Publishers Ltd®
1 Canada Square
Canary Wharf
London
E14 5AA

Our book is based largely on research and fact. Most of the principles and skills in the book reflect the research of two generations of social scientists on factors that predict real outcomes, both for spouses and for children, who have gone through divorces. Though several researchers are mentioned in the book, there are too many who have contributed to our knowledge of marriage, divorce, and post-divorce families, to thank individually.

One psychologist deserves special mention, William F. Hodges. One of Bill Hodge's first research efforts was to study the effects of divorce on children's adjustment. General opinions at the time were that divorce had horrible short-term and long-term effects on children's adjustment, but he wanted more details that were evidence-based.

He studied the school children of divorced parents in his hometown of Boulder Colorado- home of the University of Colorado. To his surprise, he found very few children negatively affected by divorce. Parents are, on average, well-educated and reasonably affluent in Boulder. The divorce rate there was also relatively high, compared to the rest of the country.

He concluded that because divorce was relatively common and that there was no social shame for the children and most of the parents had amicable divorces and cooperated regarding co-parenting. He concluded that divorce itself had no negative effects on children per se. What had negative effects was the high level of conflict and lack of communication and cooperation between divorced parents in other locations. Since then, this conclusion has been heavily supported by his and the research of others.

We offer a special thanks to Bill Hodges and the first generation of researchers (about a dozen) who pioneered the effort to understand marriage and divorce and its impact on children.

Finally, most of the examples used in the book reflect real cases that your authors have had and the invaluable input of our colleagues. For both the numerous researchers and our friends and colleagues, we offer our most sincere thank you.

Table of Contents

Administrative Notes

This publication is designed to provide accurate and authoritative information about the subject matters covered. It is sold with the understanding that neither the authors nor the publisher is rendering legal, mental health, medical or other professional services, either directly or indirectly. If expert assistance, legal services or counseling is needed, the services of a competent professional should be sought. Neither the authors nor the publisher shall be liable or responsible for any loss or damage allegedly arising as a consequence of the use or application of any information or suggestions in the book.

Nothing in this book should be considered as the rendering of legal or therapeutic/mental health advice (despite the fact that one of the authors is a lawyer-author and the other is a psychologist-author) for a specific case. Nothing in this book should be relied upon as deemed to be any such advice. Readers are absolutely responsible for obtaining such advice from their own legal counsel and/or mental health provider. This book is intended for educational and informational purposes only.

No part of this book may be reproduced, transmitted, downloaded, scanned, decompiled, reverse engineered, or stored in or introduced into any information storage and retrieval system, or distributed in any printed or electronic form or by any means, whether electronic or mechanical, now known or hereinafter invented, EXCEPT by express written permission of the authors, which will be liberally provided upon written request. Failure to comply with these terms may expose you to legal action and damages for copyright infringement.

A Picture is Worth a Thousand Words!

YOU CHOOSE!

It is a choice.

Prologue

There is a Tibetan Tale About the Road to Nowhere, Which is Worth Remembering. A story in Tibetan Buddhism tells the tale of a wealthy man who wanted to do something for his fellow villagers. He had accumulated a great deal of wealth and was reaching the age when he knew he had much more than he needed. He wanted to give back to his village. After much thought, he decided that the way to increase the wealth of the entire village was for the village to be linked to a trading route. This required the building of a road to intersect with the great trading routes in Asia.

The rich man gathered workers from the village and began building the road, knowing that the completion of the road might take years. After a lengthy period of time working on the road, a traveling monk appeared. The wealthy man greeted him as a guest and offered him a meal, as was the custom. During the meal, the monk asked about the road. The wealthy man responded that he was grateful to his village for his success and was building a road to intersect with the trading routes of Asia, so that his village would become a part of that system. The monk nodded thoughtfully and appeared to escape into his own thoughts for a while.

The monk slowly looked up and announced that he had considered keeping his silence, but then thought that would be unkind and decided to tell the wealthy man of a problem. He described his having travelled extensively, knew the area well, but, unfortunately, advised him that the road that the wealthy man was building was going nowhere and would never intersect with the famous trade routes.

Once the rich man confirmed this news, he was devastated. The monk looked sadly at the man, but shared that it is better to know this now, than to continue on a pointless task. The monk then expressed his gratitude for the meal and continued on his travels.

A year later, that same monk came upon the same wealthy man who, with his crew, had continued to build the 'road to nowhere'. The monk was astonished, and when sitting with the man at the customary meal, he raised the question: Knowing the road was going nowhere, why had the man continued to build and spend part of his life and fortune on a useless cause? The wealthy man sighed and responded,

"I understand that my road is going nowhere,
but I had put so much into it, I could not just walk away."

The monk, recognizing the foibles of human nature, nodded…

Marriage and Divorce Share Many Common Principles. This tale reminds us that people are not always rational and will do the same things over and over, knowing full well that the effort is useless. This can be especially true in marriage. Spouses start and continue the same arguments, over and over, knowing full well they will end in frustration, hurt and with a failure to resolve anything.

Contrary to what some people believe, successful marriages have just as many gut-wrenching disagreements as troubled marriages.

Arguments in marriage occur for the same reasons, whether the marriage is a successful one or one headed for divorce. Differences between spouses and disagreements are inevitable. Unresolved disagreements grow into disputes, which in turn became conflicts, which, again in turn, can become intractable conflict. By the time the marriage is dominated by intractable conflict, spouses have exaggeratedly negative opinions about one another. It is good to remember that it all began as disagreements that did not get resolved.

To some extent, this is a new problem in society. Historically, marriage had a final decision-maker, usually the husband. The husband had a role (provider), and the wife had a role (housewife). Divorces at that time were based on one or both spouses failing to fulfil their roles. With the century-long emancipation of women, and in family life the emancipation of men, marriages became egalitarian. Both spouses acquired equal power in disagreements. This new, and promising, type of marriage made it necessary for spouses to learn disagreement resolution skills.[1] The marital failure of many couples is not because they are bad people; it is because they did not have the disagreement resolution skills needed. We recognize that the marital frustrations might well have led to mistreating one another, but the core problem was difficulty mastering an egalitarian marriage.

The differences between a successful marriage and a marriage heading for divorce are simple ones.

First, in a successful marriage, arguments do not last as long. Much of the marriage goes well, and these problematic moments are limited in time. They do not last as long because spouses have skills for resolving differences and disagreements. In unsuccessful marriages, one or both spouses are weak in those skills. **Second**, there are safety nets available in a successful marriage. The

---

[1] Throughout our book, we use a descriptive phrase, "**disagreement** resolution skills" instead of the popular "**dispute**" resolution skills. A dispute arises when a disagreement is not resolved and implies that one of the spouses should prevail.

arguments in a successful marriage generally do not get as down-and-dirty. There is no crippling name-calling and scary emotional escalation. **Finally**, spouses in successful marriages have ways of recovering quickly and repairing the relationship. The frustrations and hurt do not linger and grow into bitter resentment and contempt for one another.

However, in some marriages, the difficulties do grow, occupying increasing time and emotional space in the relationship, leading to mutual contempt and deeply felt frustration, until one of the spouses gives up and makes the decision to divorce. Often, this decision is made subconsciously, even before the spouse making it, is aware of it. At that point, the apathetic spouse becomes vulnerable to the temptations of emotional and sometimes physical affairs, or, in some cases, complete lifestyle changes.

Or, the decision is conscious, but private and not brought up with the other spouse, at least not yet. Even though the spouse might be aware that a decision has been made, spouses have a hard time giving up. They maintain hope. Interview research indicates that one of the spouses has made the decision to divorce, on average, about two years before an actual separation. That might seem like the Tibetan man building a road to nowhere, but spouses often take their commitments to a marriage very seriously and hope for a turn-around.

> **For spouses considering a divorce,**
> **but who still would like to make their marriage work, see our book,**
> *"The Road to Marital Successful is Unpaved:*
> *Seven Skills for Making Marriage Work".*
> http://www.marriageanddivorce.org

In brief, the difference between a successful marriage and a marriage that ends in divorce is not that the spouses have differences about which they argue. It is in how clean they keep the arguments, recover from the arguments and focus on solving the problems, rather than blame each other as the cause of those problems.

Having a Messy Divorce is Easy. It is not difficult to have a messy (even a toxic) divorce. Typically, people who go into the divorce process have already reached the point of a messy marriage. They continue the same messy arguments, which come to them out of habit.

Remember our Tibetan tale of the wealthy man!

Going Down the Divorce Road to Nowhere, is Also Easy. It is human nature to continue the same behaviors in a divorce that led to the divorce in the first place. This happens despite knowing full well that …

"… My arguments were going nowhere, but I had put so much into them,
I could not just walk away from them…"
Sadly, the legal system can make matters worse!

The legal system inadvertently tends to foster a messy divorce,
rather than a more amicable or 'sensible' one.

Your authors have also written two books on how the current legal system inadvertently makes things worse and how this happens.[2] Of course, this is unintentional by professionals in the family law system, but unfortunately, the legal system itself is set up in such a way as to foster conflict between spouses.

---

[2] Waldron, K.H. & Koritzinsky, A.R. **"Game Theory and the Transformation of Family Law:** Change the Rules- Change the Game. A New Bargaining Model for Attorneys and Mediators to Optimize Outcomes for Divorcing Parties." Unhooked Books. Scottsdale, AZ (2015) and **"Winning Strategies in Divorce:** The Art and Science of Using Game Theory Principles and Skills in Negotiation and Mediation" (2017). http://www.unhookedmedia.com/.

The State's interest is in the distribution of property, money and child custody, which sets up a head-to-head competition between spouses.

This book offers solutions to these challenges.

Divorce Can be a Solution. It is possible to have a divorce be a solution to a problematic marriage, in spite of all of the pressures to do otherwise. A messy divorce does not provide that solution. In a messy divorce, it seems that the divorcing spouses lose the positive parts of the marriage, but retain the negative parts, sometimes for the rest of their lives. This makes matters only worse.

**This book is organized to describe how to have divorce
be a real solution for the end of most marriages.**

It is important to understand that divorced parents will still have disagreements, based on differences. These will be simpler because they do not include the stress of being housemates, financial partners and intimate. In this book, we include **Disagreement** Resolution Skills so that co-parenting does not become a source of permanent antagonism and conflict.[3]

Book Overview: In order to accomplish our mission, we will treat our subject as a *'Divorce in Four Parts'*:

1. **Part I—ACHIEVING SENSIBLE PRACTICES**. We explore the mindset of divorcing spouses, with an emphasis on a particular perspective on mindfulness as it relates to divorcing spouses. We will present some basic ideas and themes that will be helpful in understanding the focus of a sensible approach to divorce.
2. **Part II—UNDERSTANDING THE HEADWINDS AND CHALLENGES OBSTRUCTING A SENSIBLE DIVORCE.** We take a brief look at a particular perspective on marriage, in order to understand the predisposition to have a messy divorce. The roots of a messy divorce are found in the very challenges of the marriage. Control problems and dysfunctional beliefs lead to a messy divorce.
3. **Part III—MOVING FORWARD WITH A PLAN FOR A SENSIBLE DIVORCE.** We present how a sensible plan can be the antidote to a messy divorce. We focus on the approaches that work best

---

[3] See Footnote 1.

when both spouses are working as a team. We also discuss approaches that just one person can take when the other spouse is uncooperative. We introduce the skills needed for a functional co-parenting relationship and the tasks to be accomplished as separated parents.

4. **Part IV—DEVELOPING A SENSIBLE (AND EFFECTIVE) APPROACH TO THE LEGAL AND PLANNING TASKS OF A DIVORCE.** We focus on those readers with a contemplated or pending divorce (who have not yet completed their legal tasks) or on readers who are already divorced (who are having disagreements about existing court orders). Divorce includes a required legal step. The legal tasks of property and income distribution and the task of establishing child custody must be addressed. However, our approach strongly recommends not getting side-tracked with the legal tasks of the divorce and to treat them as steps in a sensible plan to reach long-term goals.

Who Should Read this Book? The answer is simple: anyone connected to divorce who wants to learn another way of looking at the issue of marriage and divorce and finding a better solution.

Mistakes might have been made, but they do not necessarily need to taint the divorce.

1. Affairs while still married. Most people who have had an affair before divorcing will later understand what a terrible mistake it was. About 25% of all divorces have an affair involved. Affairs appear to be a relatively common human mistake. We are speaking about otherwise good, empathic, even moral, people who find themselves 'falling in love' or are at least infatuated with another person while still married.

2. Meanness and even cruelty which accompany the arguments had before a divorce. Spouses heading for divorce often treat one another with increasing disdain, and at times, real cruelty. In a sense, once having given up on the marriage, there might seem little to lose in venting and making cruel statements to one another. However, the hurt inflicted on the other spouse, and the need for relief from the suffering, will likely linger into the divorce. Without children involved, this leaves a painful bitter taste in the mouth that can last a lifetime and contaminate future

relationships. If children are involved, this can lead to exposure to a lifetime of damaging parental conflict- something to be avoided.

3. Domestic violence. This is a major problem world over, but research tells us that the most common form of domestic violence is called 'separation engendered violence', which accounts for about 30% of all domestic violence. These are one or two incidents that occur at the time of a separation. They are serious and much damage can be done, so they cannot be taken lightly. However, they usually reflect non-violent people getting overwhelmed with emotion at the time of a separation and can be repaired.

Communication works!

In all three examples (whether an affair, cruel talk or domestic violence), the idea of communicating with the other spouse might seem to be abhorrent. Yet, research tells us that the sooner after a separation spouses communicate directly with one another, the more likely they are to end up with good communication and cooperation in the divorce, as well as later in life. Overcoming mistakes made can be the first step in a good plan for the divorce. The skills needed will be presented in Part III.

The key is to make rules about being honest, kind and respectful with one another (even if you don't feel like it).

How the Divorce Starts is a Good Predictor of How it Will End.[4] Few people understand the long-term implications of how they initiate a separation, and what they say when they discuss the divorce, especially the role of anger, blame and sadness in the process. When children are involved, impulsive statements or negative behavior can inflict a great deal of harm on one another and on children that can be difficult to overcome. In fits of emotion, parents can forget that they will be having a relationship with the other parent for the rest of

---

[4] One of your authors provided this advice to hundreds of clients over the span of his legal career.

their lives. To repeat a familiar refrain: '*What is temporary tends to become permanent* '!

**Once spouses enter the legal system,
they find themselves 'trapped' into focusing on
short-term legal outcomes,
as they compete for what seem to be limited resources.**

Money is important to people, but if the spouses have children, the emotions involved go to the very core of their beings. It becomes easy to see the other spouse as the enemy, not only threatening to take property and money but also limiting involvement in the children's lives. While going through this process, these people do not understand that they are increasing the odds that theirs will be a messy divorce, if it starts this way.

Magical Thinking does not Change the Final Outcome or the End of the Suffering. The long-term implications of a messy divorce can remain hidden behind the curtain on the day of the final judgment of divorce. The magical thinking is that, somehow, the pronouncement of the divorce by a judge, and the completion of all of the child-related and financial tasks associated with having a legal outcome, will be the end of the suffering. It does not. Saying '*It's over*' does not mean that it is really over. With minor children, it is just the beginning.

The next magical thought is that once the children are adults, the suffering associated with the children ends. It does not. Sadly, parents will sit by and watch the damage of their messy divorce play out in the children's adult lives, while the parents continue their destructive entanglements with one another. There are weddings and other special events to attend, grandchildren in common and holidays that can become an additional source of suffering in a messy divorce. To indulge in a messy divorce is extremely short-sighted.

One important message in this book is a simple one: LET IT GO!

Our book repeats this message for anyone considering a divorce, anyone going through a divorce, anyone who has recently gone through a divorce (that has been at least somewhat messy) and anyone who has been in a messy divorce for any length of time.

Like our wealthy road builder,
the longer one has engaged in an activity,
like a messy divorce, the more difficult it is to… let it go.

Letting go is possible at any stage. It takes two steps: first, focus on the future, about which you have control; second, stop focusing on the past, about which you have no control; second, stop doing what you have been doing and do something different. The "something different is laid out in detail in this book. It is more successful when both spouses let go of their messy divorce and practice the principles of a sensible divorce. However, even one spouse can make a dramatic difference.

A messy divorce is a dance of two co-conspirators,
and when one stops doing the dance,
the dynamic changes for both.
The best way to start a divorce
is to remember that divorce is a common life transition.

Divorce is not rare. The rate of divorce fluctuates from country to country and from time to time, but social anthropologists tell us that the average is about 30%. That suggests that on average about one-third of all marriages, whatever form that they take in a particular culture, end in divorce.

All people have major life transitions. Some are inevitable because of aging, starting school, starting a work life, dating or retiring. Some are by choice and wanted, such as getting married, having children and going to college. Some are unwanted, such as a death in the family, losing a job, getting a debilitating illness or, for some spouses, getting a divorce. Unwanted life transitions can be gut-wrenching experiences with out-of-control emotions and magical thinking (e.g., wishing to go back in time and do things differently).

There is no magic.

There is a lot of material in this book. What is absent is a magic pill for making a problematic co-parenting relationship an amicable one. Ken remembers his twins' four-year-old birthday. There was to be a party with guests, and Ken made the birthday cake. When the first bite of cake was taken, it was horrible, and literally inedible. Ken had accidentally left out a key ingredient. All of the key ingredients in this book are important. Improving a co-parenting relationship takes effort, requiring all of the right ingredients.

Trust us:
It will be well worth doing it for yourselves and for your children.

Making successful life transitions, whether wanted or not, means:

1. Getting control of Problematic Emotions and Challenging Feelings.
2. Rethinking long-term life financial and family goals, when there are children.
3. Making a Plan to reach these new goals.

This is our definition of a 'Sensible Divorce'. This is what this book is all about. With these thoughts in mind, it is time to get started.

Caution: This book is not for everyone.

Some marriages end because of a history of abusive domestic violence, criminal behavior, drug and alcohol problems, a hedonistic uncaring partner and other situations that pose real dangers.

Healing and recovering from unsafe marriages take priority over striving for an amicable post-divorce relationship with the ex-spouse.

Safety also takes priority over being sensible with a dangerous ex-spouse.

Part I
Achieving Sensible Practices

"My greatest challenge has been to change the mindset of people.
Mindsets play strange tricks on us.
We see things the way our minds have instructed our eyes to see."
(Muhammad Yunus[5])

Introduction: Throughout this book we will be focusing on various techniques and approaches that a spouse, or ideally two spouses, can take to prepare themselves for their divorce life. However, perhaps more importantly, we will be addressing the mindset that leads to healing from the wounds of a divorce and sets the stage for having a sensible divorce. Part I focuses on the necessary mindset, while the remaining chapters focus on approaches and techniques. Let's get started.

---

[5] Muhammad Yunus is a Bangladeshi social entrepreneur, banker, economist, and civil society leader, who was awarded the Nobel Peace Prize for founding the Grameen Bank and pioneering the concepts of microcredit and microfinance in 2006.

Chapter 1
Mindfulness-Its Applicability and Definition[6]

Many books, articles, classes and workshops address and define mindfulness. It is important to remember, however, that mindfulness, a clear focus on the here and now, is not the goal. Mindfulness is a means of reaching a goal: to diminish suffering by, in part, not being controlled by feelings.

Research projects into various aspects of mindfulness are on the rise, such as those occurring under the direction of Dr Richard Davidson at the University of Wisconsin. There is little doubt that mindful practices can affect various parts of our lives, and even our brains, in very positive ways. Definitions of mindfulness vary, at least slightly, depending on the point of view of the practitioner or author. However, most definitions/descriptions have much in common and are directly relevant to having a sensible divorce.

1. **Mindfulness is a form of awareness, both of ourselves and of our surroundings.** Some perspectives emphasize an awareness of the here and now. In this perspective, mindfulness recognizes that the past is gone. There is nothing we can do about it. The future is uncertain and unpredictable, and is therefore a waste of time to focus on it. Thus, the task is to focus on the here and now and to increase our awareness of it. Other perspectives include an awareness of the bigger picture, not only being aware of our place in time and in the world (meaning the here and now), but also being aware of the larger picture of how our place fits

---

[6] Mindfulness undergirds many of the principles discussed in Part I and has relevance to the Sensible Divorce.

into the whole world and how our time fits into the past, present and future.

The first step in becoming mindful, is to understand where feelings come from, because a messy divorce is dominated by problematic feelings. Feelings were, at an early point in evolution, a shortcut system for survival. At the most basic level, we had approach-feelings for things that helped us survive, and we had avoid-feelings for things that threatened us. We approached fire because warmth in a cold setting was useful, but avoided getting too close so that we did not burn up. As we progressed as a species, feelings became more complex, but still had the purpose of survival. Anger and blame were useful, even though they were not accurate. When Bubba's tribe attacked our tribe because they thought that we were hoarding the food in the area, guilt and sadness were not functional feelings. Anger and blame made more sense if we wanted to survive, even if Bubba was right.

Modern evolutionary psychologists call these obsolete urges, because they really are counter-productive in modern society. In other words, the anger and blame in a marriage gone wrong and heading divorce are counter-productive. They lead to things that are bad for the person.

Mindfulness focuses not on anger and blame, but on the sadness of an unwanted ending, the guilt for playing a part in bringing about the sad ending and a fear of what will come next in life.

It is helpful to put divorce in perspective. The hurt, frustration and sadness of a marriage ending are similar for most people. Many people go through it. You are not the first, and you are not alone. When people suffer, it is natural to become self-absorbed, thinking only about yourself. However, the bigger picture is that everyone suffers from relationships ending, whether it is a first date gone sour or a 50-year marriage where a spouse dies. Many people suffer a messy end to a marriage, and while it is not natural to think about this, it can also be comforting to know that people all share many of the problems of being alive and human, including the ending of relationships.

In relationships, mindfulness is an awareness of people who are important to us and to whom we are important. It is the awareness that we are alive, but at the same time, an awareness that we will die. It is the awareness that there are not only great pleasures in life but also inevitable suffering. It is the awareness that our actions have effects (sometimes profound effects), and that we are responsible for our actions and the effects of our actions. It is an awareness that our actions can not only cause suffering for ourselves but also cause suffering for others. In a messy divorce, when there are minor children, the behavior of the parents can cause suffering for the children. Mindful awareness is a joy and a calming of our hearts and minds, which can not only offer mental peace and contentment, but also can be emotionally disturbing and bring great responsibility.

2. **Mindfulness can shape and change who we are.** When a person practices mindfulness, the structure of his or her personality changes. Attitudes and beliefs change. Science tells us that even the very structure and functioning of our brains change. Imagine for a moment a thin, slight person, timid and lacking in confidence, even sometimes too weak to open the lid of a jar. That person decides to become a body builder through lifting weights, and over time, become stronger. The shape of his or her body changes (for the better), and the structure and chemical processes in the brain change. How he or she interacts with the world changes, and with that, the way that the world interacts with that person, also changes. He or she might become more confident with people, and because of that, his or her career improves. The people that he or she meets, and with whom he or she has friendships and even romantic relationships, change. Through the practice of body building, everything changes about his or her life.

Developing a practice of mindfulness is similar. Mindfulness takes practice, just as does weight training. Who could sit down at a piano having never played and rip off a Beethoven Sonata? However, by the time a piano student can play Beethoven, he or she has developed finger memory, a change in the brain, a non-visual memory of the piano keys, and an ability to translate the language of the music score to touching the keys. Emotional patterns change to fit to the music. Mindfulness is like this; it is the practice of reflecting on our lives and focusing awareness on oneself and one's surroundings. It does not, however, come in one day. This is identical to learning where the keys are on a typewriter.

This type of reflection requires that we take time in our lives and practice, just as our body builder has to work out at the gym or our piano player has to practice playing. Many people find meditation an effective path to mindfulness, but not everyone. Some people might find a daily practice of reflecting over a cup of coffee works better, while other people might believe that thinking during long walks or engaging in other forms of exercise, works best. Some people find keeping a journal is helpful. However, practicing reflection is essential to reaching mindful awareness. In a YouTube video on '*Letting Go*', one woman reported that every day she looked in a mirror and forgave herself, but it took a long time before she actually felt forgiven. That is how people are; we need to practice to get good at something.

3. **Mindfulness shifts our focus from blaming others to taking responsibility for ourselves.** This requires unvarnished honesty with ourselves and others. By being honest in our relationships, we are free from giving the truth self-servicing spin or even lying to defend ourselves. By mindfully focusing on others, we no longer have to take their words, thoughts and actions personally. With a mindful focus, we can react to what is really going on around us, which tends to be simple, not our imaginings when we guess what is going on, which tends to be dramatic, complicated and often threatening and hurtful.

4. **Almost all perspectives on the practice of mindfulness inform us that the practice leads to empathic concern for and a kind disposition towards others, even our enemies.** One of the goals of this book is for the reader to develop an empathic and kind disposition toward his or her ex-spouse. An angry, blaming and uncooperative ex-spouse is suffering. Kindness is the antidote to suffering. This takes practice and a new mindset, which we will discuss throughout this book.

When divorced spouses dislike or fear being in the presence of one another, never conversing about their children or enjoy being together at a child event, what beliefs are at the root?

Ken has often opened a divorce mediation when spouses or ex-spouses walk in looking terrified being in the same room together, by asking them how they met, or by asking them to tell him about what their children are like, and so forth. When he does this, he sees the tension melt away. That presents an interesting question: What were they afraid of?

5. **Mindfulness leads to dispelling false beliefs.** People sometimes believe that by treating another person a certain way, they can expect the other person to reciprocate and do the same with them. If we do a favor for another person, we might believe that if needed, he or she will do a favor for us. However, in reality, these are two separate decisions. How we will treat others is one decision that <u>we</u> make, but how they will treat us is another decision which <u>they</u> make. Some people will reciprocate, but others will not. Our responsibility ends in our decision. How we treat others is independent of how they treat us.

**Practicing mindfulness in relation to a divorce
leads to an empathic concern for and kind disposition
towards the ex-spouse, whether or not it is reciprocated.**

While being kind with an ex-spouse might change the way the ex-spouse behaves, it might not. Mindful practice is not a way to control others, although it often does influence others.

**Mindfulness is a way to control ourselves.
It is also the doorway out of suffering from a divorce.**

Chapter 2
Avoiding Four Problematic Emotions
Blaming, Distrusting, Taking Things
Personally and Thinking Inferentially[7]

Humans have developed helpful skills to survive, but these very same skills also have downsides. We will now look at the four problematic emotions (i.e., blaming, distrusting, taking things personally and thinking inferentially) that foster conflict in a divorce. We will also propose what we hope are helpful exercises for overcoming those emotions. These four problematic emotions (i.e., 'poisons') are emotionally compelling when a divorce begins. However, in many divorces, these poisons have already infected spouses, and the temptation to continue with them can be strong (whether voluntarily or involuntarily).

---

[7] In this Chapter, we address 'Problematic Emotions'. In Chapter 11, we present a comparable issue but designate them 'Challenging Feelings'. The distinction is important, which you will understand when you read our book.

**Bottom line: These emotions damage BOTH spouses
and interfere with recovering from a divorce.**

"IT'S ALL YOUR FAULT!"

Blaming others is a human trait that clearly had evolutionary value. Looking for a cause of our suffering was, at one point in human history, a matter of life and death. In modern times, this instinct can be superfluous and sometimes absurd. When we bump our toe on a table, we blame the table or whomever we believe put the table in our way. When we have ill fortune, we look for someone to blame. When we have an incident on the highway, we often first blame the other driver. In modern times, we see the horrendous destruction caused by this once very useful trait. We see the poor of one country blaming the better off of another country for the poverty they experience. The struggling middle class often blames the wealthy for that struggle and votes for candidates for office who promise to take that money away from the rich and give it back to the middle class. We see criminals blaming their parents or the neighborhood in which they grew up.

In marriages, when a person is hurt, frustrated, sad or even guilty or ashamed, they are tempted to blame their spouse, regardless of how silly it can be (E.g., "*It's your fault that I had that affair*"). This first reaction, blaming, serves an important purpose. Anger and blame focus our attention, rouse our defences and prepare us to act aggressively towards what we initially experience as a threat. At distant times in the past, this likely helped humans survive.

**While blame can be helpful in eliminating a threat,
blame does not solve problems.**

For marital partners to solve a problem, they must step back from blame, reflect objectively on their mutual contributions to the problem and develop a Plan to behave differently in the future. Blame leads to trying to control others, often a futile effort, instead of controlling oneself. It is natural to blame at the time when a spouse wants a divorce, but to continue to blame, rather than plan for a major life transition, is foolish and counterproductive.

Mindfulness is the antidote to blame and leads to solutions.

Sensible Exercise: Put blame to work for you in your relationship with your spouse. If you have had a bad experience with him or her, spend a few moments in your mind blaming your spouse. Really think through everything about him or her that caused you to have a bad experience. Make the whole experience his or her fault. When you think that you have been very thorough about this, then blame yourself. Think of everything you did or did not do that caused the bad experience. Imagine that the experience was completely your fault and that you manipulated the spouse into doing what he or she did. At the completion of this Sensible Exercise, reflect on the whole picture and dedicate yourself to focus on changing your behavior, not that of your spouse.

This might sound easy to do, but it is emotionally unsettling and challenging. For example, imagine your spouse had an affair that likely started long before you were aware of it. It might be easy to blame your spouse, and you would not be wrong. However, if honestly reflecting, it is also possible to blame yourself. Perhaps you took your spouse for granted or were not supportive of aspects of his or her life that were important. Perhaps you have been depressed and much less affectionate or upbeat than he or she needed. This is not a process of making excuses for the spouse, but is a process of being mindful and honest. Human affairs are complex, and often we all play a role in things that go badly.

Blame is the antithesis of identifying a problem and solving it, but blaming everyone involved, including yourself, can be a useful approach and exercise to seeing a problem more clearly.

"I CAN'T TRUST YOU ANYMORE!"

2. **Distrusting: In relationships, we need information to be verified.** People are by nature sceptical, which also had an important evolutionary meaning to survival in a more dangerous period in human history. Even if we tend to trust people, quick to give the benefit of the doubt, we still have doubt and quickly become leery if what a person says or does raises questions about their honesty. We are sensitive to dishonesty and dislike it for many reasons. We want verification that what a person is telling us is the truth. We get verification in one of two ways: (a) by corroborating his or her information with independent facts or (b) by reputation. If a person says it is raining, and we can see rain, we

believe them. We have a corroborating fact. However, in relationships, especially marriages, spouses tell each other much that has no corroborating facts available. If a spouse tells the other spouse that he or she is hurt or sad, there are no 'facts' that can corroborate the statement. We either believe or do not believe him or her based on reputation.

Reputation is a belief that the other person is likely speaking the truth, because by experience, the other person always or almost always speaks the truth. Developing this reputation requires the practice of rigorous honesty. Another way to think of this is to develop a reputation as honest by always being a reliable reporter of fact. To be rigorously honest, we must be aware of what is real, not what we wish was real or what we believe that it should be. We can then speak to what is real, regardless of how it makes us look or affects getting something that we want.

We do not twist reality to accomplish a goal.

A difficult but common form of dishonesty is 'spin'. Spin is the practice of not really lying but not really telling the truth either. It is giving a story a slant to bolster one's position-usually protesting innocence and blaming the other person. For example, Sarah asks Greg why he was mean when he asked a sarcastic question of her in front of dinner guests. Greg spins the conversation by saying he was just asking a question. Further, he says that Sarah takes things personally that are not meant personally. This is not quite a lie because he did ask a question, and Sarah did take it personally. However, it is not honest either. Both Sarah and Greg know that he (Greg) is not being honest, giving the situation 'spin', to make himself seem innocent, but he is developing a reputation that he is not to be trusted. This is not the recipe for a successful marriage or a successful divorce.

A mindful focus on reality leads to a reputation of honesty.

In our example, Greg could focus on his comment as it really was. He might say, "*I did not intend it to sound so sarcastic, but I can see that it did. I am sorry*". Or he might say, "*I found what you said frustrating, and I can see that I handled that poorly. I am sorry*". Or he might even say, "*I was sarcastic, but I do not know why. Maybe we should talk about it"*. Regardless of the direction the discussion takes, Greg is being mindful and building trust through honesty.

Sensible Exercise: Sit in a comfortable position and reflect on the people involved in your life. Focus particularly on to what extent they can be trusted to be honest. Think about who has to be taken with a grain of salt, because they give stories a 'spin' or out-and-out lie. Who makes excuses for themselves and who simply tells the truth? Who tells you they did not call because they got busy with a situation, and who tells you that they are sorry that they forgot to call?

Reflect on how refreshing it is to know that the person speaking to you is honest. Reflect on your thoughts and feelings when you suspect or know that the person speaking to you is giving a spin or lying. Reflect on the question: *"What is wrong with telling a lie if you can get away with it?"* When you can answer that question, you will understand the damage done by dishonesty. People make excuses for telling *'little white lies',* that somehow it is kinder than being honest. The practice of telling little white lies leads to a reputation of being dishonest. In what way is that kind? There are kind ways to be honest.

Now reflect on yourself and your level of honesty with others, especially with your ex-spouse. Do you lie? Do you give things a spin? Do you turn things around and blame your ex-spouse rather than be honest about yourself? Do you tell little white lies? Do you deny things that are true? Picture how life will improve as you develop a reputation as being honest?

A good way to practice is to correct yourself every time you are less than honest. Following a lie or 'spin' with, *"That is not really true. What is really true is…"* breaks the habit of lying or giving 'spin'.

"The advantage of being honest
is that you do not have to remember all of the lies you told people."
Mark Twain

"BOY, IS THAT THE POT CALLING THE KETTLE BLACK? YOU ARE THE ONE WHO IS REALLY LIKE THAT!"

Taking criticism personally is a major mistake. When we are being mindful, we are focusing on reality and not on defending ourselves against unrealistic threats. When a person criticizes us, we can examine what they are saying and might even decide that it is useful feedback.

"You act like I don't exist. You are so selfish.
Do you see the way the kids stare at us when you do that?"

You think about this and realize that it has useful information.

"You are not right about me being selfish. You are right that I ignored
You at the soccer match. I was afraid that the kids would see us make faces
at each other or make sarcastic remarks.
You have a good point that ignoring each other must look weird to the kids.
Can we plan our social behavior and actions to be what we would like
our children to learn, when we are both with the kids?"

We might also reflect and decide that the perception of us is incorrect. It might have nothing to do with you.

"You are a slut.
Does your new boyfriend know what a bitch you are?"

In either case, don't not take it personally.
Take it as a statement about who the other person is, not you.

This could lead to a good discussion, if it contains useful information. Sometimes, what starts out as a criticism becomes a way to identify a problem that should be solved. If there is no useful information, the criticism can be ignored.

When we are mindful,
we do not take the comments or behavior of others personally.

In a divorce, this is particularly important because most spouses who divorce have a history of taking what each other says and does personally and experiencing emotional pain, anger and blame. Refer back to our road builder.

**The habitual pattern of taking each other personally
is difficult to let go and takes mindful practice,
and yet is essential to accomplishing a sensible divorce.**

If an ex-spouse tells us that we are irresponsible because we came ten minutes late to our son's soccer game, the message is that he or she measures responsibility in part as being on time, which is something that you might or might not do. You are also hearing that he or she jumps to negative conclusions about you before hearing all the facts. If he or she did not do this, you would have been asked why you were late. The comment might also raise the question whether your son is negatively affected when you are late for his soccer games. In other words, the comment might include some useful information. You might later ask your son if being late was an issue for him.

However, you do not have an obligation to take care of your ex-spouse's feelings, and so if you do not take the comment personally, you do not have to defend yourself or get side-tracked from watching the soccer game. If your ex-spouse reacts negatively to your silence and asks, *"Well, do you have anything to say,"* you can be kind and respond and say, *"I measure responsibility by whether or not I come to the game, not whether or not I am on time."* Or you might say, *"You are jumping to a conclusion that I had control over being here on time."* Or you might say, *"I will be sure to ask our son if my being late was a problem for him."*

**The focus is not on defending yourself
and taking things personally.
It is on hearing what might be useful information.**

Sensible Exercise: Breaking the habit of taking things personally can be very challenging and takes much practice. Think of the five or ten comments or behaviors of your ex-spouse that frequently occur and upset you. Reflect on why you take those personally. What self-talk do you do after the comments or behavior that leads to feeling bad? Do you tell yourself that he or she is trying to control you? Do you tell yourself that he or she does not respect you? Think about what those feelings mean about your ex-spouse, not you, but not in a critical way. This is not an excuse to blame. For example:

E.g., "He rolls his eyes when I tell him something important about the children." What does this mean to you?

E.g., "He thinks that I am too picky and that I am trying to micromanage his parenting."

E.g., "He thinks I am just nuts and boring and is tired of listening to me."

These are the kinds of thoughts people have when they take criticisms personally. These types of thoughts lead to becoming upset, angry and wanting to avoid contact. What does rolling the eyes really tell you about him, not you?

Reflect on how you might respond differently if you did not take it personally. You might simply have no response, but you might also discover a response that might be helpful, either to you or to your ex-spouse. For example:

"You roll your eyes, and I want to understand what that means.
I want us to work as a team,
and I think that both of us should have important input
into how we do that."

Always remember that comments and behavior of other people
might include useful information, but more importantly,
tells you something about the other person, not you.

The next time you take something personally and have an angry or defensive reaction, stop and think about what you would do if you did not take it personally.

"I KNOW WHAT YOU ARE REALLY THINKING!"

Thinking inferentially can be helpful, but also dangerous, if not careful. Our minds are fed bits and pieces of reality all the time, but this almost always falls shy of a complete and coherent picture of what is really going on. Yet, we are driven to having a coherent understanding in order to know what to do. This is where inferential thinking comes to our rescue.

There are three types of **inferential thinking**:

a. The first type of inferential thinking fills in the gaps, and we are pretty sure that we are right. This is very similar to what our brains do with vision. We might look out a window that is divided into panes and outside of which is a screen, both of which break up what we see into bits and pieces. However, our minds automatically fill in all the gaps so that what we see is coherent. We see a whole tree, when in fact we see several different parts of a tree, crisscrossed with the wire mesh of the screen. Inferential thinking is essentially guesswork. We get some information from our environment, and we build a coherent understanding by guessing at the missing parts.

Fortunately, most of the time we have enough information and enough experience to guess correctly. When we see bits and pieces of a tree, we can safely guess what the other parts look like and that it is one tree, not several. When we make inferences about people, we can often be confident that our guesses are correct, but also sometimes be surprised to find out that our inference was not true. In other words, even when we are confident in our inference, it is after all a guess, and we need to be open to guessing wrongly.

b. <u>The second type of inferential thinking is cured with critical thinking, instead of guessing, when we make an inference that is likely to be wrong</u>. I might see a dark sedan pass by three times and have the impulsive inference that I am being watched by the FBI. I am likely to realize quickly that I have no way of knowing if the three sedans were the same car and that the odds of my being watched by the FBI are near zero. I dismiss the inference out of hand. The ability to dismiss unlikely inferences is called critical thinking.

In brief, the first two types of inferences are: (1) those so likely that we can proceed-believing them, and (2) those so unlikely that we can proceed-dismissing them out of hand.

c. <u>The third type of inferential thinking is when we have enough information to make a good guess, but not enough to be sure</u>. Our guess might either be true or not true, but we do not have enough information to know. I walk into my house, and my wife looks at me with a funny face. I might infer that she is upset with me about something, but I have no way to know this for sure. Thus, I do not know how to respond. One response is to believe the inference, even though it is based on incomplete information. So, I yell at her, "*Why are you always mad at me. It makes me not want to come home*". Before long, we are having an argument. The sensible response is to realize that I need more information. In that case, I ask a question, *"Are you upset about something?"* She might be angry with me, but she might be upset about something else or just have an upset stomach. The focus is on my wife's funny face, not the inference, and realizing that, I need more information in order to understand what is going on and how to respond: ask questions.

This is critical to a Sensible Divorce. A messy divorce is filled with negative inferences—bad guesses. Ex-spouses, who might have less than a few hours of direct contact in a year, often think that they really know what is going on in the other house, what the other ex-spouse really thinks and feels and what his or her motives really are! Ex-spouses in a messy divorce almost always fail to exercise critical thinking, dismissing unlikely inferences, or reality testing, meaning, checking out an inference that might or might not be true.

The danger referred to above is relying too heavily on inferential thinking, because if not careful, we can develop beliefs based on unsupported guesses.

This becomes a problem because of another human characteristic: we see what we expect to see. We have a natural tendency to screen in information that supports existing beliefs and to screen out information that is inconsistent with our beliefs.

We see what we expect to see: A Hospital Story.

Let us tell you an illustrative story. Early in Ken's career, behaviorism was relatively new, and it opened our eyes to how interactive we are with our environment, as opposed to the dominant Freudian view of humans at the time. Measures of human behavior, and the responses they provoked, were developed to analyze the stimulus-response-reinforcement cycle.

Ken was asked to do an assessment at an inpatient psychiatric hospital for children. He met with the staff who spoke with great emotion about an awful child on the ward- that everything the child did was destructive and drove others away from him. The staff was unable to say a single positive thing about the boy.

He sounded like the devil's seed. Ken went to the ward with his forms, sat in a corner at a table appearing to be totally occupied with his paperwork and was soon ignored by the children on the ward, including the child he was observing. Ken's forms were for recording what happened just before the child acted, what the act was, and what happened just after the child acted: the stimulus-response-reinforcement cycle for the child. After several days of this, Ken reported back to the staff.

To their shock, Ken reported that 92% of the child's behavior was an appropriate response to what was going on, and was either neutral or positive behavior. He also reported that there were very few reinforcements for the appropriate, neutral and positive behaviors. It was as if no one even noticed those neutral or positive behaviors. In other words, the child was getting no reward for behaving appropriately. No positive reinforcement was provided.

However, the behaviors that were inappropriate or aversive received a great deal of attention. Everyone, including the other children noticed, and the child was met with nasty looks and often direct staff intervention. The only way that this child 'existed' (i.e., got attention) was to misbehave. Otherwise, he was invisible.

Realizing this led to an entirely different Treatment Plan for the child. The point of this story is that the staff saw what they expected to see. They were completely blind to the child's behaviors that were inconsistent with their beliefs.

We see what we expect to see: A Messy Divorce.

This can happen in a divorce, where spouses are like the staff at that hospital. In a messy divorce, the tendency is for spouses to focus only on the negative, when the bulk of who the other spouse is might be very positive.

When done well, inferential thinking is human nature at work,
which helps us
develop a coherent understanding of ourselves
and the world around us.

It not only helps us figure out what to do, but also presents a pitfall if we develop beliefs based on unsupported or only partially supported guesses. In our hospital example, the staff and other children were reinforcing the negative behaviors because, for the child, that was the only time people noticed him.

There are two parts of the Tasks involved when we make an important but unsupported inference.

1. The first part of the task is to get more information—to check it out, so to speak.

If we are unable to get sufficient information to know one way or the other, mindfulness instructs us to consider our inference a 'possibility', but not necessarily 'the truth'.

2. The second part of the task is to recognize that we are prone to see what we expect to see and fail to recognize information that is inconsistent with our beliefs.

Mindful awareness specifically searches for information that might contradict our beliefs.

For example, a woman might believe that her ex-spouse is so controlling that he never agrees with what she says. Every time he disagrees, she sees that as proof, but perhaps she does not notice when he agrees. A mindful approach to this would be to pay attention every day and literally count the times that the ex-spouse agrees and the times that he disagrees. She might find that her belief is true, but there is also a reasonable chance that the balance of agreeing and disagreeing is normal. In the latter case, she will have to update her belief to reflect reality. Her belief might be wrong.

Because we have parental instincts regarding children, parents need to understand the children's experience at the home of the other parent. In a messy divorce with children, ex-spouses usually have poor communication, and as a result, have very little information about what is actually going on at the other home. They make inferences, usually negative, and these coalesce into negative beliefs. In most families, if the parents could be a fly on the wall and witness what actually goes on, they would likely discover that it is very similar to what goes on in their own home with the children. The reality is usually substantially different from the vision built on negative beliefs, when there is no information sharing about what is really going on.

Sensible Exercise: This exercise is best accomplished if done on paper. Begin listing all of your beliefs about your ex-spouse, both positive and negative. Do not do all of this in one sitting; let your subconscious mind work on this over a period of days or even longer. Leave the paper somewhere so you can easily record other beliefs over time. When you think that you have listed most if not all of your beliefs, review each belief and reflect on the foundation of that belief. What direct experience have you had that supports the belief? Have you relied on hearsay or the perspectives of others?

To what extent have you relied on your children's reports of their experiences with the ex-spouse, an often, dubious source of information, especially in a divorce? Have you been influenced by family or friends who themselves have drawn inferences and developed beliefs? Most importantly, could you prove that your belief is incorrect, by looking at other experiences, making other equally likely inferences, listening to other people describe your ex-spouse or even remembering back to your impressions of your ex-spouse when dating and in the early part of the marriage? Finally, what additional information would you need to have more confidence in the beliefs that you have developed?

**The real challenge here is to be willing
to change beliefs about your ex-spouse.**

Clinging to our beliefs, especially when they blame other people, has the tendency to preserve our sense of wellness. If we see our ex-spouse as a jerk, we can pretend that all the problems are his or her fault; when the reality is that we are both probably acting like jerks and that both of us likely have many positive qualities that are being ignored and not being acknowledged. Remember the hospital story.

Summary:

In brief, Mindfulness, as it applies to divorce and sensible practices, involves:

1. Shifting away from the blame-frame to solving problems, including reflecting on your own responsibility.
2. Being completely honest.
3. Resisting taking criticism personally, but also possibly including some useful feedback.
4. Avoiding developing beliefs based on unsupported inferences, especially negative beliefs about the ex-spouse.

Almost every messy divorce includes: blaming, distrusting, taking things personally, thinking inferentially and developing beliefs based on unsupported inferences.

A Sensible Divorce shifts from blame to solving problems,
not taking criticism personally, checking out inferences
with critical thinking and communication, and
discarding beliefs based on insufficient information.

These are principles that will reappear many times in this book. We will even challenge some of these principles to test their metal as general guidelines to a Sensible Divorce.

In order to accomplish our mission, and realize the very core purpose of this book, we want to emphasize that soon-to-be ex-spouse is likely exhibiting one or more of the four Problematic Emotions (i.e., 'poisons') presented in this Chapter.

One spouse can commit to being sensible and healthy, and not 'messy', whether or not the other spouse makes the same commitment. However, in order to understand the solution, we must first understand the problems (which we call the headwinds and challenges obstructing a Sensible Divorce). This will be the focus of Part II of our book.

Part II
Understanding the Headwinds and Challenges Obstructing a Sensible Divorce

"Captain, it is not important how we got here.
What is important is knowing where we are
and what we are going to do."
(Mr. Spock, Star Trek.)

Chapter 3
The Decision to Marry; the Marriage; the Pitfalls Present in Marriages; and the Decision to Divorce

1. The Decision to Marry.

A wedding is not a marriage; the marriage is everything that happens after the wedding. The wedding is just the legal event that changes a person's legal status from single to married, triggering in a number of laws and social expectations. It is both a happy time and a sad time.

1. **The happy times:** The decision to marry is a choice, but undergirding that choice is deciding what type of person should be the partner in the marital relationship. It is good to think of a marriage as presenting positive possibilities leading to a marriage that we all hope for ourselves. We have a promise of companionship and a teammate with whom to share the challenges of life and a romantic partner. We might really like

many of our in-laws and new friends. Two can live more cheaply together than one alone. We might want children and can realize the dream of parenthood. We have the carrot of a long-term happy marriage dangling in front of us.

2. **The sad times:** At the same time, there are sad losses and not so happy times. It is a sad time because we are losing our status as single, which includes a great deal of change. We can no longer make unilateral decisions about how to spend our money. We cannot flirt with anyone we wish, pursue other relationships or have sex with other people. We lose some of our ability to choose with whom we will associate. We accumulate a whole set of in-laws and friends of our spouse with whom we will be having relationships, some of whom we might not like. We can no longer organize our residence the way we want or how we used to do it, or sometimes, not even live where we want to live. We lose all of the advantages of being single.

The problems faced by divorcing spouses
have their roots in the marriage.

Therefore, in order to construct a sensible divorce, we first need to back up and understand the pitfalls inevitably present in all marriages. In addition, there are known pitfalls leading to doom in a delicate marital balance. In a sense, it is important to be aware that a marriage can go, or at least begin to go, either way at any time.

While the losses give us second thoughts about marrying, the promises of happiness are hard to resist, if we have reasonable encouragement and assurances that the person, we are marrying offers that prospect.

Most people approach their wedding with trepidation,
balanced with hope and joy.

2. The Marriage.

A marriage does not involve a single decision. We wake up every day and decide to remain married, not only out of habit but also by choice (perhaps subconsciously). Most people make the decision to marry (i.e., to stay married) (again likely subconsciously) every day.

The reality is that each day might be the last day of the marriage or might be the first day leading to the last day. In some marriages, spouses might on occasion wake up and discuss whether or not to stay married for another day. However, this would be emotionally exhausting if done daily, and not surprisingly, most people do not do it. Instead, people take their marriage for granted, partially because of momentum, until something happens that makes them aware that the decision to stay married is tentative and can go either way. You might be married for ten years and feel secure until your wife comes home at 1 AM in the morning and tells you that she went out for drinks with Ed (from work), who has just separated from his wife. Then, and perhaps only then, you realize that you and your wife have some decisions to make, which might include whether or not to remain married.

In some marriages, we might not discuss whether to stay married or divorce, but we are aware that we could. We might even realize that we not only decide this every day, but also, decide it every minute. When we respond to our spouse, we are deciding to respond in a manner that encourages or discourages the marriage. If our spouse is sharp with us, we can respond by being sharp with him or her, discouraging the marriage, or we can ask, "*What's wrong?*" encouraging the marriage. When we are at work and know that our spouse is upset about something, we can take the time to call, encouraging the marriage, or not call, discouraging the marriage.

In some schools of Buddhism, the monks and nuns have lists of hundreds of '*right behavior*' prescriptions, but they generally boil down to avoid violating themselves or others and being kinder and less selfish. In a marriage, we make moment-to-moment decisions to engage in right behavior (and be kind) or wrong behavior toward our spouse (and be selfish). Our spouse might put up with a few instances of wrong behavior, but not with a pattern of wrong behavior over a lengthy period of time. Some wrong behaviors can even be deal-breakers.

Think of a marriage as one long date.

When people go on a date, they are deciding whether to go on a second date, but so is the other person. If the date goes well, that is, if both people are a good date for the other person, they agree to go out again together. If it is a bad date, they think of how to decline further dates. If most of the dates go well, even if there is a brief period when it does not, people might decide to give it another try. A date usually has both promising and discouraging experiences, but both people are usually on their best behavior. A marriage is somewhat like this.

3.   The Pitfalls Present in a Marriage.

Emotional capital builds during a marriage,
as does the commitment.

To say that a marriage is like a first date, where staying together is as tentative as a decision to go on a second date, is simplistic and ignores the influence of experience. However, once people date for a while, and especially when they marry, they begin to build emotional capital in the relationship. One bad experience on a first date can be the end of the relationship, but one bad experience after ten good ones might not. In a sense, relationships build emotional capital, like putting money in a bank. The more capital in the bank, the easier it is to absorb the ups and downs of real life. Capital can not only include positive experiences with one another but also include many intangibles, like mutual friends, children, in-laws to whom we have become close and so on.

A marriage can have some problematic patterns,
but be so rich in other emotional capital,
that the marriage persists and perhaps is even very strong.

People who marry also make promises to one another, and this creates a sense of commitment that by itself can carry people through rough periods in the marriage. The balance of marital experiences might be negative for a long period, but the commitment and hope help people stick it out, at least for a while. People might go through periods of great happiness, but most spouses also go through periods when they are just tolerating things for a while. Emotional capital and commitment are what gets us though difficult periods in a marriage. Altruism also builds during a marriage.

4. The Decision to Divorce.

As we point out in Chapter 5, marriages go through developmental stages, and the final stage is dominated by an altruistic connection with the spouse. When marriages reach that point, even long periods of difficulties in the marriage are tolerated because of a truly altruistic interest in the welfare of the spouse. Likewise, the spouse might even tolerate long periods when the value of the marriage to them is very low.

The decision to divorce can be a predictable outcome
when the emotional capital is insufficient to absorb
the negative experiences of the marriage, for a long enough
period of time, or when a 'deal-breaker',
such as an affair, has occurred.

Social anthropologists tell us that historically and across cultures, about one-third of all attempts at marriage, or comparable customs, end in separations or divorce. In other words, although it might be named differently, or might or might not even include an actual legal marriage, about one-third of the time, the effort at a union between two people does not work, and people separate.

While many people think of a divorce as a failure,
it is not. It is simply a common occurrence and
predictable about 30% of the time.

As we also point out in Chapter 5, in many cases a mismatch of control strategies is the problem- not something involving bad people or involving people who fall out of love. Some marriages can run into a problem that has no solution (e.g., one spouse wants children and the other does not), again with good people involved. Some problems, such as the development of an incurable drug addiction, develop in a marriage that make divorce the best solution.

Sensible living includes an awareness of impermanence, including relationships. In fact, all relationships end, including those that include marriages. All endings are sad.

A relationship might end after one date. That is only a little sad. Most people who go on a date are aware that the odds are stacked against the date leading to a long-term committed relationship. They only have a small bit of hope. Discovering that the date does not lead to further dating is only a little sad. Some relationships end after a long period of dating, and that is sadder. It is possibly even very sad, especially for the one who did not want the relationship to end. Some marriages end in the early stages, and that is even sadder. However, the biggest sad is when the relationship ends because one of the spouses gets old and dies. Paradoxically, that is what most people hope for- the long-term marriage until '*death do us part*', and yet, that is the saddest ending.

The divorce rate goes up and down and is different in different cultures at different times for a number of different reasons. Interestingly, one of those reasons is the role and impact of women's property rights. In cultures in which women have few if any property rights, the divorce rate remains fairly low. If women gain property rights, the divorce rate goes up. In other cultures, the divorce might reflect other oddities. In Ireland, for example, divorce was not a legal option until fairly recently, so in the past, the divorce rate was essentially zero. Yet, many married people were living separately, sometimes with new partners, and when Irish law changed to allow divorce, quite a few people got in line. Costa Rica boasted one of the lowest divorce rates in the world. However, it turns out that many of the people who present themselves as married, had never had a legal service and were merely living together. Some did so successfully for a long time, and some separated, but there was no registered divorce because they were never legally married.

Divorce is just an ending.
When a marriage ends in divorce,
it is not a failure.
It is a sad ending of a relationship,
which happens about 30% of the time.[8]

Divorce is simply an ending of the relationship, earlier than at least one of the spouses wishes and sad for both spouses who hoped for a marriage that would last until death. If both spouses tried to make it work, at least for a while, and the marriage ended in divorce, it is not a failure. It is a sad ending.

Earlier, we wrote that a wedding is not a marriage. The marriage is everything that happens after the wedding. The wedding is just the legal event that changes the legal status of the participants from being single to being married. We recognize that a wedding can also have religious and social implications, but for our purposes, let us keep the focus on the legal event.

A divorce is not the day of the Judgment of Divorce.
The divorce is everything that happens after that day.
The day of the divorce Judgment is just the legal event
that changes the status of the spouses from married to single.
Like a wedding, divorce is both sad and happy.

It is sad because of the many losses involved, and if there are children involved, because of the complicated logistics of raising children when the parents live in separate residences. It is happy because the suffering associated with a marriage gone bad ends, or should end. Both spouses are once again free to make unilateral decisions and pursue other relationships that might be more fulfilling.

Having a sensible divorce, and not a messy one, is a choice.[9]

---

[8] We again offer a special thanks to Bill Hodges and the first generation of researchers (about a dozen) who pioneered the effort to understand marriage and divorce and its impact on children.
[9] Remember the photos at the beginning of our book, reminding us about this choice!

Just as people marrying make choices about what type of marriage they would like, people divorcing can make choices about what type of divorce they would like. For starters, they usually need to tangle with the momentum of the problems in the marriage that led to the divorce. In addition, the need to encounter a legal system that can make getting a divorce very unpleasant, which might be as bad or worse than the problems they faced while married.

However, couples can choose to have an amicable or sensible divorce. They can communicate and cooperate as parents, share family income in various forms of support and treat each other with courtesy and respect. They can let go of the marital problems. Looking to the future instead of the past, and choose a sensible divorce.

However, instead of having a sensible divorce, others struggle breaking ties with the marital problems. In addition, they continue to engage in problematic behavior with one another. The important fact is a simple one: these couples choose to have a messy divorce.

**At first blush, choosing to have a messy divorce
sounds like an absurd thing to do.**

Why would anyone choose to have a messy divorce? Why would anyone choose to continue to suffer? The research evidence is incontrovertible: people do choose to perpetuate suffering, inflicting harm on one another and on their children, if they have children.

Here we harken back to evolutionary psychology and mindfulness as a cure.[10] The emotions in a divorce cover up the real feelings, which are dominated by sadness, but often include guilt, shame and fear. Ken often began mediation sessions with divorcing spouses by saying something similar to: "*I know that when you married, you did not think that you would end up here in my office to plan your divorce. I know this is incredibly sad for you. I hope to help you make a good Plan for your divorce, but I want you to know that I understand how sad this is for you.*"

There are messy divorces, and there are functioning amicable or at least peaceful divorces. In fact, research tells us that about one-third of all divorces are sensible, where the ex-spouses get along reasonably well, communicate and

---

[10] See Chapter 1 on Mindfullness.

cooperate if they have children and treat each other with courtesy and respect. A messy divorce is not inevitable, so there must be a choice.

Although choosing a messy divorce and a toxic dance seems a self-defeating choice, there are reasons for it.

People are tricked, by themselves and/or by their spouse, into doing what we call a 'toxic dance' with one another. People choose to have this toxic dance. In the Prologue, we touched on one of the tricks: When people have put a good deal of effort into a pattern, it is hard to let go of the pattern. [Remember the road to nowhere!] Sometimes, it is easier to stick with a familiar negative relationship than to try to establish a new sensible relationship.

Familiar conflict might be painful, but predictable.

Summary:

In Part I, Chapter 1, we expanded on the toxic dance by pointing out that people can choose to go to the dark side of blame.

In Chapter 2, spouses sometimes say that they want to be amicable but blame the other spouse for perpetuating the toxic dance. By blaming, they make themselves helpless to choose a different way. When people blame someone else for their problems, the problems can only go away if the other person changes. Blaming gives other people control (i.e., meaning they give up control) over their own happiness.

In Chapter 2, we also introduced the problems of distrust in a divorce. In the toxic dance, neither spouse trusts the other spouse, often for good reason. Your authors have noticed over the many years of our practice, in amicable divorces, spouses are typically open and honest with one another. In messy divorces, spouses try to keep secrets, rarely communicate, and share information with 'spin' and sometimes outright lies. We also introduced the problems associated with taking things personally. This is endemic in messy divorces.

Finally, in Chapter 2, we introduced the pitfalls associated with inferential thinking, especially falling into the well of intractable conflict, when inferential thinking coalesces into negative beliefs.

In Chapter 9, we are going to explore other reasons how people are trapped into choosing a messy divorce. We also want to posit that the traps, temptations and pitfalls of natural human tendencies can lead to self-defeating choices and suffering.

We all know that there are bad people in the world, and there are mentally disturbed people in the world, where many of them might choose to have messy divorces. However, in the experience of your authors, by far, the majority of those who choose divorce are good people, without mental disturbance, but end up in messy divorces.

Why? Because they have been 'trapped',
by themselves, by others
and/or inadvertently
by the family law system itself.

HOWEVER, THERE IS A WAY TO AVOID A MESSY DIVORCE.
AND, IF YOU ARE IN A MESSY DIVORCE,
THERE IS A WAY OUT:
CHOOSE A SENSIBLE DIVORCE!
(Please read on.)

Chapter 4
The Decision to Control the Headwinds and Goal Based Planning to Have a Sensible Divorce

A divorce relationship between spouses often appears to have a life of its own, as people take for granted the habits and patterns of the marital relationship. When practicing 'sensible divorce', people are aware that every day, they make choices with regard to that relationship. This awareness gives them freedom to choose behaviors and habits that are self-defeating and hurtful, or to choose other behaviors each day that change their relationship with their ex-spouse for the better.

**Therefore, they can control their happiness
if they control the headwinds and
challenges obstructing a sensible divorce.**

To do this, however, we need a deeper understanding of both marriage and divorce. We will continue down that path in the next Chapter, but for now, we want to emphasize that spouses everyday may choose to have a messy divorce or to change direction and have a Sensible Divorce.

A Messy Divorce continues only if,
like our road to nowhere,
people do not let go of the old relationship
and begin a new way of relating to each other
in a new and improved relationship.

People do not choose to suffer, but suffering can be an inevitable outcome of the choices they make. The reason for this is that they continue to make the same mistakes they made in the marriage, without realizing it.

In order to understand the choices
that lead to a sensible divorce,
we need to explore the mistakes made in the marriage.

If you are getting impatient, reading about all of the challenges faced when getting a divorce, or even thinking that choosing a sensible divorce sounds way too complicated, that sounds pretty normal. However, we thought that a little promise and reassurance here might be helpful and encouraging. If we could leave out all of the descriptions of where a messy divorce comes from, we would have done that. Sorry. However, we will continue to delve into the reasons that people end up in messy divorces when most would love to have an amicable divorce.

In Chapter 6 [11], we describe our researched-based **Ten Disagreement Resolution Skills Needed for a Sensible Divorce** and our **Four Step Planning Template for Making Collaborative Decisions**.

---

[11] Other important research-based Skills are introduced in Chapters 6-9 and in Chapters 15-17.

**Here's the good news: Understanding the problem is complicated, but
the solutions are modest and easy.
It "only" requires learning skills!**

WE PROMISE!

We will begin to keep this promise, before we get back to the headwinds and the challenges obstructing a sensible device, by reminding our readers that the title of the book begins with the word, 'Planning'.

What do we mean by 'planning'?

Planning is the very first skill that amicable and sensible spouses must exercise, whether or not they are also co-parents and even whether or not they have children. Effective planning means following our simple **Four Step Goal Based Planning Template.**

**Managing the emotions involved in the planning process
is complicated, presenting additional challenges.
When people have messy endings to a marriage,
they are almost always facing in the wrong direction:
they are <u>facing the past</u>.**

They remember every detail of the hurt inflicted on one another, every broken promise and every unfinished argument. They are full of blame, both of themselves and each other, for the marriage having gone wrong. They become convinced that they now finally see what each other are *'really like'*, instead of the person that they used to like and even love.

Of course, the problem with this thinking is that time keeps moving forward no matter what happened in the past. Worse yet, people do not get *do-overs.* In other words, spouses facing the past cannot change what happened. They are facing in the wrong direction.

Don't get us wrong; there are some good reasons to react by looking at the past. Reacting to an unplanned and unwanted end to a marriage, or any other life crisis, always begins with facing the past, trying to make sense of what happened and looking at the past differently. The purpose, though, is to learn from mistakes and do things differently in the future.

After that initial reaction of looking at the past, the emotional task is to turn around 180 degrees and face the future.
Spouses cannot change the past,
but they have a great deal of control over the future.
Control over the future comes from planning.

We will introduce two important characteristics of planning in this chapter:

1. Using our **Four Step Goal Based Planning Template for Making Collaborative Decisions**[12] and

2. Recognizing the importance of planning for the accomplishment of goals for both spouses. This is it! The moment when you turn around from facing the past and focus on controlling the future.

Four Step Goal Based Planning Process for Making Collaborative Decisions: Our Template

1. Describe in detail the current situation.
2. List each spouse's long-term goals, specific to the decisions being made.
3. Plan the steps for reaching long-term goals.
4. List the obstacles and steps to overcome them and create a Plan.

Step #1: Describe the current situation.

What is important to this Step is being honest and thorough. Both spouses must describe in detail the starting point for him and her. Very likely, there will

---

[12] Dale Carnegie came from very poor roots and became one of the most successful people in history. He was obsessed with how he did it and commissioned a number of research studies on how people become successful. His research discovered that there is nothing special about successful people: they are not any smarter than everyone else, or better looking, or more charming, or even better mentally adjusted. They just follow a simple decision-making process, comparable to the Four Steps described in this chapter. Since then, further studies have added little to the "Carnegie Formula" (our term; not his), other than the importance of persistence.

be significant differences in those explanations, particularly with the intangibles related to parenting. Property and incomes are quite a bit more concrete. It is pretty easy to get relatively accurate figures regarding property values and current incomes and expenses. Some incomes might be more challenging, when they fluctuate, as is the case with most sales jobs and self-employment situations. Parenting starting points can be even more challenging.

Children's ages, grade levels, special problems, performance levels and so on can be fairly objective, but parents might disagree about the needs for discipline, levels of expectations, chores and responsibilities and estimations of each other's parenting strengths and weaknesses. Surfacing those differences can spark new and old arguments, but it is important in this first Step to surface those differences, without focusing on who is 'right' or even whether or not they are accurate. Those differences might require specific planning to avoid future conflicts, beyond the scope of Step #1 at this juncture.

Step #2: List each spouse's long-term goals, specific to the decisions being made.

The Four Steps apply to big goals and little goals, and they apply to children's issues and financial issues.

We posit two major sets of **Goals** using our **Goal Based Planning Template** in a divorce, which should answer the following questions:

1. What kind of family life do the parents want to give their children when their parents will be living in separate residences?
2. What kind of financial lives do the divorced spouses want to have in the future, whether or not they have children?

More regarding the importance of goals: (1) If the parties have children, a little goal related to their post-divorce family life might be what kind of experience the children should have with their parents involved in their activities (e.g., school concerts, parent-teacher conferences, attending sports events, etc.). (2) A little financial goal might be how the parents will pay for an extracurricular activity agreed to by both parents.

This sounds easy, but it can get pretty emotional. For example, when planning attending events, the subject of remarriage might come up as an obstacle. What role will stepparents play? What will it be like to see a stepparent hugging one of the children?

Here is where the importance of goals comes into play. If the goal is for the children to have good experiences at their events, with both parents attending, the parents might, at times, have to overcome emotions and behave sensibly. The plan might include greeting a stepparent with a smile and courtesy, smiling when the stepparent hugs the child and keeping the focus on the child's experience. As they say in children's books, parents sometimes have to *put on their grownup pants*.

Another little financial goal might be whether or not to retain a house for one of the spouses. Again, this can be very emotional. A house can have a great deal of emotional meaning to spouses. At times, it might also seem to have connections to other future financial goals and often to other goals related to the children (e.g., keeping children in their current schools).

Most important is that all of the little goals
fit into the Plan
for the spouses to reach the big
long-term financial and family goals.

For example, a long-term family goal might be for both parents to be very active in the lives of the children. That might be financially impossible if one of the spouses retains the family home in order to keep the children in the same schools. In order to accomplish the family goal, the spouses might have to sell the house and find a location where they can live near one another. The short-term stress of changing schools might be worth it in order to accomplish a long-term family goal.

Step #3: Plan the steps for reaching
long-term goals.

Many or the long-term goals of spouses might be the same or at least similar. For example, both parents might have the long-term goal of the children experiencing their parents getting along well and cooperating with one another. Both spouses might have the goal that both of them are living in stable residences in the future.

However, spouses might have different goals, particularly when addressing little (short-term) goals. When there are differences, they must remember that:

It takes two to tango!

Trite as this sounds, it reflects a profound reality. One person cannot tango by themselves. The only way for two people to do the tango is to work together as a team.

You might ask, quite reasonably,
what does this have to do with planning a divorce?
The anwer is: EVERYTHING!

Significant research has shown that the best solutions are achieved when two people bargain cooperatively, with the goal of getting the best solutions for BOTH PEOPLE. And, guess what? Going through a divorce is a bargaining experience. Bargaining over the legal tasks that need to be accomplished and bargaining over other issues important to accomplishing long-term goals is what a divorce is all about. But keep in mind that our definition of bargaining is "planning to reach long term goals."

And guess what again? If the divorcing spouses have children, they will be bargaining with one another for the rest of their lives. They will be bargaining even when their children are adults. Assume that one of the long-term family goals is for the children never to have loyalty conflicts. Example: Planning for holidays. This requires bargaining between the parents. Parenting never ends. Bargaining never ends. Much of that bargaining will be pretty easy. One parent wants to sign a child up for basketball, and the other parent likes the idea. The only bargaining is on the logistics of how that will work, how both parents can be involved and supportive of the child and so on. However, sometimes a decision will come up or a problem will arise, and the parents will initially disagree about what to do. Oh-oh!

When most people disagree about something, their first reactions are, "*I am right (which means that you are wrong)*" and "*How am I going to get my way*". Oops. They forgot that it takes two to tango. This means that the best solution will be one in which both people '*get their way*'. A key in that endeavour is for both parents to be asking, "What are you trying to achieve with your proposal?" That opens the door to solutions that accomplish both parents' goals.

Step #4: List the obstacles and steps
to overcome them and create a Plan.

At this point, spouses have described in detail their starting point, including all of the relevant financial factors and the factors related to their children. They will have described in detail their long-term family and financial goals, and also some short-term goals that are suggested by their long-term goals.[13] They will have defined steps to take to reach their goals. In this fourth and final Step, they identify obstacles to taking those steps, which might include what appear to be incompatible goals, and come up with a plan to overcome those obstacles.

Maybe a couple of examples, one regarding parenting and one regarding financial issues, will help.

A Parenting Example:

Step #1: Current Situation: Dad wants to sign Jimmy up for football. Jimmy wants to pay football. Mum forcefully objects.

Step #2: Future Goals: Dad identifies his goals. His father coached football, and Dad also played football. It became a special connection between Dad and his father. Dad wants to be, and found out that he can be, the assistant coach for the parks and recreation departments football league for children. He wants Jimmy to have that special connection to him like he had with his father. Dad

---

[13] For example, a long-term goal might be to minimize the children's confusion by having rules, routines and enforcement similar in both homes. Because they differ in their discipline styles, they might have a short-term goal of making those styles more similar with the help of a counselor.

knows quite a bit about football and feels that he can be an asset to the team and a model for his son.

Mom is sympathetic to Dad, but believes that football is simply too dangerous. Recent news has identified children who go through life with serious football injuries. She is also concerned that if Jimmy does well at his age, he might play in high school and even college, magnifying the risks of life-long damage. Her goal is to keep Jimmy as safe as possible from what she perceives are real risks.

Step #3: Steps to Accomplish Goals: Both parents propose steps to take, but cannot come up with mutually agreed-upon steps because their apparently incompatible goals do not merge. For example, Dad proposes that Mom speak with the high school football coach to find out how common football injuries really are. Mom proposes that Dad read a recent article in Parent's Magazine about football injuries to children.

The underlying problem is that the steps that they each were proposing were aimed at convincing each other to change their minds. The conflicting goals were important to them, and after arguing for a while, they were stuck.[14]

Step #4: Obstacle Discussion and a Plan: Overcoming the obstacle of what appears to have been conflicting goals was accomplished by redefining the goals themselves. Rather than Dad wanting to repeat an experience he had with his father with football, the goal was redefined as having the *same type* of special father-son experience, but not the exact same one. Mom's goal to keep Jimmy safe from physical harm was redefined to keeping Jimmy safe from *serious long-term* harm. This opened the door to Planning Steps.

The outcome was the following: Step 1: The parents planned to enrol Jimmy in soccer on a team on which Dad could be the coach or assistant coach. Step 2: Mom agreed to accommodate soccer schedules so that Dad could take Jimmy to practices, independent of the custody schedule, and Jimmy could play games, also independent of the custody schedule. Step 3: Mom, with a smile, suggested that she could be the team mom and would bring the refreshments. Step 4: Dad, also with a smile, said that he better learn more about soccer.

Notice that the solution above was better for both parents than either of their initial proposals. Notice that no time was spent arguing about who is right and who is wrong. The focus was on the goals, not the opinions or positions.

---

[14] This is a real case that was sent to Ken for mediation in hopes of avoiding a hearing with a judge to make the decision- a clear win-lose situation.

**This is how our Four Step Planning Template
for Making Collaborative Decisions works,
even when people initially disagree.**

A Financial Example[15]

Step #1: Current Situation: The husband has been the primary income earner in the marriage. He makes four times the income that the wife is earning as a store clerk. He is likely to pay a high level of both child and spousal support. While the level of spousal support is likely to be high, the term is likely to be limited because of the length of the marriage. Both spouses would like to be financially independent of one another, but the wife sees herself as in a bind and needing as much support as she can get so that she can not only continue to work but also take steps to get a higher paying career. Those steps are likely to be slow, given that they have a child, and she currently works full time.

Step #2: Future Goals: The spouses share the goal of both not only being financially independent of one another, but also both doing financially well, living in owned residences with similar lifestyles. The wife would like to have a more professional career in order to substantially increase her income.

Step #3: Steps to Accomplish Goals: The husband will pay a high enough level of spousal support, substantially higher than is likely to be ordered if contested, to allow the wife to quit her job and enrol in a training program to develop her skills in an area of interest to her for a self-employment career. At the completion of the one-year training program, the wife will start her own business. As her income increases, spousal support will be offset. As an incentive to the wife to build her business, an expectation of three years is set as the potential point of termination of spousal support and the re-calculation of child support.

---

[15] Again, we have chosen a real mediation case.

Step #4: Obstacle Discussion and a Plan: The primary obstacle to the Plan is that the rate of business growth for the wife, in spite of her best efforts, might be slower than expected. The Plan: if the wife's income does not reach the level needed at the end of three years, the spouses agreed to meet again, with the husband having the final decision as to whether to continue to pay spousal support. Remembering the shared goals, which included his wanting her to have a good lifestyle, to which they both agreed.

Sidenote: In this real case, the parties returned to mediation as the three-year limit approached because the wife's business was growing more slowly than hoped. The husband was convinced that she had and would continue to be making a sincere effort and would ultimately be successful. They agreed to an extension of spousal support, which by this time was substantially less than was paid earlier.

Notice that the plan was independent of what a judge might have ordered and much more likely to achieve long-term goals. Note too, rather than being adversarial, the planning was cooperative. In other words, it was sensible.

Summary:

In this chapter,
we show what kind of choices people make and
what kind of patterns develop every day.

Even if a divorce has gone badly, people have control over changing their choices and their patterns. Changing a messy divorce to a sensible can be accomplished by:

1. Overcoming the emotional momentum to keep the messy divorce going.
2. Turning around and focusing on the future, not the past. A famous golfer was once asked what the secret to his success was. He answered, "*I have always been able to play the next shot, not the last one*". In other words, rather than focus on his last bad shot, which he could not change, he focused on the next shot over which he had control.
3. Planning means applying the Four Steps of our Goal Based Planning Template. Memorize the Four Steps and apply them every time you and

your spouse, or later you and your co-parent, have a decision to make or a problem to solve.

4. Aiming at solutions so that both spouses reach as many of their goals as possible is a win-win situation.

Take-aways:

There are several important take-aways in this Chapter, but the critical one is a simple one:

The only situations that are hopeless are when
both people involved are dead.

The reason is simple: Every day, people can make different choices. A 20-year serious alcoholic can join Alcoholics Anonymous and choose not to drink that day. Tomorrow could be the first day when a messy divorce begins to become a sensible divorce.

It all begins with a Plan!

Chapter 5
Everything Is About Control

The Marriage and Divorce Challenges.

The Marriage Challenges.

Control issues are often at play. Marriages have an emotional cycle or developmental path that predicts what will be the primary focus at different periods in the marriage. It begins with dating and checking each other out. When that process goes well, it includes what is called *The Honeymoon Phase* and ultimately, that dating becomes a marriage.

During the marriage, *Control* issues surface when the parties have their first argument. Spouses understand that marriage involves control. In fact, there were control issues before in the Honeymoon Phase, but they were overshadowed by attraction, positive experiences and hope.

A wide range of control issues surface in a marriage.

Control issues might not come up in some aspects of the relationship because of what the spouses have in common. If both people are tidy, for example, control over how tidy the residence is might never surface. If both people are similar in their needs for physical affection, control of the kissing, hugging, neck rubs and even sex might not be an issue.

However, control issues can be challenging (and possibly ugly) when people have differences. Those can be simple, such as making sure that the toothpaste tube is put away after brushing (mildly challenging), who does what residential chores (more challenging), or when to start having children or how often to have sex (extremely challenging). Another challenging control issue in marriage is the very question of what is open to mutual control and what is not.

Some issues are better left in the unilateral control of just one spouse. For example, if marital parties agree that the wife's career is an important part of the long-term success of the marriage, then her choices about her career, with or without the husband's input, should remain under her control. If the husband wants to keep activities with his long-time friends going during the marriage, the wife might have to relinquish any control over that. If the wife enjoys flirting, but is faithful to the marriage, the husband might do well to let her flirt and enjoy that aspect of her personality.

**Trying to control everything in a marriage
is usually (if not always) a mistake.**

Fantasy comes into play related to the control issue. The control issue in marriage can be characterized as the fantasy life of the spouses, although most people do not recognize this. Deeply cemented in people's brains is a template of what a happy marriage should be.

There is an important Template at play. This template has (1) historical and cultural foundations, (2) foundations in their personal history, especially families of origin, and (3) foundations in the spouses' underlying personality structure and temperaments.

Let's unpack each of these three Principles applicable to the Template at play:

(1) **Historical and cultural foundations.** People have historical and cultural experiences that are not only built into their genetic make-up, but also modelled to them when they were growing up. In other animals, this is called patterning, and is a way of learning about how the world works and what we should do in the future. If people marry someone from their own culture, differences might be minor. They might find themselves compatible, without fully understanding why. If they marry someone from a different cultural background, they are likely to run into differences. Some of those differences might be attractive, but some might present challenges and provoke control struggles. A man from an Irish background might find very attractive that his wife, with a Spanish background, is so comfortable with being openly sexual in her appearance. However, at the same time, the man might find her effusive temperament very difficult to handle.

(2) **Foundations in their personal history, especially families of origin.** Two spouses might have grown up in similar cultural areas, but their families of origin might have influenced them in very different ways. For example, both spouses might have grown up in the 50's and 60's. The man's family might have modelled a male- dominated marriage (i.e., Father Knows Best), but the woman's family might have been more ignited by the woman's movement and the goal of an egalitarian marriage. A control issue in this type of marriage might be around his assumption of primacy in making decisions and her assumption of mutual and equal control of decisions. Others in families, especially parents, also modelled how to resolve disagreements. Those models affect how they approach disagreement in their own marriage. If their parents had a mature healthy strategy, the spouses will likely apply the same to their marriage, but the reverse is also true if they modelled immature or destructive approaches to disagreement.

(3) **Foundations in the spouses' underlying personality structure and temperaments.** Differences in personality structure and temperaments might also provoke challenging control problems. Imagine that one of the spouses is very outgoing and thrives on social interaction, while the other spouse is much more comfortable alone, with less social interaction, or with just a few close friends, likely making one of the

spouses uncomfortable. However, both of them like to be together rather than doing what they like alone.

The major challenge in a marriage
is resolving the control issues.

The Template and the Fantasy. A different way to look at this control issue goes back to a fundamental issue, which is that people have a template of what would make for a happy marriage. Their fantasy wish is that the other spouse would just play his or her role in a fantasy movie—the template of a good marriage. In other words, in people's fantasy, they want the other spouse to be an actor or actress in a supporting role in their movie of the happy marriage, in which they are the star. When parts of the other spouse's template clash, because he or she has his or her own needs and interests, people try to get the other spouse to shape up and play the role the way they want him or her to play. However, the other spouse is doing exactly the same thing- trying to get his or her spouse to play their bit role in his or her movie.

This is the Control Phase of the marriage,
which is quite different from the Honeymoon Phase.

However, this is a necessary phase or stage in the marriage, as difficult as it might be, in order to make the marriage the best that it can be for both spouses.

However, control struggles have a dark side
and can ultimately lead to a divorce.

We are exaggerating to make a point: that all control problems arise from differences and disagreements about what each spouse wants to happen in the marriage. Because there are always differences and disagreements in every marriage, because no two people have exactly the same backgrounds, expectations, needs and wants, there will always be control challenges.

**The difference between successful marriages
and marriages that end in divorce
are not whether or not there are differences and disagreements.
The difference is how those differences and disagreements are handled.**

The Divorce Challenges.

A marriage is a series of decisions made every day, including the decision to continue to be married. A deal breaker, like an affair or an unresolved gambling addiction, is something that might prompt a decision to divorce. However, the most common cause of divorces is that differences and disagreements do not get resolved well or at all, and include emotional damage to each other and escalate into unresolved conflict. Sometimes the approaches to disagreements are just so bad that they are doomed to fail.

Maybe a spouse is a bully and always has to get his or her way. Most often, though, the approaches to control of two spouses just clash. They might work with someone else, but not with that particular spouse. When that happens, the failure to resolve differences and disagreements builds up into conflict, with escalating arguments or a cold war, both of which are very hurtful. After a while, one or both spouses start toying with the idea of a divorce, and more and more, divorce seems like the only escape from the pain of the marriage. By that time, divorce might be the only solution.

**Not everyone succeeds in mastering the control issue in a marriage,
and some simply crash into deal-breakers.**

In fact, given the temptations and pitfalls of marriage, it is remarkable how often marriages succeed. By the time people divorce, they are usually in pretty bad shape. While the marriage might have been dominated by anger, frustration and blame, the really tough feelings are the sadness, guilt, disappointment and shame. Nobody going into a divorce wanted to go in that direction, at least at one point. Even marriages that started with serious problems were usually filled with hope. A divorce dashes that hope. It is no wonder that many people go into the divorce process with a 'messy' relationship.

The bad news. The bad news is that, when people divorce who have children, they still have control challenges. They will still face differences and disagreements in how to raise the children. Many parents try to avoid control clashes by ignoring the differences, by ignoring what goes on in the other home, ignoring each other as much as possible, and sadly, even ignoring their children when they are with the other parent. Parents often desperately try to get involvement with the children by struggling to get the most custody time possible. This is in part what leads to a messy divorce.

The good news. The good news is that control challenges are much easier to resolve at divorce, especially because of the absence of the intimacy issues of a marriage. As we will show in the next two chapters, we introduce our Ten Disagreement Resolution Skills (Chapter 6) and our Five Tasks and Rules (Chapter 7) for parents. Once learned, they provide extraordinary guidance and assistance for the parents, which in turn creates a much better living environment for their children. This is a very satisfying and successful family experience. Better yet, this skill development will occur in a new and different setting- where they no longer face the challenges of living with each other, jointly managing money and in the absence of the intimacy needs of each other. They are no longer responsible for the feelings of each other, except as co-partners in parenting.

More bad news and good news.

- The bad news is that the spouses need to change their approaches to control, so that differences and disagreements get resolved in a healthy way.
- The good news is that this is much simpler to do in a co-parenting relationship than in a marriage.

Summary and a Good Roadmap to other Book Chapters:

1. A decision to have a sensible divorce can happen at any time, regardless of what has happened in the past.

2. A functional and sensible co-parenting relationship involves: (a) learning our Four Step Goal Based Planning Template for Making Collaborative Decisions, which we introduced in Chapter 4 and presented again in Chapter 6, and (b) committing to apply those Steps to every decision that needs to be made and every problem that needs to be solved. (**Note**: we also introduce our Four Step Goal Base Planning Template for making decisions regarding legal and planning tasks in Chapter 14. Please stay tuned.)

3. A functional and sensible co-parenting relationship involves learning how to make decisions when people disagree and how to solve problems together that they or their children face.[16]

4. Having a functional co-parenting relationship is a major part of having a sensible divorce. To do so well includes learning some new skills and making a Plan to apply our Five Tasks and Rules for Successful Co-parenting (Chapter 7).

5. Accepting that all relationships include control, a marriage has the most complicated challenges with control issues because of deep insecurities and important interpersonal needs.

   A co-parenting relationship also has control issues, although much less complicated unless parents continue to battle over their deep insecurities and important interpersonal needs. **Note**: If they do, they will have a messy divorce.

6. Our Ten Disagreement Resolution Skills address the issue of co-parents making decisions when they disagree (Chapter 6).

7. As mentioned above, control issues in a co-parenting relationship can be addressed by applying our Five Tasks and Rules for Successful Co-Parenting (see Chapter 7)

---

[16] Here is another preview of coming attractions: We will be addressing the second and third tasks of Successful Co-parenting mentioned above in Chapter 6. All this also involves learning our Disagreement Resolution Skills, which we also begin to describe in Chapter 6.

We hope we have not tricked you into thinking that this will be easy. It is not. Remember our example of the alcoholic of 20 years changing his mind and starting a life of sobriety by not drinking today. Starting each day with a commitment not to drink is not easy. In fact, to think this way would be foolish. Ninety percent of all alcoholics have at least one episode of heavy drinking in their first year of sobriety, even those who eventually get and remain sober for the rest of their lives. However, by year three of sobriety, the rate of alcoholics who go back to drinking is down to about 10%.

**While it might not be a perfect fit,
it is possible that an effort to have an amicable divorce
might include serious problems in the first year,
but have a 90% chance of running very nicely by year three.**

If someone were to ask children who were raised in a functional family with separated parents who had a sensible divorce, they might respond with something like the following:

"The first year was pretty rough. They tried to get along, but there were lots of problems. We hated it. But then it started going really well. They got along, were both there for us at all times, were very flexible with the custody schedule and backed each other up when we were being jerks. It went very well and still does. They were both at our weddings and even danced together. Both are now involved with helping take care of our kids. It is great."

Make sense?

Chapter 6

Ten Disagreement Resolution Skills[17] Needed for a Sensible Divorce and Our Four Step Goal Based Planning Template for Making Collaborative Decisions

History and rule-making—in brief. Throughout history, differences and disagreements were handled by rules, and when people broke the rules, wars, murder and abandonment resulted. One set of the rules, regarding marriage, was that men and women play certain prescribed roles, and, in almost all cultures, men controlled women and set the rules.

For example, in most cultures, until the late 19th and early 20th century, women could not own property. Even today, Opportunity International, a micro-financing charity group, tells us that women do most of the work in poor cultures, but men own almost all of the land. Differences and disagreements were settled easily: men made the final decisions.

---

[17] We also refer to our Ten Disagreement Resolution Skills as our "DR Skills".

There was no such thing as an egalitarian marriage in which both spouses have equal say-so, until very recently, and only in a few cultures. In the United States, and in some other countries, the rules began changing at the beginning of the 20th century with women being designated as primary caregivers of children. This was true in marriage, although with fathers often having the final say in a disagreement, but even more so, in divorce. Mothers almost exclusively got the children in a divorce.

The evolution of rule-making- again in brief. Throughout the 20th century, the egalitarian marriage and the egalitarian divorce took hold. This meant that both men and women began to have equal say-so about what happened in the marriage and what happens in a divorce. The implication is that humans had to develop skills for dealing with differences and disagreements because there were no rules about who had the final word. This cultural development has been not only a boon in many ways, but also has presented special challenges.

It took years to begin to figure out what skills people needed to resolve differences and disagreement successfully. It has also taken years to understand how to raise children with separated parents successfully. That research is ongoing, but already we have learned a great deal.

**There are ten Disagreement Resolution Skills
needed for a sensible divorce,
especially when the spouses have children.
They fall into four categories.[18]**

1. Having the Right Mindset:

SKILL #1: Overcoming personal bias
SKILL #2: Bridging the gap between realities
SKILL #3: Getting perspective

---

[18] Having the right Mindset is covered in Skills 1-3. Learning to manage feelings and emotions are covered in Skills 4-6. There is still the task of resolving disagreements. The final four Disagreement Resolution Skills are covered in Skills 7-10.

2. Managing Feelings and Emotions:

SKILL #4: Identifying and processing core feelings
SKILL #5: Developing the ability to be vulnerable in relationships
SKILL #6: Hearing criticism in a healthy way

3. Implementing Effective Problem-solving and Decision-making Techniques:

SKILL #7: Identifying a problem in a way that leads to a solution
SKILL #8: Resolving a disagreement when both people are 'right'
SKILL #9: Making decisions that accomplish both people's goals

4. Recovering from Destructive Conflict Quickly:

SKILL #10: Keeping it short and clean, resolving the disagreement and repairing the relationship damage

Before introducing and defining our Ten DR Skills, we need to address some preliminary issues.

When spouses divorce, there are three major mistakes (see below) that are very tempting to make. When parties are divorced but have a messy divorce, unfortunately, they usually continue to make these identical mistakes.

To have a sensible divorce, these three major mistakes must be avoided, or if already present, corrected:

1. **The waste of psychological energy to dwell on the past.** Humans are lucky enough to remember the past because this gives them useful information on decisions to make for the future. However, '*living in the past*' robs people of a future. Instead of remembering the past, about which people have no control, they should be facing the future, where decisions and actions shape their lives.

Maintaining a focus on a past marriage taints the future, and yet this is exactly what ex-spouses do in a messy divorce. New experiences are just added on to the past and are more fodder for the cannons that they keep firing at one another.

2. **Negative reconstruction of spousal identities.** Janet Johnston, a prominent divorce researcher, identified a common pattern in messy divorces that she labelled *"the negative reconstruction of spousal identities"*.[19]

In order to 'explain' a failed marriage while blaming the other spouse, ex-spouses actually rewrite history, reinterpreting their marriage and their ex-spouse in increasingly negative ways. They pretend that all the good that they saw in one another early on was fake.

This might provide temporary comfort to a wounded ego, making the failure entirely the other spouse's fault and oneself as the innocent victim. However, this creates a delusion that makes it impossible to work cooperatively with a co-parent.

3. **Blame-frame.** If you blame someone else for your problems, you are by definition making yourself powerless to fix the problem. Only the person blamed can fix the problem. Making your happiness completely dependent on your ex-spouse, who might not care whether or not you are happy, is a serious mistake. Blame can temporarily restore a personal sense of being okay, but the price is very high. Because blame points the finger at the other spouse, making him or her the focus, the core feelings of sadness, guilt and shame never get processed. When this happens, people get locked into an emotional box and cannot get out.

This is the reason that people who have been divorced for many years talk about their divorce like it just happened. They are emotionally stuck in the blame-frame.

Ten Dispute Resolution Skills

Next, we return to our Ten Dispute Resolution Skills.

1. Having the Right Mindset.

---

[19] Johnston, J. (1988) *Impasses in Divorce.*

Skill #1. Overcoming Personal Bias:

This skill sounds a little complicated, but it is not. Humans developed natural tendencies that were important to survival at one point in our species' history, but they can interfere in relationships.[20]

These tendencies are:
1. Overconfidence Bias
2. Us-Them Tribal Warfare Bias
3. Judgment Bias

What Are These Three Natural Tendencies?

Overconfidence Bias, is just what it sounds like. People tend to think of themselves as better than they objectively are. People have a very difficult time seeing themselves objectively. When they hear a recording of their voice, it does not seem to sound like them. We have a psychologist friend and colleague who videotapes his patients while they describe difficulties they have in their marriage, and he then shows the recording to the patients. Most patients are very surprised at what they look like. More important, they soon begin to understand why their spouse reacted a certain way. When people disagree with another person, they tend to think that they are right and the other person is wrong. Because people are overconfident, if they have a problem in a relationship, they tend to think that it is the other person causing the problem, which leads to anger and blame. In addition, because the other person is also likely overconfident, he/she does the same thing and ends up angrily blaming. Both people think they are the one trying to cooperate, where the problem rests with the other person. Round and round they go.

Us-Them Tribal Warfare/Bias was key to surviving when resources, like food, were scarce. Early humans were not only competing with other species for those resources, they were also competing with other groups of humans. Usually organized into families and tribes, one group would attempt to get the resources, sometimes warring with other tribes in the same area. Whole versions of our species went extinct as a result of this thinking.

---

[20] Sapolsky, Robert. (2017) *Behave: Human Behavior at our Best and our Worst.*

For example, one hypothesis is that Homo Sapiens killed off Neanderthals, or at least crowded them out of areas with resources. In parts of the modern world where resources are not scarce, people channel Us-Them Tribal Warfare into less destructive activities, such as sports, lawsuits and divorce. Most divorces start out with a competition for resources: property, future income and time with children.

A once loved spouse becomes 'them', along with those on 'the other side', such as his or her attorney and any friends or extended family members who took the ex's side. 'We' of course are the 'us'. At the same time, the ex's perspective is that they are 'us' and we are 'them'. The gravitational pull leads to litigation that feels like warfare, sometimes which can last well beyond the divorce itself. Sound familiar?

Judgment Bias, is a little subtler. Social researchers, such as Robert Sopolsky, point out that people judge others by their actions, but judge themselves by their intentions. Because of this, a parent might judge their ex for an action negatively, but judge themselves positively for the same action because they had '*good intentions*'.

For example, a mother thinks she is being honest with the children and that the father is '*badmouthing*' her, but they are both doing the same thing. In another example, one parent is viewed as '*hitting*' the children, but the other parent is viewed as '*spanking*' to teach a lesson. In other words, '*hitting*' is wrong when it is done by the other parent, but '*spanking*' to teach a lesson is okay, because the intention is good.

Overcoming personal bias is accomplished by seeing through these natural tendencies and being objective about ourselves and our CPP.[21]

Most people are ordinary and not superior to others. When people have problems in their relationships, they are usually at least part of the cause. When they blame, even if they are at least partially right, it does not solve the problem. Respectful cooperation solves problems. Even though people are tempted to take an 'Us-Them' perspective, they can step back and remember that they probably

---

[21] Throughout this book, we will generally use the acronym "CPP" when referring to Co-parenting Partner.

share similar long-term goals with their CPP, which are goals that can only be reached through cooperation.

Destructive actions are destructive, no matter what the intention is. People should judge themselves by their own actions, not their intentions.

> **Overcoming personal bias is no easy task,**
> **but doing so simply means learning**
> **and practicing the skills involved**
> **and mentioned in the above paragraphs.**

Summary: Even when the CPP fails to develop these skills, one parent can learn and use them to prevent or escape destructive conflict. If one CPP angrily says that she or he is helping with homework and the CPP had better do the same, the other parent can respond by saying that they both want their child to do well in school and should talk about how they can accomplish that. Goal: To be humble, avoiding tribal warfare and judging actions, not intentions, might seem challenging, but is healthy and effective.

Skill #2. Bridging the Gap with Different Realities:

This skill involves bridging the gap between two different realities and is closely related to Skill #3 (below). People live in their own world, which differs dramatically from the world where others live. This is because we all have experiences not shared by others, different ways of interpreting our experiences, and even have unique differences in what we pay attention to and to which we give value. When people see that another person is living in a different world, they sometimes judge them as not understanding what is *'really'* going on or even lying. People have a hard time accepting that what is going on in the other person's world can be true, especially when it differs from what is going on in their world (which can also be true). Inevitably, they say things like, "*That is not what happened,*" instead of recognizing that it really did happen in the other person's world.

> **People are able to bridge the gap between two different realities**
> **(i.e., worlds) with effective communication and rules.**

In effective relationships, there is usually a little of both: effective communication and rules. Good communication involves listening and asking questions, so that two people can understand each other's world and get the whole picture. However, sometimes it takes a rule. For example, one spouse might have come from a family in which teasing includes swearing, but the other spouse might react very negatively and feel denigrated as a person. These parents might never understand each other's world and might simply need to make a rule that there is no swearing when communicating with each other. Why are rules so effective? If everyone knows the rules, people can have high functioning relationships, even when they do not understand the other person. Think of a card game. If everyone knows the rules, they can play without understanding or even knowing anything about the other person.

Summary: Effective communication takes a good deal of patience and a genuine interest, both of which might be in short supply during or after a divorce. However, when there are children involved, learning to listen, ask questions and, when necessary, make rules, is a must. For example, one parent might react very poorly to any disrespectful behavior (e.g., *rolling the eyes*), and the other parent might not understand why the CPP gets so upset. Thinking the other parent is '*wrong*' for getting so upset is an example of personal bias (see Skill #1). A rule to be respectful of one another, including not rolling eyes, should solve the problem.

Skill #3. Getting Perspective:

Getting perspective is looking at a situation from another person's point of view. This sounds like Skill #2, but takes it one step further. The challenge of this skill is using imagination. Even when they agree on reality, people have very different points of view because of their histories, personalities, values, differing information and even what they pay attention to and what they don't. In order to be effective in relationships, people have to have the skill called perspective-taking. This means looking at a situation from another person's point of view. Research shows that this skill can be learned.

In 1990, Howard Zehr introduced restorative justice in the United States.[22] Beginning with delinquent criminals, the delinquent child meets with the victim of the crime, with a mediator and often with others who were affected, such as family members. The mediator solicits the perspectives of both the victim and the delinquent, and others present who were affected by the crime, and they work out reparations (e.g., the delinquent might mow the victim's lawn ten times at no charge).

Actual outcomes have included the following:

1. The victims were able to see the perspective of the delinquent, and the delinquent was able to see the perspective of the victim.
2. Both the victim and the delinquent developed empathy for one another.
3. Victims reported that the process resolved the bad feelings.
4. Delinquents were much less likely to re-offend in the future because they learned to see the perspective of victims.

This is a true win-win. These findings led to research on teaching perspective-taking simply by presenting situations (e.g., a photograph of a person is some situation) and asking subjects to report what they think people in the situations might be thinking and feeling. Clumsy at first, subjects became better and better at perspective-taking. Perspective taking can be learned, but takes practice.

Summary: The Mindset of getting perspective undergirds most of our other Skills. It also turns the tables on conflict. Assume one parent accuses the other parent of something. Rather than getting defensive, by asking a few questions, the accused parent can say something like, "*I can see from your point of view that what you're saying makes sense*". The accused person might add something like, "*But you are missing some information from my perspective*".

This approach will in most situations deflate the anger and make problem-solving possible, particularly if the people involved are humble, resist the temptation to engage in tribal warfare and judge themselves by actions, not intentions. Most people facing differences try to get their point of view across, but do not really listen to the other person.

---

[22] Restorative justice had been practiced in other cultures for a long time, such as Maori in New Zealand.

To get the other person's perspective means asking something like, "*I want to understand your point of view about X, but I need a little more information*" and then really listening.

2. Managing Feelings and Emotions.[23]

Skill #4. Identifying and Processing Core Feelings, Including the Ability to Have Mixed Feelings and Ambivalence:

It is so simple to blame another person for our suffering, to be angry at them and even hate them. This is because anger, blame and hate are Defensive Emotions. This means they are the emotions people would **rather** feel when compared to the **core** feelings under the surface. The dominant Core Feelings involved in a divorce are sadness, shame, fear and insecurity. These are difficult feelings to focus on, so people jump to blaming and anger instead. Anger and blame can feel so real, but they are just cover-ups for the Core Feelings.

When a meaningful relationship ends, it is sad. The longer people had that relationship, the sadder it is. A divorce might include, or at least the hope for relief from pain, but a divorce really means giving up each other and even giving up the hopes and dreams people had of a life together. They lose the family experience that they wanted for their children. They lose some friends and often beloved extended family members of their spouse.

A divorce also ignites people's fears. They are unsure how money will work out. i.e., how raising children as separated parents will work out and whether or not their children will be '*scarred for life*'. They also wonder if they will want another relationship, and if they do, will they find one that works? Going on the 'dating market' raises fears and insecurities. Although people might blame their spouse, most people know that they played a part in what feels like a failure, so a Core Feeling is guilt. People are often ashamed of having a 'failed marriage', which they also try to cover-up by blaming the ex-spouse.

---

[23] Avoiding our four problematic emotions: blaming, distrusting, taking things personally, and thinking inferentially are introduced and discussed in detail in Chapter 2. Sensible solutions for processing challenging feelings are introduced and discussed in Chapter 11.

When people fail to resolve these core feelings, they stay on guard and are sensitive to and quick to blame their ex-spouse. The key is to work on the sadness, guilt, shame, fears and insecurities.

This means going back to painful experiences. Asking questions, *"What were our hopes when we decided to have children?"* *"What am I afraid of?"* *"What have I lost?"* *"What are my insecurities about my future?"* and so on.

The goal is to resolve those Core Feelings and leave behind the anger and the blame.

Sadness is resolved by going through grief. Guilt is resolved by forgiving oneself and asking forgiveness from the spouse. Shame is resolved by being open and taking some responsibility for the failure. Fear is resolved by developing a plan for going forward. Fear and insecurities are resolved by being humble and open with people.

Summary: Most divorcing spouses have mixed feelings about each other. However, the good feelings are hard to handle when losing someone once loved. By being aware of the mixed feelings, good and bad, people can maintain a healthy balance. When a person can say that they have mixed feelings about their CPP, that they just got stuck in the marriage and that they both did the best they could do at the time, a person can let go of the shackles of a messy, perhaps nasty, divorce.

Skill #5. Developing the Ability to be Vulnerable in Relationships:

This skill is quite simple, and yet is probably the most emotionally difficult skill to practice. In order to understand this skill, we take a look at insecurity versus confidence. Insecurity in relationships comes when we fear losing control of a situation because we do not know what will happen next. For example, imagine that you are at the end of a first date with someone you like and to whom you are attracted. Do you ask for a kiss? Do you ask for a second date? When you do ask, you are out of control and do not know what will happen. If you get a "yes," you are happy and relieved, but what if you get a "no?"

Most people grow up with insecurities but develop ways to avoid experiencing the fear undergirding those insecurities. People develop ways of creating a social image that they think will get people to like them, or take them seriously, or be attracted to them. People rehearse conversations with potential employers or memorize a speech. People might learn to make excuses for behavior or failures and give 'spin' to stories to try to convince other people that they did not really make a mistake or do something wrong.

If people age in a healthy way, they learn that being rigorously honest with others, being who they really are, saying what they are actually thinking, being open about mistakes, admitting to wrong-doing and apologizing and taking responsibility, reduces insecurities and develops confidence. As people slowly move into adulthood, they feel more confident and less insecure. When mistakes are pointed out, they can admit to them and laugh at themselves. They do not blame other people, make excuses or lie for wrong-doing or failures.

Not everyone learns that taking responsibility
and being rigorously honest resolves insecurities.

Many people maintain defence mechanisms to avoid being vulnerable in relationships. As they do, they continue to be insecure and afraid of losing control. Often, these people have good reason to feel afraid, because of bad experiences while growing up.

The solution to those insecurities
is to practice being vulnerable in relationships.

Summary: Practicing this skill involves being rigorously honest, in a respectful manner, taking responsibility for yourself, and being humble. Being humble simply means acknowledging that you are a flawed person who makes mistakes, being selfish when you shouldn't be, saying and doing things you shouldn't, not looking perfect, and so on. The reason this resolves insecurity is two-fold: First, people find out that bad things do not happen often when you are forthright. In fact, people will generally find you refreshing and attractive. Second, people find out it is not so bad when bad things do happen. In other words, people become confident.

In cases of divorce conflict, both CPP's generally have difficulty being vulnerable with one another. During the marriage, both have experienced real pain with each other and fear more pain. Yet, the path out of this quagmire is by practicing being vulnerable.

Skill #6. Hearing Criticism in a Healthy Way:

Criticism comes in many flavors. Sometimes a criticism is very direct (*"You are such an a**hole"*), sometimes they are a bit subtler (*"If you loved the kids, you would be on time"*), and sometimes there are no words involved at all (just a sneer and/or rolling of the eyes). Some criticisms are implied, but not directly communicated, such as when a parent greets the other parent and the other parent ignores the gesture. In divorce conflict, these criticisms often provoke angry responses, like defensive behavior, angry criticisms of the other person, or ignoring the other person.

The root of all these inappropriate responses is in taking criticisms personally.

The skill here is in not taking criticisms personally, because criticisms generally are not personal. They tell us more about the person doing the criticizing. There is no rational connection between loving children and being on time. A sneer and a rolling of the eyes is an ineffective way of dealing with hurt or anger. Most criticisms are a poor way of identifying a problem because they do not suggest a solution. Criticisms generally say something more about the person making the criticism, not the person being criticized, and therefore, they are not personal.

It takes practice to get used to not taking criticisms personally, but when accomplished, people find that they escape the negative reactions to them. For example, in response to the *"You are such an a**hole"* comment, you might respond: *"I am truly sorry that you think that"*. Sometimes a polite smile will be sufficient.

Caveat: Some criticisms have useful information, so, it is worth listening, even though you are not taking it personally.

Here is the twist. Because some criticisms have useful information, it is worth listening. For example, "*If you loved the children, you wouldn't be late. The children were really upset*". Here, you would not take the criticism personally, but there is useful information about the children. You might respond, "*Thank you for telling me this. I will talk with the children about it*". In another example, "*You are such an a**hole for telling your sister that I am a liar*". If it is true that you told your sister this, this is useful information. You might respond, "*You are right. Neither one of us should be saying bad things about each other to other people. I am sorry and will try to correct this with my sister*". Here, the response is to the useful information, because you did not take the name-calling personally.

Summary: In short, it is a useful skill to avoid or escape divorce conflict by not taking criticisms personally. Instead, listen carefully and respectfully to the criticism in case it contains useful information. It can take time to get good at this skill, but it is well worth it.

3.   Implementing Effective Problem-solving and Decision-making Techniques.

Once a person has the right Mindset and learns to manage feelings and emotions well, there is still the task of resolving disagreements. The final four skills are our Disagreement Resolution Skills.

Skill #7. Identifying a Problem in a Way That Leads to a Solution:

When a problem comes up that a person would like to solve, it helps to define the problem in a way that leads to a solution. While this sounds simple, in human relationships, people can identify a problem and define it in a way that leads to conflict **or** to solutions.

Assuming that solutions are better than conflict, being skilled in defining problems makes a good deal of sense. For example, compare the following before and after re-framing:

Before the Reframe:

"You fought so hard to get your precious daily calls, but your telephone call last night really upset Sally. I told you it was a bad idea. That is the end to those calls."

After the Reframe:

"Sally was very upset by your call last night. She cried and kept saying that she missed you. We should try to come up with a way that she does not miss us so much when she is at the other house."

In the first example, the problem is identified, but not in a way that leads to a solution for the actual problem. Sally is not going to miss her mother less just because her mother does not call. The second example can lead to a solution because the problem is identified in a way that can be solved.

The first example leads to more conflict, while the second example promotes cooperation on a problem that both parents likely care about *and are willing to solve.*

Let's try another example.

Before the Reframe:

"You kept the good jeans that I bought and sent him back in his crappy old clothes. I expect him to come back with the clothes that I send."

After the Reframe:

"I can see that the logistics of clothing going back and forth is complicated. We need a system for getting the right clothes at the right house at the right time. We will probably need a system like that for sporting equipment, school work and who knows what else. Let's come up with something?"

In the first version, the person is demanding his or her solution, which is unlikely to work and puts the burden on the child to wear the exact same clothes back and forth. Anger and blame are trumping common sense. In the second version, the person took time to identify the underlying problem and defined it is a way that can lead to a solution. They can now find a way to deal with the logistical problems of the child spending time in two homes.

In both of the above examples, the skill is to step back from impulsive emotional reactions and really focus on the underlying problem. Then, the problem has to be defined in a way that leads to a solution.

Let's take one more example, but follow it through the process of applying this skill.

Parent A is thirty minutes late and has a habit of being late. Parent B had plans and has been scrambling to change plans because the child is late. Parent B gets upset. Rather than saying anything when Parent A arrives, Parent B decides to think about the problem and come up with a Plan.

A couple of days later, Parent B sends an email:

"When you are late bringing the children, any plans that I have can get disrupted, as happened a couple of days ago. No one can be on time all of the time, and some people have more difficulty with that than others. However, we need to come up with a way that plans are not disrupted by the other parent being late. Can you put some thought into what you could do to avoid disrupting plans, and I will put some thought into what I could do and then maybe we could talk?"

This changes the definition of the problem from a parent is late to the definition that transitions from one parent to the other should not disrupt plans. That definition leads to solutions.

An important feature of defining a problem in a way that leads to solutions is that while cooperation is promoted, it is not required. If the problem is defined as Parent A as being late, Parent B has no control of the solution, and the problem is only solved if Parent A is always on time. If the problem is defined as transitions should not disrupt plans, a cooperative solution will be more effective. In addition, just Parent B can solve the problem without any cooperation from Parent A. A Solution emerged: It could be proposed that Parent B pick the children up or Parent B could always allow extra time before plans are finalized in case Parent A is late.

Summary: Rather than reacting based on emotions when a problem comes up, it is important to take time to come up with a definition of a problem that has solutions.

Skill #8. Resolving a Disagreement When Both People are 'Right':

This Skill is also challenging, but not for emotional reasons. The challenge is about life assumptions. Most people assume that there is only one 'right' answer. Thus, if they disagree with someone, and believe that they are 'right', they try to prove the other person is 'wrong'. If the other person believes that he or she is 'right', that person (of course) does the same thing. This can be a healthy first step, because sometimes, one person is 'right' and can prove the other person is 'wrong'. If the other person is healthy, he or she will admit it. Likewise, the other person might prove us 'wrong', and, if he or she is healthy, will be vulnerable and admit it.

However, often in relationships, after attempts to prove who is 'right' fail, people are tempted to escalate the argument. This can lead to very destructive conflict. Instead of discussing a topic, people start personal attacks on each other, develop increasing hostility and create emotional distance. They might even run to their attorney and try to get a judge to agree with them.

The challenge is to resolve a disagreement when both people are 'right'. This is not the bogus, "*Let's agree to disagree,*" where the person secretly still thinks that he or she is 'right' and the other person is 'wrong'. That is a stand-off, not a resolution. People must really accept that both people are 'right'. The difference is the result of different values, what people focus on, differing histories, new but different information and just plain old human nature.

To resolve these disagreements, the first Step is trying to prove that they are 'right' and that the other person is 'wrong'. The next Step is to discuss the differences that led to their opinions, including the values that affect the topic, histories, what is considered important and unimportant and the differences in the information that people have. They come to an understanding of the larger picture and the differences undergirding the disagreement. If they need to make a decision, and the disagreement is about what will be decided, people have to step back and consider options that accomplish as much as possible of what both people feel is important and what best fits both people's values,

There are three possible alternatives:

1. **There is more than one way to 'skin a cat'!** As gross as that saying is, it also is true. There are usually many more options to consider when people get stuck on just the two options about which they are arguing. They can step back from the argument and brainstorm other

options that accomplish more of what is important to both of them. Real 'winning' an argument is when both people feel that what is important to them was included in the solution, even if they do not get everything that they want.

2. **Different levels of importance matter.** It can be helpful to measure these differences. Some arguments do not have a third option. For example, Judy wants to abort a pregnancy, and Bob disagrees. They first argue about who is 'right', but after a while, they realize that both are 'right'. They then discuss the values, points of focus, histories and information that they each have. This is an intense discussion, but does not resolve the question. They decide to measure the level of importance on a scale of 0 to 10. Judy says that she is an 8, because of the disruptions to her life having a child will bring. It is very important. Bob says he is a 10, and could not live with himself, which would likely mean ending his relationship with Judy. They do not abort the baby.[24]

3. **Pace is important.** If two people want to run together, they have to run at the pace of the slower runner. For example, Jim wants their 2-year-old to start day care and Sally does not. She wants to stay home with the child for at least one more year before starting day care and going back to work. They stop arguing about who is right, but instead, share information, histories, values etc. Ultimately, it comes down to Sally just not being ready leave the baby and return to work. They hold off on day care. Jim has to accept that if they are going to work together, he has to operate at Sally's pace.

Summary: The Skill here involves what to do next when both people continue to believe that they are 'right'. If people believe that there is only one 'right', arguments escalate and become increasingly destructive. On the other hand, if they believe that there can be more than one 'right', the disagreement can change directions and generate a solution. If a decision must be made, they will search to find one that works for both people.

The Skill here is one Mindset (that there are two 'rights') and applying the technique of asking questions about what the other person is trying to accomplish and coming up with ways to accomplish what both people think is important.

---

[24] One can see the importance of honesty here.

Skill #9. Making Decisions that Accomplish Both People's Goals:

The focus of this skill is on making joint decisions. Collaborative decision-making, meaning how decisions are made when more than one person is involved, has been heavily studied. Much of that research discovered flaws in the way that people made decisions, but some of that research uncovered the secret to successful decision-making.

Separated parents must make many collaborative decisions, well beyond what is dictated by law. If separated parents have difficulty collaborating on decisions, they often put the burden on the shoulders of their children by each making unilateral decisions in their separate homes. For example, teaching good work habits involves establishing good routines with rules, so that the child just does it out of habit. In order to do this, the routines and rules have to be similar in both homes.

What happens if the routines are different in the two homes? Instead of learning good work habits, the child tries to learn how to adapt to the two settings. This can get even crazier when one parent works hard to establish a routine and the other parent leaves it up to the child to get the work done. This child grows up knowing he or she should be getting some things done, but cannot seem to force themselves to do it.

Of course, the solution is that parents should coordinate their routines, but this involves making decisions together. Decisions that work best are those that are made collaboratively. Deciding how much say-so to give the child in the selection of extracurricular activities, and how much time each week can be spent in those activities, are just two more practical examples of working together to make collaborative decisions, even including input from the children.

The obstacle for separated parents is having difficulty collaborating on a decision. Sadly, it rarely has to do with who is right. It mostly has to do with people wanting to win arguments. For example, the habit of doing homework immediately after school is not superior to doing it immediately after dinner. What matters is doing it the same way in both homes. The goal is to teach good work habits.

As we presented earlier in Chapters 4 and here in Chapter 6, making collaborative decisions, has been studied. Again, it involves following our Four Step Goal Based Planning Template for Collaborative Decision-Making.

Four Step Goal Based Planning Process
for Making Collaborative Decisions

A Family Planning Example.

Step #1: Describe in detail the current situation.

1. **Make an appointment and discuss the current situation. This should be the easiest of the Four Steps.**

"Melanie [12-year-old daughter who has shown some talent playing soccer] says that she wants to join a summer soccer league. Some of her teammates are also planning to join. When can we have a telephone call to discuss this?"

2. **At the initial appointment, share information and decide what additional information is needed and how to get it.**

At the telephone call: *"We know that she loves playing and is quite good at it. I think that we both want to support her interests. But a summer league might interfere with vacations and the logistics of getting her to and from practices and games might be complicated."*

"I will get the league schedule. We should also find out from the coach if she can miss a game or two for family vacations."
"I would like to know if there is some traveling to games and what the costs will be. Can you check that when you get the schedule or talk with the coach?"
"Sure. I'll give you a call when I have that information."
"I will nail down the dates for our trip up north. I won't make any other plans until I hear from you."

At the second phone call: *"Did you get the schedule and signup sheets that I faxed you?"*

"Yes. It looks doable because it is over by the end of July. Our trip up north is in August."

"Our vacation is over July 4th week, but the coach said that she can miss a game for that. It is pricey though, and there is some travel on Saturdays. Money is tight here right now. It is more than twice the spring league."

"If we decide to do it, I can pay a little more. Practices are a little early though. Might be tight for me getting out of work. Can she bike over?"

"We can ask her if she will bike to practices, but in a pinch, I could take her. If she is at your house, I can pick her up and take her. One of the advantages of working from home, I guess."

Step #2: List each spouse's long-term goals, specific to the decisions being made.

Note: Remember, the best decisions are those that accomplish both parent's goals. List the options and the pros and cons of each option.

"I think that we both want to support her in soccer. It is good for her social development with teammates, her sense of responsibility and commitment and who knows, maybe she has a real future with soccer. Might even help pay for college."

"I really like the skill building, and boy it will be nice if she gets really into it as she goes through her teen years. I also heard on public radio that kids who are involved in extracurricular activities tend to do better in school across the board."

"I suppose that we could look into another summer league with less travel, but I think Melanie has her heart set on this league because her friends will be on it. I think that is important too."

Step #3: Plan the steps for reaching long-term goals.

Choose an option. If unclear which option is the best, just choose one and agree to evaluate the choice when there is more information.

Note: If disagreement persists on the options, go back to each parent's goals and what they are trying to accomplish and come up with another option that accomplishes as much possible for what both parents want to accomplish.

"Okay, I'll sign her up and pay for it. You agreed to take her to get her uniform and pay for it."

"Thanks, by the way, for covering this. I really appreciate it. I'll talk to her about biking to practices."

"You're welcome, but you would do the same if you could. Maybe we should get another bike for my place, rather than taking her bike back and forth. I will look into that."

Step #4: List the obstacles and steps to overcome them and create a Plan.

"We need to set up a system for Melanie getting to practices and calling you if she is going to need a ride. I am also thinking that we are going to have to be pretty flexible on the weekends in case Jimmy does not want to go to a game. We should touch base every week in case we need him to go to the other house on game days."

Some parents might read the above and say, *"I wish"* or *"If we could talk like that, we'd still be married."* It might be true that if parents had this skill, they might still be married, but intimacy is much more complicated than a business-like relationship with a CPP. That the marriage did not last is sad, but the focus should now be on developing a good future for the co-parenting relationship.[25]

The solution is to agree on rules for this process and having meetings together to discuss the issue and come up with a solution. Rules can be developed for these meetings. One rule might be to discuss one decision at a time. Another might be to stay on topic and agree on a way to get back on topic if they get off. Another might be to be courteous and respectful by listening to each other, not interrupting, not making denigrating comments and so on. Parents must always

---

[25] If you get serious about salvaging your marriage with the information in this book, you might like to buy our book applying comparable skills to marriage: *The Road to Marital Success is Unpaved: Seven Skills for Making Marriage Work.* Austin McCauley. The book is available, including in digital form, at most retailers. www.marriageanddivorce.org or www.Amazon.com.

have the goal of accomplishing as much for both parents as possible, rather than trying to be 'right' about something.

Summary: Like any other skill, this takes practice and there will be lots of mistakes in the early stages. However, it is well worth sticking to it. The first few times will be anxious, but in a year, the parents will look forward to this collaborative process because of the improvements in their lives and the child's family experience. A side benefit for parents is that it will teach their child this skill by modeling it, so that their child can take the skill into adulthood.

4.   Recovering from Destructive Conflict Quickly.

Skill #10. Keeping it short and clean, resolving the disagreement and repairing the relationship damage:

While simple in theory, in practice this Skill requires all of the other nine Skills—especially looking at the other person's point of view and having healthy reactions to criticism and blame by each other.

The first point is to recognize that all substantial relationships have disagreements, whether that is with a friend, an extended family member, an ex-spouse or even children. Disagreements are unavoidable. Studies comparing successful marriages with unsuccessful ones discovered that successful relationships have as many, and, often as intense, disagreements with each other as people who get a divorce. The difference is how the disagreements are handled.

In successful relationships, the spouses keep it mostly clean and stay on topic. In unsuccessful relationships, people get way off topic, get personal and fight dirty. They have the same problem over and over because they never arrive at a solution. When a successful relationship gets personal and dirty, they stop and repair the damage with apologies and taking responsibility for their mistake.

However, successful relationships take one more step that is extremely important: they keep the disagreement contained in time by having a way to recover quickly. The reason this is so important is very practical. If a relationship spends about 10% of their time in conflict, this frees them up to spend 90% of their time conflict free with one another. If they spend 90% of their time in conflict, there is far too little good time left to absorb the pain and frustration of conflict.

In a co-parenting relationship, limiting conflict time by recovering quickly opens the door to enjoy raising children together, with both being at activities and happy to see one another. Whether or not the other parent is cooperative, at least one parent can take the initiative-keeping disagreements clean, taking responsibility and apologizing when it is called for, asking questions to try to understand the other parent's point of view, taking blame and criticism from the other parent in a healthy manner and always looking for definitions of a problem that have solutions. This can make a big difference.

When co-parents have disagreement, they need to cool down, look at the situation from the other person's point of view, be honest with themselves about their part in it, pledge to work on improving their part in the co-parenting relationship, and acknowledge this to each other, including an apology, if warranted.

Summary: Co-parenting relationships can improve by working on the ten skills presented in this chapter and working on the Five Tasks and Rules for Successful Co-parenting presented in the next Chapter.

It is best if both parents work on these skills, but even if only one of them works on the skills, the co-parenting relationship can improve. If both parents learn and use these skills, the co-parenting relationship can and will improve dramatically. This is accomplished by:

1. Having the right Mindset
2. Managing feelings and emotions
3. Implementing effective problem-solving and decision-making techniques
4. Recovering from destructive conflict quickly

Chapter 7
Five Tasks and Rules for Successful Co-Parenting

Successful co-parents perform Co-Parenting Tasks[26] on a regular basis.[27] by applying our DR Skills described in the prior chapter Those Tasks are:

1. **Sharing Information:** In order to parent well as a team, co-parents must communicate regularly so they can share information, and not solely by texting and emails (which should not be the primary method of communication). The goal is for both parents to have all of the relevant information that they need to parent well as a team. That includes:

    a. **General information:** General information should be shared in a once or twice a week meeting or telephone call.

    b. **Emergency information:** Emergency information is essential when both parents want to know what is happening in an

---

[26] In this Chapter, we provide a detailed treatment of the Five Tasks for Successful Co-parenting. In our Chapter 9 Summary, we reframe the Five Tasks in a slightly different manner to highlight the identical issue.

[27] For a detailed Guide to these tasks, at a modest cost of approximately $20, you can order our *Coparenting Training Workbook,* authored by Dr Kenneth H. Waldron from www.unhookedmedia.com.

emergency. This includes the means to getting in contact as soon as possible, possibly with the use of texting in this situation.

c.   **Transition information:** When receiving a child, there might be information that helps the receiving parent know what to do. This could also be done by texting or at the transition.

d.   **Paperwork:** Parents should ensure that both of them see all relevant paperwork (e.g., activity schedules).

2. **Having Access and Flexibility in the Parenting Time Schedule:** A custody schedule is a must, which primarily means that the parents know who is responsible at any given time for the children. It should not be a rigid schedule that locks the other parent out of the children's lives. As a general rule, parents should have access to the children, and the children should have access to the parents independent of the custody schedule. Part of that is not only just a chance to talk (e.g., phone calls or stopping by after work) but also real flexibility in the schedule (e.g., changing the schedule for events and opportunities). Access can also include others, such as grandparents.

3. **Planning Child-focused Transitions:** Going from house to house can be stressful for children, and even for their parents. Successful co-parents put a lot of energy into planning transitions that are as smooth as possible.

There should be no dropping the kids off at the curb, and the like. They also plan getting important 'stuff' back and forth smoothly (e.g., sports gear). They should ask the children if there is anything else they can do to make transitions work better (e.g., come into each other's homes when the children invite them in to show them something).

4. **Coordinating Homes to be Similar:** A simple but important fact about raising children is their need for structure and discipline. This includes clear rules, routines, expectations, chores and responsibilities and a well understood system of rewards and punishments. This provides training for children so that they can eventually become confident, competent and independent adults.

A major risk to children when parents separate is that the training methods in their parents' homes will be substantially different. Instead of internalizing the skills of good training, children have to learn to adapt to the two different settings. This might not be so bad if the differences are small and matters of style, rather than of completely different approaches. The basics should be the same or very similar.

Successful co-parents design a system that is similar or the same in both homes. One outstanding study was done in California on young children with separated parents. Only about one-third of the children were developing normally. Two-thirds had moderate to serious problems. The parents with the one-third of the children doing well were amicable and made the effort to make the two homes the same or very similar with regard to rules and routines. A couple of sets of parents even went so far as to buy the same furniture for the children's rooms.

Successful co-parents have those discussions and agree: What should be bedtimes? How much screen time should there be? What chores and responsibilities should the children have? What should a homework routine look like? And so on. They continue to have those discussions as the children get older and need different approaches.

5. **Making Decisions, Solving Problems and Taking Action:** The final task for co-parents is to decide what decisions should be joint decisions and develop a successful decision-making procedure for those decisions and what problems will be best solved with the involvement of both parents. This may also include a procedure for solving those problems successfully.

Rules make it work!

When people interact with one another, in any setting, they establish rules of conduct. Even when enemy nations sit at the table at the United Nations, there are rules of conduct, such as taking turns talking, staying on topic, keeping voices down and so on. Roadways are dominated by rules. The point is, successful co-parenting relationships must have rules of conduct in order to work well. In messy divorces, spouses/co-parents do not establish effective rules and inadvertently give themselves permission to break conventional social rules.

To perform the **Five Tasks for Successful Co-parenting,** CPP's must establish Rules.

There can be General Rules that apply to all five Tasks:

1. Be pleasantly respectful at all times.

2. Never make demands and always make polite requests.
3. Be completely honest at all times.
4. Never blame and always identify problems or decisions to address.
5. Always check first if it is a good time to talk before launching into a discussion.
6. Only ask personal questions if you have already gotten permission to do so.
7. Always apologize for missteps.

AND

There can be Specific Rules that apply to a Specific Task:
1. When sharing information, cover everything on the list.
2. When sharing information, if a problem or a decision comes up, make a separate appointment to address it.
3. If a CPP gets too upset to talk reasonably, end the discussion, but the upset CPP must make the appointment to get back to the discussion.
4. Always take turns talking and listening, and never interrupt or escalate before the other CPP is finished.
5. When access or flexibility is requested, always try to grant it, and if impossible, look for alternatives.
6. Never bring up a problem or a decision at a transition. Stay focused on a smooth transition for the child.
7. Before initiating a new routine, rule or expectation with the children, make an appointment with the other parent to discuss it. As a goal, make every effort to have both homes be organized as similar as possible.
8. If a CPP defines a problem in a way that has no solution, coach the other parent on coming up with a different definition of the problem that does have a solution.
9. All problem-solving and decision-making should include attempting to accomplish the goals of both CPP's.

The above are, of course, only general suggestions, but CPP's should not take setting rules for interactions lightly. Additionally, setting rules is always a work-in-progress. Whenever there are the beginnings of a breakdown in the co-parenting relationship, try to develop a rule or rules to improve the situation.

Understanding the importance of our Ten Disagreement Resolution Skills is also critical.

Summary. The Five Tasks of Successful Co-parenting obviously require an ability to resolve disagreements, at least most of the time. Again, when co-parents agree, there is no problem, as long as they are thorough. Disagreements are inevitable, and the Ten DR Skills Model and Template discussed in the prior Chapter make disagreement resolution not only possible, but also rewarding to the parents. Decisions and problem-solving solutions, which include the input of both parents, are almost always superior to what each parent does on his or her own.

Chapter 8
Ten Traps of the Traditional Family Law System: Additional Challenges

A quick trip through history. In the current/traditional family law system, the focus is on legal outcomes. Legal systems were originally established in order to handle disputes between people. Based on the limited information that we have, early on, either the tribal leader or an elder might have listened to disputes and dispensed justice based on what he believed was wise and fair. Some cultures in Africa developed rules, such as the murder of a member of one tribe, must be compensated with the delivery of a certain number of camels. Kings, or their staff, came to settle disputes during the Middle Ages. In the sixteenth and seventeenth centuries, after popular uprisings that limited the power of kings, systems of justice relying on written law and judges were developed.

The theoretical principle undergirding modern judicial systems is that if two sides of a dispute present their best evidence, an impartial judge can settle the dispute with a fair conclusion. Humans, being a bit imperfect, have made this a little messier than was contemplated, but overall, it is a system that works fairly well.

However, we go back to the basic assumption: that the judicial system is for the settling of disputes. When people come into the system, it is assumed that they have a dispute and their interests are in conflict with one another. This is the reason that parties must have their own attorney. One attorney cannot represent both parties to a dispute.[28]

This assumption is certainly true in most disputes, but is it universally applicable in family law?

The focus in the legal system is on the legal outcome. This is also the focus of judges and the focus of attorneys. It is true in the current family law system, if the focus continues to be on legal outcomes, there probably will be a dispute, at least on some of those legal outcomes.

The current legal system inadvertently traps people into a negative and often painful adversarial divorce relationship.

In a dispute, the most rational approach is to take an aggressive competitive approach and attempt to prevail. However, the effect of doing so ignites a win-lose attitude. It generates a perspective that the other divorcing spouse is at least a competitor, if not an enemy, which generates bitter feelings about legal outcomes. In other words, the traditional family law system inadvertently traps people into a negative and often painful adversarial divorce relationship.

Added to the assumption of a dispute, the interest of the State in divorce is in the distribution of property—who gets what. This interest also has a long history in human affairs. First there were tribal rules, then religions and the nobility took over, and more recently the State took over with law and courts. In western cultures, men got the property because women could not own property. Historically, children were property and awarded to men. That all changed in the 20th century and is still changing. Most people do not think of children as property, for example, and women have established property rights. This made

---

[28] We recognize that disputes might have more than two parties, but for simplicity, we will assume two parties, as is the case in most divorces.

divorce law complicated. Every case has to be decided on the facts of a particular family.

Divorce is about the distribution of property. Children are no longer awarded, but time and control of children is awarded on a custody schedule. In other words, parents share ownership, but on an alternating/sharing schedule. Future income is awarded in the forms of child support and spousal support. However, distribution sets up a competition between people, in this case spouses, and turns the Non-zero Sum Games of financial planning and co-parenting into the Zero Sum Game of win and lose. In other words, the legal outcomes of distribution come to dominate people's minds and actions, instead of making a good Plan for a major life transition, based on long-term goals.

In this Chapter, we take a close look at the 'traps'[29]
of the traditional family law system.
However, we first want to discuss the assumptions
undergirding our legal system.

The general functioning of the traditional family law system seduces divorcing parties into assuming that they have a dispute, triggering the natural human desire to prevail, focusing on legal outcomes instead of long-term financial and family goals, with vague, ambiguous and sometimes contradictory standards by which to measure outcomes.

Within this climate, the system
traps people into making irrational choices.

Perhaps the most impactful of those choices is to see one another as rivals and begin a lengthy divorce relationship filled with frustration and wrath. Divorced parties often will engage in open conflict with one another or avoid each other like the plague. Ex-spouses, who might have been married for many years, and who have children together, might sit in the same room or go to a child activity acting like they do not even know each other. This is very sad.

It is in this context that we now focus on our ten Traps in the current/traditional family law system:

---

[29] These traps are inadvertent, but are nevertheless traps. Read on!

TEN TRAPS IN THE TRADITIONAL FAMILY LAW SYSTEM.[30]

Divorce is not about the law. It is about the future lives of spouses!

1. **Trap #1: In the traditional family law system, the parties are directed to and often pressured to focus on legal outcomes, not life goals.** Legal outcomes are not goals. Legal outcomes should be tools for the parties to reach their goals. If focused on the legal outcome, it makes sense that a property distribution should be equitable. It also makes sense that income should be shared in a manner that gives both parties a sufficient amount to live their lives. In addition, if focused on the legal outcome, it makes sense to identify who has what authority to make major decisions about the children and to establish a schedule for the child to be with each parent. Short-term thinking makes sense when focusing on legal outcomes.

    However, if the focus is on the long-term financial outcomes for both of the spouses, the division of property and income should be one that increases the chances of a long-term positive outcome for both parties, whether or not that means an equitable division at the time of the divorce. If the focus in on long-term goals for the children, such as that they have a positive experience of family life with separated parents, then how decisions are made and how each of the parents will be involved with the child are the questions to ask and answer. The focus should not be on what physical and legal custody will control the family. The legal outcome might be a rigid physical custody schedule, when we know that positive long-term outcomes for children need flexibility in the schedule. A bitter competitive win-lose approach to a physical custody schedule makes sense if a favourable legal outcome is the focus, but we know that the quality of the post-divorce parental relationship is far more important to outcomes for children than the physical custody schedule. Co-parenting and parenting is not a win-lose competition!

---

[30] See also Chapter 10, "Dispelling the Ten Illusions." In order to have accurate thinking, and before moving forward with a Plan for a Sensible Divorce, we need to face reality and recognize these Ten Illusions, which can distract us at best, and be our ruin at worst.

**Trapping divorcing spouses into focusing on legal outcomes
distracts them from their long-term goals
and leads to self-defeating choices.**

Financial planning and parenting are not Zero-Sum Games!

2. **Trap #2: The traditional family law system turns Non-zero-Sum games (e.g., raising children and financial planning) into Zero Sum Games (e.g., dividing the children's time and dividing property, debt and income).**[31]

    A Zero Sum Game is when a limited resource is to be 'won' by one of two people. If we put $100.00 on a table and tell one person to propose a split, and if the other person accepts the proposal, the money is split like that. However, if the other person rejects the proposal, no one gets any money. Every dollar one person gets is a dollar the other person loses. This is a Zero Sum Game. If we place $100.00 on the table and tell two people to decide where to go together for dinner and use the $100.00, this is a Non-zero Sum Game. They are both winners.

    What effect does this have on spouse in a divorce? Zero Sum Games promote competition, a win-lose mentality, often accompanied by bitter feelings. Zero Sum Games also promote competition, dirty tricks and dishonesty as winning strategies, causing sometimes irreparable damage to the parenting relationship- and too often to their children. In the Zero Sum Game of distributing custody, any day one parent gets is a day the other parent loses. In the Zero Sum Game of distributing property and income, any dollar one parent gets is a dollar the other parent loses. A Non-zero Sum Game promotes cooperation and planning to reach goals. They are likely to have some disagreements, but both can be winners.

---

[31] For those unfamiliar with Zero Sum Games, a Zero Sum Game is one in which the prize is a limited amount (e.g., 7 days in a week). A Non-zero Sum Game has no artificial limit (e.g., participation in a child's activities).

Trapping people into viewing co-parenting and financial planning as Zero Sum Games promotes competitive battles and dirty tricks, rather than cooperation and planning for the future.

Divorcing spouses are parents, not enemies!

3. **Trap #3: The traditional family law system assumes that disputes exist and that the interests of the parties are in conflict.** This unquestioned assumption pervades every aspect of the family law legal system. Every question, lawyers ask, pounds this assumption into the minds of their clients. Even the paperwork reflects this assumption. In most jurisdictions, the name of the case labels the parties as in a dispute: the name of the case is so-and-so <u>versus</u> so-and-so. The language used reinforces this view: 'the other side', 'opposing counsel', 'the litigants', 'dispute resolution', 'settlement negotiations', and so on. What is the basis of this assumption?

    The development of the legal system focused on the primary purpose of resolving disputes: innocent or guilty, where the property line is, who is responsible for an injury, etc. When the State took an interest in marriage, which previously had been a private and/or religious matter, it also took an interest in divorce and began to apply the same thinking— the assumption of a dispute.

Why don't people need to hire attorneys to have a wedding? [32]

This trap is fundamental to the family law legal system and to the training of lawyers. This is their mindset. In fact, it is more than a mindset; it is their definition of reality. Transactional attorneys have a very different mindset. While they still focus on legal protections, representing one party to the transaction, they do not assume there is a dispute. They believe they have a deal to close, and they implement a Plan to accomplish this agreed-upon goal. Why are family law attorneys not transactional attorneys, instead are litigation attorneys? It is because of the fundamental assumption that the parties are in a dispute.

---

[32] For the sake of simplicity, and to make our basic point, we are ignoring the fact that some parties hire lawyers at the time of the marriage to negotiate the terms of a Premarital Agreement.

When spouses enter into the traditional family law system, they quickly are absorbed into the assumption that they are in a dispute. The difficulties in the marriage make spouses particularly susceptible to this temptation. They might even already see one another as enemies- as the reason that the marriage is moving to a divorce. Neither could prevail in their marital struggles, and now they can hire professional fighters (i.e., divorce attorneys) to try to prevail over one another.

However, if we take the emotion out of the situation for a moment, do spouses really have a dispute? When we ask divorcing spouse what are their long-term goals for their children, there is rarely much difference. When we ask divorcing spouses if they would rather prevail on legal outcomes, even if that damaged the future of the other spouse, or if they would rather have legal outcomes that helped both spouses reach long-term financial goals, the answer invariably is the latter. This prompts the question: what would the legal system look like if it did not assume a dispute?

**Trapping people with similar long-term goals
into believing that they have a dispute with one another
leads to escalating conflict and poor post-divorce relationships.**

Children are not property to be won and owned!

4. **Trap #4: Children are treated as property in the traditional family law system.** Historically, children were treated as property because for eons, they were property. It was only in the late 19th and early 20th century that children began to be treated as a special class of citizens with legal protections. Rather than awarding children to a party, which for over hundreds of years is what happened, our legal progress now awards time with the children to the parties. What impact does this have on the parents?

    Evolution selected traits in parents for the protection and training of children. In order for people to reproduce, their children have to reach at least their mid-teens. Getting children to that age was not easy. Prior to the last hundred years or so, and especially prior to the invention of antibiotics, only about fifty percent of children lived to five years old. The selection pressure on parents to be protective was very high.

Distributing children like property triggers millions of years of evolution to want to do battle with the threat. The traditional family law system inadvertently identifies the other parent as the threat. It is the other parent who wants to take your time with and control of your children away from you, or at least that is the impression that the legal system creates. See how silly this is?

The trap of treating children like property, restricting the involvement and control of parents, flies in the face of fundamental instincts. These instincts might not even be part of the consciousness of the parties, but will drive the competition between them. If you doubt this, think about why we do not object to our children spending days in school, hours of soccer practice, music lessons, spring break with grandparents, sleepovers with friends and so on, but fight in court to try to get an extra day or two away from the other parent. When parents send children to school and put their rearing in the hands of teachers, they do not feel locked out of their lives and out of control of what happens.

Sadly, it is the traditional legal system that traps people to feel locked out and out of control when the other parent has parenting time with the children enforced by a court order. In a sensible divorce, both parents are parents one hundred percent of the time, although not always spending time with their children.

Trapping co-parents into viewing children as property to be distributed triggers battles, and even hatred, based on unconscious evolutionary based instincts.

Being sensible means looking for solutions that are good for both people!

5. **Trap #5: Selfish strategies permeate the traditional family law system.** Petitions and Affidavits focus on what parties want for themselves, not on what will be good for everyone in the family, especially the other spouse. Lawyers often see their task as getting their client what the clients say they want. Having already been trapped into focusing on legal outcomes, parties often say they want what appears to be a favourable legal outcome, even when those outcomes, and the

process of getting them, are self-destructive. How would 'winning' one more day with the children or paying a little less spousal support compare to a miserable co-parenting experience for the rest of their lives and watching this damage their children?

Research demonstrates that a balance of narcissism (selfishness) and altruism (concern for the outcome for the other person) in the bargaining process improves the outcomes for both parties. In other words, the bargaining between parties should include not only focusing on what is good for him and her but also what is good for the spouse. Many attorneys ask their own clients about their goals, but few, ask their client about the goals of the other spouse, also trying to help reach those goals too.

**Trapping people into being selfish reduces the value
of the outcomes for both spouses.
Don't compete. Plan!**

6. **Trap #6: Winning on legal outcomes is most important.** Playing a game with someone is fun, win or lose, but it is more fun to win. Evolution selected humans who win and who have a natural desire to prevail, whether in enjoyable activities like tennis or serious activities like battle to the death.

**The traditional legal system inadvertently promotes
this desire to prevail in a family law case.**

Lawyers also get drawn into not only wanting to win desirable legal outcomes on behalf of their client but also on behalf of themselves. Not only can they pat themselves on the back if they get a 'win', but also their social or professional status might improve. They might even end up with more clients and more income. The proof that this is a fantasy is that fewer and fewer people are willing to hire attorneys. In family law cases.

Trapping people into a win/lose mindset ignites the competitive desire to prevail and not to lose, which promotes continuing conflict.

Work on the sadness, and often the guilt and shame, that goes with it!

7. **Trap #7: Escalating anger and blame, rather than resolving sadness, permeates the traditional family law system.** A divorce is the culmination of the failure of spouses to give each other their dreams. We all enter marriage with an idea of what we think will make us happy. In the Honeymoon Stage of a relationship, we often think that we have a good chance of that coming into being. Sadly, over time, however, our spouse usually ends up being a real human being, and not a bit player in our movie. We start trying to get our spouse to make our dream 'come true', so that we can have a happy marriage. This is where the Control Stage of the marriage begins. In a successful marriage, the spouses manage to resolve many of the control issues, but we never get our whole dream. We learn to tolerate those losses because the rest of the marriage is worth it.

However, when people fail to get enough of their dream to make the marriage worth it, they move to divorce. The losses involved are very sad. The loss of hope and the dream of a happy marriage and an intact family are perhaps the saddest.

Most divorcing parties do not focus on the sadness.
They focus on being angry at the other spouse
for failing to give them their dream.
Simply stated: they *'fall in hate'*.[33]

The family law system often fans the flames of anger rather than redirects spouses to focus on the sadness. Attorneys, thinking that they are being supportive, might inadvertently fan the flames of anger and even take action, like accusatory letters to 'the other side', which only increases the anger in the divorce relationship between spouses.

---

[33] This is opposite of "falling in love."

117

Trapping people into anger and blame,
instead of resolving sadness,
promotes a dysfunctional post-divorce relationship.

Build a good Plan piece by piece!

8. **Trap #8: Deductive decision-making and bargaining is encouraged from the beginning of a divorce in the traditional family law system.** Bargaining begins with the big picture issues and then drilling down into the details. 'Every other weekend' is decided on, without looking in detail at the start and stop times, or even if that is the best way for the particular family to handle weekends. Holiday schedules are lumped together in a Template that the lawyers (or mediators) give their clients: one parent gets the odd years and the other gets the even years, without a look at whether or not that will provide the family with good holiday experiences. The decision is made as to whether the schedule will be 50/50 or a 9/5 or some other distribution, before looking at the best way to arrange days. This is called Deductive Bargaining.

Inductive Bargaining produces a better plan.
Inductive Bargaining ignores the big picture issues and
builds a Plan step by step, focusing on the details.

What follows is an example of Inductive Bargaining:

- The parties might start with each holiday and any time off of school and work associated with each holiday.
- They develop a Plan for each one to optimize the experience of themselves and their children.
- For example, they might spend time planning the best possible Thanksgivings and Thanksgiving break from school.
- Then they focus on vacations, with the same goal of optimizing the experiences.
- Then they plan summers, meaning the best ways to organize the summers to provide themselves and their children the best summers possible.

- Then they plan weekends and other days off of school.
- By the time they get to school days, they have already planned, depending on the school district, about 200 days of the year.
- Even days can be broken down into parts. After-school time might be different from evenings in a good plan.

This is the process of building a physical custody schedule inductively, focusing on long-term goals instead of legal outcomes. When the attorneys write down and submit the schedule to the Court, they are submitting a Plan for the parties to reach long-term family goals.[34]

The same inductive approach also works for financial issues, especially when using our **Four Planning Steps for Making Collaborating Decisions**[35] and focusing on long-term financial goals.

Trapping people into bargaining deductively
ignores the long-term goals of the parties-
financially for themselves and as co-parents for their children.

The day of the final Judgment of Divorce is just
day one of the divorce life!

9. **Trap #9: The day of the final Judgment of Divorce is the end of the case for the spouses, as well as for the attorneys, mediators, judges and other professionals involved.** This creates the illusion for parties that the day of the final Judgment will be the end of their relationship, and parties are often shocked, starting the day after the final Judgment, that this is not true. In fact, rather than getting relief, they often find that the divorce process made the relationship worse than it was before. The trite prescription that attorneys and judges give to divorcing parents, usually including some version of *"Get along with each other,"* does not

---

[34] In Part IV of this book, we flesh out this planning principle in much more detail when discussing each of the legal and planning tasks of a divorce.

[35] We first introduced our Four Step Goal Based Planning Template for Making Collaborative Decisions in Chapter 4 and presented it again in Chapter 6 when discussing Skill #9. Making Decisions that Accomplish Both People's Goals. See also Chapters 15-18. Hopefully this context is helpful.

pervade the process in ways that encourage parties to develop a sensible relationship. To the professionals, the case is over; to the ex-spouses, it has just begun. The divorce is everything that happens after the day of the final Judgment of Divorce.

Trapping people into focusing on the final Judgment of Divorce as the end leads to the shocking realization that this is a fantasy and being unprepared for what follows.

Fault and blame are irrelevant, and often are obstacles, to making a good Plan for the future!

10. **Trap #10: The attribution of fault and blame has a long history in the traditional family law system.** Lawyers are sometimes referred to as 'professional blamers. This can fit like a hand in glove with divorcing spouses who, as we point out in Trap #7, are already blaming each other for the failure of the marriage to provide them with their dream. Fault and blame have little relevance to making a Plan for the parties' futures. Focusing on sadness and focusing on planning for the future is critical. A good financial planner does not focus on blaming people for getting into financial trouble. The planner focuses on how to use current resources to have a better future. Parties could (perhaps should) do the same.

Trapping people into focusing on fault and blame distracts them from focusing on sadness and planning for the future.

Summary:

Because the traditional family law (divorce) system focuses on the interests of the State, people often get trapped into making bad choices. The traps grab their attention and fool people into focusing on the needs of the legal system, instead of facing their life transition with a Plan to reach long-term goals.

Lawyers, mediators, mental health professionals and judges make the legal tasks of distribution appear to be what is important. The legal tasks are largely irrelevant to whether or not people have a sensible divorce and healthy divorce lives. The professionals often (but inadvertently) side-track spouses into making major mistakes, greatly diminishing the quality of their lives and the lives of their children.

A divorce has to include decisions about the legal tasks, but those decisions should be based on what decisions on legal tasks are most likely to get a sensible divorce off to a good start.

Chapter 9

Summary of the Headwinds and Challenges to Planning a Sensible Divorce; Roadmap to Planning a Sensible Divorce

There are lessons learned about achieving a Sensible Divorce. By way of a Summary, we have learned the following:

- To choose a Sensible Divorce, we must have an idea of what sensible practice is and is not.
- In all marriages, there are pitfalls, and most marriages are a delicate balance of opportunity on one side and pitfalls on the other.
- The decision to marry is not a one-time decision to have a wedding. It is a daily decision depending on the balance of emotional capital, commitment and altruistic love on one side of the scale, and negative traits and aversive experiences on the other side of the scale.
- There are not only deal-breakers that can lead to a divorce, but also the wear and tear of long periods of aversive experience with one another, which can bankrupt the emotional capital and wear down the commitment.
- Most people do not understand the implications of many of the decisions they make as the marriage is heading down the path to a divorce, during the divorce and following the divorce.
- Choices can be made that prolong the suffering of the marital and divorce problems for the rest of people's lives, OR spouses can choose a Sensible Divorce, which is a solution to their marital problems. [We introduced some Sensible Practices in Part I and throughout the book].

There are challenges and obstacles
in the way of achieving a Sensible Divorce.

By way of a Summary, we have also learned the following:

- Spouses live in two different worlds that can only be bridged with effective communication in which both spouses are rigorously honest.

- Ex-spouses also live in two different worlds that are even more divergent, because they spend very little time with one another. However, we learned that effective communication is still the only way to bridge that gap.

- Most divorces are the result of difficulties in mastering the control issues that all marriages face. Often, efforts at control escalate to include bullying, withholding, and other problematic behaviors until apathy sets in, where one or both spouses give up, and one or both make the psychological decision to divorce. Thus, spouses enter the divorce process with existing bitterness and low empathic concern for one another, making them vulnerable to being trapped by the legal system and other headwinds.

- Once the decision to divorce is made, at least one of the spouses loses all incentives for continuing to try, and it is only a matter of time before the spouses separate and divorce. This can create a serious obstacle in the divorce process because the efforts to control each other might continue. Despite failing to get the other spouse to act 'right' in the marriage, many spouses try to get the other spouse to act 'right' in the divorce, often escalating to litigation in order to gain the power of the Court in this effort.

- We learned that the focus on the past relationship is a psychological waste of energy, that the blame-frame defends us from threats but does not solve problems, and that spouses are vulnerable to unsupported inferential thinking. The allure of intractable conflict can be hard to resist.

- Divorcing spouses have the internal obstacles of guilt, shame, anger, trauma triggers, distorted perceptions, intractable conflict and sadness of loss. To avoid addressing these core feelings, spouses often adopt the

Defensive Emotions of blame, anger and even hatred of one another to try to restore a sense of wellness.

- Finally, we have seen that the traditional family law system tempts and (inadvertently) traps divorcing spouses, especially with children, into making irrational, self-defeating choices that reduce the chances of a positive post-judgment relationship and helping them reach long-term financial and family goals.

The antidotes

- o Focus on planning for the future, not on legal outcomes.
- o Don't fall for turning the Non-zero-Sum games of financial planning and co-parenting into Zero-Sum Games of distribution.
- o Don't assume disputes—long-term goals might be similar or even the same. There might be disagreements about the steps to take, but those are only disputes if they do not get resolved with our Four Planning Steps for Making Collaborative Decisions.
- o Don't treat children like property to be distributed. Be parents 100% of the time.
- o A balance of concern for each other and for oneself leads to the best solutions, not selfishness.
- o Don't turn planning for the future into a competition to win short term legal outcomes.
- o Work on resolving sadness, instead of getting caught up in anger and blame.
- o Engage is Inductive Planning to reach goals, not Deductive Decision-making about legal tasks.
- o The day of the final Judgment of Divorce is not the end of suffering; it is the beginning of life after divorce.
- o Avoid getting stuck focusing on fault and blame for the past by focusing on resolving sadness and planning for the future.

ROADMAP FOR PLANNING A SENSIBLE DIVORCE:
AN INTRODUCTION
**With all of these headwinds and challenges,
we might wonder how it is possible
to have a Sensible Divorce. It is!**

In spite of the obstacles, it is possible to have a Sensible Divorce, but as the saying goes, '*It ain't easy*'. If you were reading a book on financial health, the book would start with a look at the current situation. That might describe a financial mess, created by many mistaken ideas about money and many stupid decisions. It might seem hopeless. Then the book would focus on long-term financial goals, followed by a Plan on how to reach those goals from the current situation.

Just like a hypothetical book on financial health, this book focuses on 'divorce health' (i.e., having a sensible divorce) and follows the same model. Success means following a Plan. Mistakes should be avoided. Don't dwell on the past, as it is a waste of psychological energy, where nothing can change the past. Don't make up increasingly negative things about each other. Avoid the blame-frame.

We introduced our Four Step Goal Based Planning Template for Making Collaborative Decisions and our Ten Disagreement Resolution Skills in Chapter 4. Both are also mentioned throughout various parts of the Book. As a reminder, we repeat each of them here as part of our 'Roadmap for Planning a Sensible Divorce'.

FOUR STEP GOAL BASED PLANNING TEMPLATE
FOR MAKING COLLABORATIVE DECISIONS

Step #1: Describe in detail the current situation.
Step #2: List each spouses' long-term goals, specific to the decisions being made.
Step #3: List the steps for reaching long term goals.
Step#4: List the obstacles and steps to overcome them and create a Plan.

TEN DISAGREEMENT RESOLUTION SKILLS

1. **Having the Right Mindset:**

SKILL #1: Overcoming personal bias

SKILL #2: Bridging the gap between realities

SKILL #3: Getting perspective

2. **Managing Feelings and Emotions:**

SKILL #4: Identifying and processing core feelings, including the ability to have mixed feelings and ambivalence

SKILL #5: Developing the ability to be vulnerable in relationships

SKILL #6: Hearing criticism in a healthy way

3. **Implementing Effective Problem-solving and Decision-making Techniques:**

SKILL #7: Identifying a problem in a way that leads to a solution

SKILL #8: Resolving a disagreement when both people are 'right'

SKILL #9: Making decisions that accomplish both people's goals

4. **Recovering from Destructive Conflict Quickly:**

SKILL. #10: Keeping it short and clean, resolving the disagreement and repairing the relationship damage

Note: When separated parents face making a decision or solving a problem and disagree, we encouraged the use of our Four Planning Steps for Making Collaborative Decisions and using the Ten Disagreement Resolution ('DR') Skills. As part of our Summary, we mention the Tasks for Successful Co-parenting, previewed below and covered in more detail in Chapters 7 and 9.

TASKS FOR SUCCESSFUL CO-PARENTING:[36]

1. **Sharing information.** Share information so that both parents are well-informed about the children's lives.

---

[36] See Chapter 7 for a detailed treatment of the Five Tasks for Successful Co-parenting. In the Summary Chapter 9, we reframe the Five Tasks in a slightly different manner to highlight the identical issue.

2. **Creating expectations.** Use the custody schedule to create expectations, but have easy access and flexibility at all times.
3. **Having child-friendly transitions.** Try to provide transitions where the entire focus in on the experience of the child(ren).
4. **Coordinating similar homes.** Coordinate the homes to be organized as similar as possible.
5. **Solving problems as a team.** Make decisions and solve problems as a team.

We are reminded of a great story about Apple. Simply summarized, Steve Jobs was involved when the company was started, but he and Steve Wazniak, were ousted early in the company's history. Apple languished for many years and never developed more than a 3% market share, in spite of the fact that most expert computer users thought the product was better than the PC's made by other companies. The only problem with Apple was that you had to be a 'geek' to use it.

Apple finally invited Steve Jobs back to discuss his coming back into the company. Jobs walked into an 'exploratory meeting' with all of the top brass, including the engineers, who were about to explain all of the company's troubles and their current situation. Before being accepted back as CEO, and before anyone at the table unloaded on Jobs as to why the company was not going anywhere, Jobs said:

"We are going to make four computers: a desktop and a laptop for
professionals; and a desktop and a laptop for everyone else.
They are going to be intuitive, easy to use, high quality,
expensive and 'cool'. Go figure out how to do that."

Witnesses report that everyone in the room smiled and ran out the door to get to work. Steve Jobs became the new CEO, and Apple became the biggest company in the world.

Recognize our Four Step Planning Template in action?
We hope so!

In Part III of this book, Moving Forward with a Plan for a Sensible Divorce, we look at where we are going, which includes developing a Plan to get from here to there and overcoming the obstacles along the way. In other words, regardless of the starting point, success only means getting a clear vision of describing the current situation, listing long-term goals, developing steps to reach those goals, overcoming the obstacles, and following the Pl

Part III
Moving Forward with a Plan for a
Sensible Divorce

*"If you don't know where you are going, you cannot know
how to get there."* (Irish Proverb)

In order to have accurate thinking, and before moving forward with a Plan for a Sensible Divorce, we need to face reality and dispel the fact that there are illusions about reality that can distract us at best and ruin us, at worst. Our Ten Illusions are discussed below and summarized in a Table at the end of Chapter 10 and again as one of the Documents in Chapter 19.[37]

---

[37] See also Chapter 8, "Ten Traps in the Traditional Family Law System: Additional Challenges" In order to have accurate thinking, and before moving forward with a Plan for a Sensible Divorce, we need to face reality and recognize these "Ten Illusions," before falling into them.

Chapter 10

Dispelling Ten Illusions: More Obstacles to a Sensible Divorce

Illusion 1. "My spouse is so controlling, and that is the marital problem."

We have already addressed some illusions in Parts I and II. We have seen that a view of the spouse as 'controlling' is simplistic and focuses on just one aspect of the normal Developmental Phases of a Marriage (Part II, Chapter 3). In fact, during the Control Phase of a marriage, both spouses are generally attempting to control one another, the purpose of which is not servitude or emotional abuse, but rather the initial attempts at making the marriage better. Because we have all learned different ways to try to control, those sometimes clash with one another. In some marriages, spouses are able to adapt their strategies to work better, but in some, the clash of control strategies leads to an escalation of problems and eventually a divorce. Thus, the view that the spouse is controlling and that caused the marital problem, is an illusion.

The marital problem is that the control strategies of both spouses clashed, and escalating efforts to control were damaging.

There are certainly marriages in which one or both of the spouses have inherently damaging control strategies. One might be a bully; one might be compulsive and need everything done a certain way; one might be engaging in coercive control because of fear; and so on. However, in most divorces, spouses view the other spouse as controlling and abusive, when that is not the case. It simply feels abusive when control failures escalate into repeated conflict.

Illusion 2. "We live in the same world."

Another illusion we have already addressed is the belief that we all live in the same reality. We hope that we have been convincing that in fact, we all live in different worlds. How different are those realities depends on our cultural heritage, our experiences with our families of origin, our personalities, temperaments and even our physical ability. To have conflict over whose reality is 'right' is fruitless and a wasted effort. We bridge the gap between our realities with communication. We share our reality with the other person, and we listen closely when they share their reality with us. We do not focus on who is right; we focus on getting the whole picture that includes different perspectives and sometimes even different facts.

Surprisingly, even money, which seems to be so objective ($10.00 to Jim is identical to $10.00 to Sally) and about which there are such common assumptions (more money is better than less money), is truly very subjective and means very different things to different people. Not all people even make the same assumptions about property and money. For example, $10.00 to Warren Buffet is not the same as $10.00 to a hungry homeless woman, and more money is not better than less money to a person who wants a simple uncomplicated life.

Our point is that the realities of spouses relative to children, property and money are almost always different, and to understand the whole picture in a divorce, spouses must communicate.

Illusion 3. "When is he/she going to change?"

We all, to some extent, start out a marriage with an idea of what a good marriage is, and we struggle when the spouse does not play their part in our movie. Our spouse struggles when we do not play our part in his or her movie. We sometimes spend years trying to change our spouse. In some ways, we change and play at least parts of the role in order to make our spouse happy and reduce the friction. However, we can never fulfill the fantasy that we will be the complete mate that our spouse wants or that our spouse will be the complete mate that we want.

It is only as the Control Phase of the marriage begins to wane that we begin to appreciate being with a real person, not an actor or actress in our movie. We come to understand that the wish was, in the first place, an illusion. That the other person needs to change for our relationship to be sensible is another illusion, especially after a divorce. Note: You can be sensible, whether or not your spouse or ex-spouse changes.

In addition to these first three Illusions, we will address seven additional Illusions below that are particular to a divorce.

Illusion 4. "Time heals all wounds."

Time does not heal all wounds! Engaging in a messy divorce perpetuates the suffering and pours salt on the marital wounds. The fantasy that, given time, the pain will stop, is an illusion. The illusion is sometimes made more complex by adding that time and a final Judgment of Divorce by a judge will be the end to the suffering. Expecting relief when the divorce is finally granted is wishful thinking **and** an illusion.

If there are no children involved, and no continuing financial obligations between the parties, there are still sources of distress. There is grief and sadness. The end of a marriage means the end of hope and is likely to feel more like a death than a new beginning.

Connections with in-laws and some friends are likely to be lost and might be sad by themselves. Most people feel some guilt for a marriage that ended in divorce, some feel shame, and some feel both. There might be loose strings that might never be tied up. There might be unfinished arguments playing over and over in the head. Knowing that your ex-spouse might move on (which is likely), got into new relationships (which is also likely) and look back at his or her time with you as a mistake (which is very likely) might hurt. To be described as a mistake is like having a big eraser wipe you away as a person.

If there are children involved, the situation is even more complex. Then, if the ex-spouse has moved on and gotten into a new relationship, you actually see it. You interact with the ex-spouse through the children and sometimes directly. Seeing the ex-spouse might trigger both attraction and hate- a toxic combination of feelings. The loss of control over how children are being raised is an emotional challenge. Having your children fall in love with a step-parent can feel threatening.

Even when there are no children, a property settlement can seem so unfair to one of the spouses such that anger, and even desires for revenge, can linger for a lifetime. Ken was with a friend of his brother, who, at one point, told the story of his 14-year-old divorce. [38] He bitterly described the 'unfair' settlement regarding his professional business, acting as if it had occurred in the more recent past.

If time and a Judgment of Divorce do not heal wounds, what does? In simple terms, what heals the wounds of a marriage that ended in divorce is having a Plan. The first step to making a Plan is having a very clear and very specific vision of the outcome of the Plan. It is a waste of psychological energy simply to continue to engage in the same types of conflicts with your ex-spouse that you had in the marriage and in the early phases of the divorce. This is all about making and acting on that Plan. However, first, it is important to realize that hope and that time, by itself, will heal the wounds is another illusion.

Illusion 5. "Trusting lawyers as guides will always lead to success. Lawyers know what is best for us."

Lawyers are crucial to structuring a divorce. We have a very high opinion of family law attorneys. There are always some bad apples, but most family law attorneys are genuinely good people, sincerely interested in the well-being of their clients and are knowledgeable about many (but not all) aspects of a divorce. This knowledge gap is a serious one for lawyers, especially when it pertains to what is required to have a sensible divorce, and is even more pronounced when the clients do not understand or even know about it.

---

[38] He had been happily remarried for 10 years.

Attorneys are trained in the law, of course, and also in the economic implications of many of the decisions that people make at the time of the divorce. They are also trained and skilled in the alternative ways to organize the details of the divorce and often in the research on children and families with divorcing parents. However, they are not trained and are likely unaware of what is required to have a sensible divorce.[39] Of course, read on to learn our suggested requirements of a Sensible Divorce.

Divorcing without attorneys is like
taking a hike in the jungle without a guide.[40]

Despite the serious need for lawyers in this process, there is a good reason to resist the temptation to live in the world of the lawyers and not blindly trust lawyers and assume that lawyers always know what is best for clients. Why? There are three reasons:

1. The first reason to resist the temptation to live in the world of the lawyers is that lawyers live in a world dominated by legal outcomes, not by the goals and hopes of their clients. The temptation, then, is for the client to become seduced into focusing on legal outcomes as goals. Lawyers often start the conversation by asking questions about what legal outcomes the client wants. The legal outcome appears to be the goal. Legal outcomes are not goals. At best, they can be tools for reaching goals.

2. The second reason to resist the temptation to live in the world of the lawyers is that, in their world, there is an assumption that the two clients are in a dispute and that their job is to help their client prevail. They see the divorce process as a competition over limited resources-property,

---

[39] We concede this is a very bold assertion, but we assert it is sincerely believed by your authors.

[40] In our books, "*Game Theory and the Transformation of Family Law*: Change the Rules- Change the Game. A New Bargaining Model for Attorneys and Mediators to Optimize Outcomes for Divorcing Parties." Unhooked Books. Scottsdale, AZ (2015) and "*Winning Strategies in Divorce*: The Art and Science of Using Game Theory Principles and Skills in Negotiation and Mediation. (2017)," we address changing our new Mindset of lawyers to better serve the interests of their clients.

money and time with children. Every dollar the other client gets is a dollar that his or her client loses. Every day that one spouse gets with the children is a day lost to the other spouse. We refer to this as a Zero Sum Game, played by the parties and joined in (usually inadvertently) by the lawyers.

3. The third reason to resist the temptation to live in the world of the lawyers is that they cannot and do not really know what is good for their client. Most people are aware the 'Scientific Method' as a way of making a decision: (1) get information, (2) list the alternatives, (3) list the pros and cons of each alternative, and (4) pick the best one. In fact, people rarely use the 'Scientific Method' to make a decision. Instead, they use what is called 'Bounded Rationality'. In our minds, we have stored a great deal of information, much of which is not even conscious to us. Through millions of years of evolution, our brains have learned to make complex calculations and decisions that might mean life or death. It took until Sir Isaac Newton to figure out how to calculate what will happen to objects in motion, but our prehistoric ancestors were also making those calculations in split seconds when they threw spears or rocks at animals for dinner or figured out where to dig for food.

Sample Questions: Children's Life Goals.
(Lawyers are usually not trained to ask these questions.)

To create a vision of life goals and long-term outcomes regarding the children, some sample questions might be helpful:

1. *"What type of relationships would you like your children to have with both parents by the time they reach adulthood?"*
2. *"When your children are twenty-five years old, how would you like to hear them describe their lives after their parents divorced?"*

3. *"What type of divorced relationship would you like to have with your ex-spouse?"*

4. *"Would you like to look back someday and be proud of how you handled your divorce?"*

5. *"Would you be proud that both parents were very involved in all aspects of the children's lives?*

6. *Are there advantages to the children in having both parents involved in their lives, independent of where they sleep?"*

One can easily imagine both spouses answering these questions very similarly, if not the same way. Notice that not one of these questions is about a legal outcome. To emphasize this point, the following is the result of a great deal of research on outcomes for children with divorced parents.

Factors Predicting Outcomes for Children Following a Divorce:

The following factors, from most important to least important, predict how children will turn out after divorce:

1. Level of conflict and the degree of effective communication and cooperation between the parents and other important adults (e.g., step-parents, grandparents, and so on), i.e., meaning the quality of the co-parenting relationship
2. Quality of parenting in each home
3. Pre-divorce adjustment level of the child
4. Social capital of the family (e.g., grandparents and other adults to help; stability of the parents in the community, and so on.
5. Mental health of the parents
6. Socio-educational-economic status of the parties' post-divorce at or below the poverty line

7. Physical custody schedule

Note: See also below for additional comments regarding this seventh and least important factor predicting outcomes for children following the divorce.

Sample Questions: Financial Life Goals.

(Lawyers are usually not trained or experienced to ask these questions.)

Notice that the legal outcome (e.g., the physical custody schedule) is the least important factor, and even then, only a factor if the schedule is grossly problematic for the child. Equally important, and likely surprising, if the other six factors are in place, the custody schedule has almost no effect.

To create a vision of life goals and long-term outcomes regarding financial issues, some sample questions might be helpful:

1. *"How far along are you on your retirement planning?" "What about planning regarding your property, debt and income?"*
2. *"What kind of financial shape would you like yourself and your spouse to be in five years down the road? Ten years down the road?" "What about planning regarding property, debt and income?"*
3. *"Have you thought about the types of activities that the children might be in down the road, and the expenses involved?"*
4. *"Have you and your spouse thought about college for the children and the expenses?"*
5. *"Both of you having stable homes for the children so that they have easy access to friends and a stable school experience is going to be expensive. Have you been planning for that yet?"*
6. *"It is usually pretty tough financially right after a divorce, but down the road you are going to want both of you to have vacations. Do you have a vacation fund or are you planning one?"*
7. *"Would you be proud that both you and your ex-spouse did well financially in the future?"*

More on decision-making and the helpful role of lawyers. In most marriages, spouses did not sit down and use the Scientific Method to decide on buying a house, a car, or deciding who would help the children with their homework, retirement planning, and so forth. Bounded Rationality came into play. Some of the decision calculations included consciously considering some factors, but at the same time, unconscious calculations were also at work.

Spouses might buy a house that might be a little too expensive for them, but trust that they will work hard to reach the point when they can afford the house easily. They know each other and themselves, and know whether or not they are ambitious and will put in the hard work to reach that goal. People drift into parenting roles because of interest, skill, temperament and logistics (e.g., availability). They do not sit at the dinner table and use the Scientific Method to decide who will be the soccer parent or who will take the children to the dentist or what employment or career choices make the most sense for the family.

Lawyers can give clients important legal information
or information about legal or financial implications
of certain decisions. However, they cannot know what will be
good for the client or what legal outcomes will be best
to help the client reach long-term life goals, without
getting valuable facts and information directly from the clients.

The decisions that need to be made regarding the divorce are best made by the spouses, based on which legal outcomes will help both of them reach life goals, which they probably have in common. Believing that lawyers know what is best is an illusion.

The parties truly know what is best for them.

Lawyers know how to inform clients of important information from research on children, on budgeting and financial planning, of the implications of decisions and how to draft the legal documents memorializing the agreements, once reached by the spouses.

**It is a two-way street to get this information on the table.
It is an illusion to believe that this information will
automatically appear.**

Illusion 6. "The divorce is final."

To return to an earlier analogy, to say a divorce is final, is like saying a marriage is final on the day of the wedding. It is almost meaningless and certainly an illusion. With the wedding, the single status of those getting married is over. In that sense, it is final, but beyond that, it means nothing. The same is true of a divorce. All of the legal outcomes, except for the termination of the marriage, are decisions that might fit reasonably well at the time of the Final Hearing, but might not fit in the future. For example, a legal outcome might be three years of spousal support at a certain level. The plan was for one spouse to get further education and earn more by the three-year mark, changing the support need. However, at three years, what if the spouse needs three more months (or more) to reach the goal? A different decision and agreement might have made more sense.

Likewise, if there are children involved, there will be many times that circumstances warrant a change in the schedule. Some of those changes will be temporary-perhaps one or two-time changes. In those cases, just some flexibility with the schedule will work fine. However, in order for that to work well, two things are very important to put into place in the final settlement agreement: (1) agreed-upon procedures for you and your ex-spouse to follow, when one of you wants to make a temporary change, and (2) a commitment for a positive tit-for-tat arrangement. Let's unpack each of these alternatives:

1. **Agreed-upon procedures.** Procedures are needed in the agreement to address possible future changes in circumstances. All procedures should

have clear rules. For example, it might be a rule always to contact the other parent before discussing a possible change with the children. Another rule might be always to support one another if the children know about the possible change or even initiate the request themselves. For example, if a child initiates a request, there might be a rule that the child first needs to discuss this with the custodial parent in case there is a reason that the change cannot occur.

Or, if a child knows about a possible change and the change cannot happen, both parents need to explain why it cannot happen and teach the child to deal with disappointment. Another important rule might be never to blame or criticize the parent who objected to the change. One more rule might be that if the change includes an overnight, there is a procedure for switching so that no one loses an overnight. That might seem silly. What is the problem having one less overnight in a child's life? However, separated parents have to live with a lot of loss, and one overnight can have a lot of emotional meaning and value. It is also much easier to say yes to a request if there is no net loss of time with the child. Why is having these procedures in place a good idea? Because the divorce is not final.

2. **Positive tit-for-tat rule.** A procedure for a positive tit-for-tat rule should be set forth in in the agreement. This procedure will only work if the parents are committed to such a positive rule. This means that when a change is requested, the parent receiving the request always says yes, unless there are competing plans that cannot be changed. In a negative tit-for-tat situation, parents say 'no' just because the other parent said 'no' last time. This leads to inflexibility in the schedule. A positive tit-for-tat rule leads to flexibility, and when the answer is a 'no' because there are competing plans that cannot be changed, the 'no' is easier to accept.

Some schedule changes are permanent changes, or at least permanent until the next reason for a change arises. For example, a schedule for a toddler might not be a good schedule when the toddler starts school. In another example, if one of the parents remarries and would like the children on the same schedule as the step-children, a change might be needed. Research finds that teenagers have particular needs in the custody schedule which might warrant making a change when a child reaches that age. As another example, a parent has a change in employment that makes them available after school for the children. Having that parent available to take the child to activities, or simply be able to take care of them until the other parent is available, could be a good idea.

Note: This same type of arrangement can (and should) be built into the settlement agreement regarding certain financial issues.

Again, the key is to have a procedure for making certain changes in the future regarding certain issues in the settlement. This is important for several obvious reasons:

    a.   Flexibility in the future for certain financial issues (not likely property division but certain support issues) might be appropriate.

    b.   Flexibility regarding the children allows parents and children to take advantage of more opportunities. The 'back and forth' of a rigid inflexible schedule is mitigated by the smoother feel of a flexible schedule.

Interestingly, in a follow up research study, twenty-five years after the original study, the now adult children were surveyed. The most important factor to those children was whether or not their parents got along with one another. The second most important factor to the children was whether or not they had flexibility in the schedule. (Based on this study, it is assumed that the children would feel the same way regarding certain financial issues.)

A sensible approach to divorce includes an awareness of the child's experience regarding the divorce. A rigid schedule determined at the time of the divorce, which never changes as family circumstances change, is problematic for everyone in the family. (Based on this same study, it is assumed that modest and sensible changes could be made to the support agreement, and children would feel the same way regarding certain financial issues. For example, a dad telling a child that "*I could not afford the basketball training session at the university, so your mom offered to pay for the whole thing. You might want to thank her.*")

All this implies accepting that a divorce is not final.
It is the beginning of the next phase of family life,
and the need for change is inevitable.

Why is having a positive tit-for-tat rule place a good idea? Because the divorce is not final. In most cases, especially when there are minor children, many things are not final, and to believe otherwise is an illusion.

When no children are involved, having a divorce be final includes both spouses being satisfied that they are each on their way to achieving long-term financial goals. Remember that while attorneys typically represent their own client's interests and goals, optimal outcomes are enhanced when the focus is on both spouses' interests and goals.

Illusion 7. "People don't change."

We could deal with this subject in a very general way, but here we will focus on this illusion solely as it applies to divorce. In a phrase, people do change, but slowly over time. Some of this change is relatively predictable, because humans, like most animals, go through predictable developmental stages, not only in childhood but also in adulthood up until old age and death. Some change is unpredictable and affected by experience. Interestingly, most spouses who divorce witnessed change in themselves and each other during the marriage. What is important here is to recognize that ex-spouses will likely continue to change after the divorce. However, many ex-spouses behave towards each other as if the ex-spouse is exactly the same person he or she was when they divorced. This is a big problem.

In fairness, some of this is natural. When we get together with old friends whom we have not seen for a while, we often quickly regress to what we were like the last time we were together. Relationships, like people, have personalities, and with a lack of exposure, those personalities do not change much over time. However, we see some evidence of change. Our friends look surprisingly older. We know that they likely changed. We know that their children are grown. However, it is natural to begin to act the same as the last time together. It is an illusion to think that our friend or we have not changed. They have, and we have.

The pitfall in divorce is that there is often insufficient interaction between ex-spouses to see the changes, and because of this, it is easy to regress to the personalities that were in play at the time of the divorce. While this might be 'natural', in a Sensible Divorce, the ex-spouse recognizes that this is an illusion and that the other person has likely changed, perhaps quite a bit.

For example, in many marriages, one parent will be deeply interested in parenting, and the other parent might be quite a bit less so. Perhaps that other parent will be focused on work or hobbies, often to the exclusion to paying as much attention to the children as they perhaps should. However, in many divorces, the less interested parent '*falls in love*' with their children and becomes much more interested in parenting, during or after the divorce. However, his or her ex-spouse might not be aware of this change and might look for and inevitably find evidence that the old perceptions are still accurate. (In other instances, his or her spouse will flat out ignore any signs of any such change.) In another example, a deeply hurt spouse because the other spouse had an affair might be bitter in part because the ex-spouse never took responsibility for the hurt caused. The other spouse, once the messy divorce was over, might have stopped blaming the hurt spouse for the affair and might have become deeply guilty and apologetic. However, because they do not communicate, the hurt spouse might not see this change and continue to be stuck with bitter feelings.

In a Sensible Divorce, although ex-spouses might have insufficient communication and exposure to see the changes in one another, they recognize that to imagine no change is an illusion. In a Sensible Divorce, hopefully both spouses are more open to recognizing signs that the ex-spouse did change. In one of our examples, one can look for and inevitably find proof that the other parent is still not interested in the children, but if open to mindset change, that same parent might find proof that the other parent has become much more interested in the children. In our second example, the hurt spouse might ask the ex-spouse for an apology for the affair, and perhaps get it.

Illusion 8. "The children are not watching."

One of the ways Ken was involved in family law for 35 years was to do family evaluations as the court-appointed neutral expert. When Ken interviewed children in the families he was evaluating, he usually asked, *"How do your parents feel about one another?"* The children were remarkably aware and accurate in answering this question, even in situations in which the parents tried to protect them from the conflict. Ken heard many times that, *"They try to act like they like each other, but they don't. In fact, they hate each other"*.

There are two implications, suggesting that the children are watching:

First, part of the development of children is first to internalize into their own identity the identities of their parents. Later they internalize characteristics that they see in teachers, coaches and peers, but the foundation is the identities of their parents. Because children internalize the identities of their parents, unfortunately they are also internalizing the conflict between their parents. The conflict and the behaviors of the co-parents towards one another become part of the structure of the child's personality. Unfortunately, they are likely to behave that way as adults.

An interesting study chose, as subjects, teenagers whose parents had divorced at least five years earlier. There was remarkable symmetry between the relationship between parents and social success of the teenager. If the parents avoided one another and had as little to do with each other as possible, the teenager tended to avoid social interaction and spend a great deal of time alone, often playing video games. If the parents engaged in open conflict with one another, the teenager tended to have behavior problems in social situations, including bullying. The teenagers who were most successful socially were those whose parents got along at least reasonably well with one another. Children become what they see in their parents.

Second, another part of the development of children relates to parenting skills, which will impact the outcomes for children, based on research. We list these co-parenting skills below:

FIVE CO-PARENTING SKILLS AFFECTING
OUTCOMES FOR CHILDREN

1. Authoritative parenting, including protection and limit-setting [juxtaposed with permissive or authoritarian parenting]
2. Nurturance, warmth, pride and affection
3. High standards and clear expectations
4. **Good instruction, teaching negotiation of control issues in relationships (e.g., effective bargaining), and modeling social maturity** [Please see below.]
5. Intellectual stimulation and exposure to diverse activities, including monitoring those activities

The first two skills are the big ones. Here, however, we want to focus on the fourth skill set. Parents who engage in a messy divorce are modeling social immaturity and irresponsibility. Those children have a harder time succeeding in life. They are also learning control strategies from their parents' interactions that put them at high risk for having a similar negative experience when they are adults. A research example of this replicates the divorce rate for children with divorced parents: If the divorced parents got along well with one another, the divorce rate for their children is about 30%. If the parents engaged in ongoing conflict, the divorce rate for them is about 65%.

Sometimes, parents will misbehave in front of very young children, thinking that they can do this because their children will not notice, or at least will not remember. Research disabuses us of that illusion. The children who are most affected by parental conflict are infants, toddlers and pre-schoolers. Not only are they the most affected, but also they are the least likely to recover from the damage. They might not remember those experiences, but instead they are stuck with having serious problems their entire lives. Worse yet, because they do not remember, they do not know why they struggle so much.

The illusion that children are not watching unfortunately, though inadvertently, this gives parents' permission to engage in behavior that greatly harms the children involved. Not only are the children watching, but also, they are sensitive to the undercurrents in their parents' relationship, even when the parents try to hide it. Not only does parental conflict make children feel uncomfortable, but also it becomes part of their personality, which can be carried into adulthood in the form of personal problems.

Illusion 9. "I just want my child to be happy."

Most parents prefer children to be happy rather than unhappy or suffering, but it is unrealistic, misleading and misguided to make decisions with this goal.

- **It is unrealistic** because life does not offer pure happiness. At all ages, and at its best, life presents not only periods of relative happiness and occasional episodes of pure joy, but also periods of unhappiness and occasional episodes of intense suffering.
- **It is misleading** when a parent strives to make their child happy, because they fool the child into believing that such a thing is possible. This creates a sense of entitlement, as if the child believes that because pure happiness is possible, they should not have to be unhappy or suffer. Striving to make children happy is like striving to make them fly and getting the child to believe they can fly.
- **It is misguided** because research tells us that successful children reach young adult hood with confidence, competence and independence, but not happiness. In other words, the goal should not be to make a child happy; it should be to help them develop competence, confidence and independence. One set of competencies is how to cope with unhappiness and suffering, rather than creating the illusion that those can be avoided. In fact, a child must go through periods of unhappiness and suffering in order to develop competence and confidence. In order to be confident as a roommate and eventually a spouse, the child must learn chores and responsibilities in the home, often causing the child unhappiness and sometimes suffering. In order to be intellectually competent and confident, the child must do homework and study for tests. In order to be socially confident and competent, the child must learn to deal with rejection and social disapproval.

In a sensible approach to divorce, a parent should focus on teaching the child to be confident, competent and independent—not happy. Ironically, children who learn this lesson are most likely to have the most moments of happiness and pure joy. Rather than try to protect a child from the hassles involved in having parents who live in separate households, the task is to teach the child skills for dealing with those hassles. Rather than clinging to a child because it is sad for the parent when the child leaves to go to the other household, the task is to teach the child to deal with sadness, in themselves and in others around them, and learn the independence of not having to take care of the parent's feelings. This is the antidote for wanting your child to be happy.

Illusion 10. "Vengeance is sweet."

Vengeance, like so many other pitfalls in relationships, had a useful evolutionary purpose. Survival often depended on getting even with other people or tribes who caused suffering. However, then and now, it was and is not sweet. Vengeance is sour and typically leads to more hurt and more suffering.

The rise of Hitler and World War II was the result of vengeance, chiefly of France, against the Germans following World War I. It is alleged that the conditions of surrender and the reparations following the end of the first war were pure vengeance against Germany, setting the stage for the conditions in Germany that made the promises of Hitler appealing.

In messy divorces, we often see a string of ex-spouses' efforts to enact some vengeance on one another. A simple example is the negative tit-for-tat situations mentioned elsewhere in this book. When one parent asks to have the children off schedule and the other parent says 'no', the parent making the request says 'no' next time, simply because of the prior 'no'. That is, the parent says 'no' to get even because the other parent said 'no' last time. And on and on it goes. In another example, the ex-spouse and the person with whom they had the affair break up. Instead of being sad for him or her or sad for the children who seemed to like that person, the ex-spouse might be happy that it did not work out. This is pure vengeance. Repeated litigation is often simply spouses seeking vengeance for the way that the last round of litigation went. Vengeance is not sweet.

We are often touched by a story of someone forgiving another who caused great suffering. Why is that? In truth: forgiveness is sweet. In sensible relationships, people acknowledge their faults and mistakes and apologize. This might even include taking some sort of action to make amends. The other person forgives and forgets. That is the sweetest form of forgiveness.

Almost by definition, in a divorce, both spouses have much to apologize for and much to forgive. The human temptation is to seek vengeance. The illusion is that vengeance will provide relief, but it does not. Vengeance creates more suffering for both ex-spouses. We will be addressing forgiveness later in this book, but for here, we wanted to focus on the illusion of vengeance being sweet and introduce forgiveness as truly sweet.

As we stated at the beginning of this chapter, we need to face reality as it is, not as we think it might or should be. This includes facing the fact that there are illusions about reality which can distract us at best or ruin us at worst.

Chart: Summary of Ten Illusions: Obstacles to a Sensible Divorce		
#	ILLUSION	REALITY
1	"My spouse is so controlling, and that is the marital problem."	Both spouses are trying to change each other to fit his/her Template of what a good spouse does. The problem is not that they were controlling. The problem is that they were unsuccessful in their positions because their strategies clashed. **Let the blame go**.
2	"We live in the same world."	We do not. We share much of what we think of as reality, but we also have realities that are different from one another. **Communication is how we bridge the gap.**
3	"When is he/she going to change?"	In a messy divorce, we are tempted to continue to try to make the ex-spouse fit our Template of what a good ex-spouse should be. This is a waste of psychological energy. **Our focus should be on what type of ex-spouse we are.**
4	"Time heals all wounds."	Time does not do it. **A Plan plus action heals wounds.**

5	"Trusting lawyers as guides will always lead to success. Lawyers know what is best for us."	Lawyers are indispensable to achieving legal outcomes that help divorcing spouses begin their Plan to reach long-term life goals. However, only the spouses can determine what those goals are, and only the spouses can keep the focus on legal outcomes as tools for reaching goals, not as goals in themselves. **The parties, not the lawyers, lead and set goals.**
6	"The divorce is final."	The Judgment of Divorce finalizes the end of the legal status as marriage, but the divorce is everything that happens after that Judgment. Realizing this sets the stage for the spouses to decide every day what type of divorce to have. **The divorce is never really final.**
7	"People don't change."	To act as if the ex-spouse has not changed (when he or she has), is a self-defeating strategy. Communication bridges the gap between who our ex-spouse has become and what we believe is true. **People do change.**
8	"The children are not watching."	Children are sensitive to the goings-on between their parents and are heavily affected by the quality of the parental relationship. **In a Sensible Divorce, ex-spouses imagine (correctly) that the children are watching and learning from everything they do.**
9	"I just want my child to be happy."	Focusing on whether or not a child is happy is unrealistic, misleading and misguided, and doing more harm than good. **The focus should be on promoting confidence, competence and independence, not happiness.**
10	"Vengeance is sweet."	Forgiveness is sweet. **Vengeance is sour and creates a perpetual cycle of suffering.**

Chapter 11

Sensible Solutions for Processing Challenging Feelings and Practicing Kindness

Part One: Sensible Solutions for Processing Six Challenging Feelings[41]

Now with your feet firmly on the ground after dispelling the Ten Illusions (i.e., one of many obstacles to having a Sensible Divorce), it is time to tackle the next obstacle: processing challenging feelings and practicing kindness.

It is a well-known fact in scientific circles that about 50% of the population in the United States makes most of their decisions on the basis of feelings. That might be fine when choosing a movie, but can be problematic when making choices in a divorce. This is particularly true because a divorce is frontloaded

---

[41] In this Chapter, we address 'Challenging Feelings'. In Chapter 2, we present a comparable issue but designate them 'Problematic Emotions'. The distinction is important, which you will understand when you read our book.

with challenging feelings that are likely to lead to really bad choices, particularly the following six challenging feelings:

SIX CHALLENGING FEELINGS

1. Guilt
2. Shame
3. Anger
4. Trauma Triggers
5. Distorted Perceptions
6. Sadness of Loss

In this chapter, we explore each of these six challenging feelings and include Sensible Solutions for overcoming them. For most of these feelings, simply saying "*Get over it*," is not very helpful or a sensible solution. Real feelings are a little more complicated. The goal is to process the feelings so that they do not dominate choices.

This discussion opens the door for choices being made with critical thinking, that is, with our **Four Step Goal Based Planning Template for Making Collaborative Decisions** presented earlier in the book.[42]

1. Guilt

Guilt sometimes gets a bad rap,
and there are ways to make things better.

Guilt is a feeling that we have when we attribute a problem that someone else is having to our actions or lack of actions. [For simplicity, we will call both of these 'actions'.] Whether the action was deliberate or not, we feel guilty, or should, if we did something that hurt another person.

---

[42] See Chapter 6: Ten Disagreement Resolution Skills Needed for a Sensible Divorce, See also our Four Step Goal Based Planning Template for Making Collaborative Decisions in Chapter 6 and our Four Step Goal Based Planning Template for Making decisions regarding the Legal and Planning Tasks in Chapter 14.

Guilt springs from Empathic Compassion. Empathy is the imaginative exercise of putting ourselves in someone else's shoes in order to understand their experience. Compassion is caring about what that experience is. Empathy without compassion is what manipulative, sometimes sociopathic, people have. They understand the other person's experience, but do not care. Empathy with compassion is altruism.

Some guilt is not healthy guilt. Some people feel guilty, even though it was not their actions that caused another person to suffer. We often see this in abusive relationships, where the abuser blames the victim for the abuse, and the victim feels guilty.

When feeling guilty, it is important to reflect on whose fault is the suffering.

Some people react to another's suffering by immediately thinking of what action could have been taken in the past to prevent the suffering and then feel guilty for not having taken that action. Most reasonable people can think of action that they could have taken in the past to prevent suffering, but it is not reasonable to do so in all cases. One might feel guilty if the action not taken is action that most people would have taken. For example, if a parent learns about a special event at school, but fails to tell the child, and the child, surprised by the event, suffers, the parent probably should feel guilty. However, if a person decides that had they not driven to the store, they would not have had an accident that hurt someone, it would not be reasonable to feel guilty.

Guilt is sensible when based on empathic compassion and is an accurate reflection on reality.

This can be very difficult to do in relationships, because in relationships, there is so much ambiguity. We do not always know if it is realistic to feel guilty or not. For example, a spouse says to the other spouse, "*I feel really hurt that you did not ask about my doctor appointment yesterday*". Should the spouse feel guilty?

It is always important to check out inferences. We should say, "*Did you expect me to ask?*" If the answer is yes or something like, "*I didn't expect it but wished you had,*" then we ask. "*What does it mean to you that I did not ask?*" or

153

"*Why do you wish I had asked?*" As you can see, again, we are recognizing that we live in two worlds. In our spouse's world, our asking about the appointment means something, but in our world, it might not. Both are true. We are also getting useful information. Our spouse's idea of cooperation includes being asked about appointments. In our example, the cause of the hurt was the spouse's expectation, not failing to ask.

Applying this to divorce, usually both spouses have reason to feel guilty for causing suffering. Often, one spouse can point out the manner in which the other spouse caused suffering, but has more difficulty reflecting on his or her own contributions to the suffering of the other spouse. This is the blame-frame about which we wrote earlier in the book. We suggested the sensible practice of putting blame to work, first by exhausting the list of reasons to blame the spouse, but then doing the same reflecting on oneself. Here we take it a step further. We borrow this sensible approach from Alcoholics Anonymous.

Sensible Practice:

(1) The first step is to **take an inventory**. What does this mean? We reflect honestly on our behavior and our contributions to the suffering in the marriage and in the divorce. We do not make excuses. We do not minimize what we have done or rationalize our behavior. We do not sugar coat it. We face it down with honesty. If we called our spouse a horrible name, we are guilty, regardless of what he or she did or said to make us angry. If in our apathy about the relationship from which we withdrew, we were not emotionally supportive or responsive to requests for help, we are guilty. The focus is on ourselves and what we have done to cause or contribute to the suffering of the spouse.

(2) The second step is to **make amends**. This is often just a genuine apology, but at times, further action is required in order to make amends. Let us give an example of each of these. A simple apology for a pattern of behavior might be sufficient when there is no other action that can be taken. For example, we might say, "*I owe you an apology. I called you some horrible names, and there is no excuse for that. I am truly sorry. I cannot take those names back, but I would if I could. You did not have it coming. I am sorry*".

If additional action could help heal, then it might be important to both apologize and make amends. For example, we might say, "*I told some of my family, some of your family and some of our friends' horrible one-sided stories about you. That was cruel and selfish on my part, and I am deeply sorry. I plan to correct that by speaking to everyone with whom I talked and correct it. We both messed up, but portraying you as the bad one was both untrue and wrong"*.

(3) What is the next sensible step when dealing with guilt? If someone makes a genuine apology to us, we will **forgive and forget**. If we have something to add to making amends, we suggest doing so. In our above example, we might say, *"Would you please really make an effort with my sister? She has not talked to me since we separated, and now I know why"*.

What do we do if we apologize, and our spouse does not forgive and forget? Nothing. We have behaved in a sensible way, which is the goal. The goal is not to get our spouse to do what we want him or her to do. By our actions, we increase the chances that our spouse will respond in a sensible way, but the goal is to shape our behavior, not that of our spouse.

Summary: This means there are ways to overcome guilt:

1. Take an inventory and honestly take responsibility for actions that hurt the spouse.
2. Make amends with a sincere apology and any additional action that might correct the wrong.
3. Forgive and forget.
4. Do nothing if you apologize and your spouse does not forgive and forget. Your spouse (or ex-spouse) might not respond, but your actions likely register with him/her anyway.

2. Shame

Shame can be helpful.

Healthy people often feel both shame (and guilt) when they have broken a social rule. To understand how to overcome shame, we should understand why humans feel shame in the first place. Humans are social animals, but social groups can only exist with an understanding of common rules. The fundamental purpose of rules in social groups is to enhance the chances of survival and reproduction. The rules of any given social group are learned.

The avoidance of shame serves a purpose in having people follow rules. Shame also serves the purpose of punishing those who break the rules.

Shame avoidance also serves an important role in preserving the social order. Shame also serves an important role for the group when dealing with rule breakers. Not long ago, public shaming practices were common in most cultures. This not only served as a warning to the rule breaker but also modeled for others in the group what will happen if they break the rules. For shame to work, members of the group must be somewhat self-conscious, that is, must monitor themselves and try to stay within the limits of the social rules. People don't tell jokes at a funeral.

Differentiating between shame and guilt is complicated, because there is much overlap. As stated earlier, healthy people often feel both shame and guilt when they have broken a social rule.

Guilt is the dominant emotion when harm has been done to someone else, whereas shame is the dominant emotion when a person has simply strayed from commonly accepted rules of conduct, but not necessarily where any harm was done to any other person.

Some shame and shame-avoidance are healthy. Without a fear of shame, people can engage in socially inappropriate behavior that causes social difficulties. The fear of shame makes us more careful when we make choices.

However, unhealthy shame can mask healthy behavior. Being ashamed of a divorce is unhealthy. Feeling sad, disappointed and acknowledging mistakes are healthy reactions that can be covered up by trying to avoid shame. For example, a person might try to avoid shame by lying to people about problems in the marriage and blaming the spouse.

It is important to recognize that the original social rule prohibiting the break-up of a marriage was a mistake because the rule failed to recognize the reality of the human condition.

Humans, on average, are only able to make permanent commitments to one partner about two-third of the time. Social anthropologists inform us that about one-third of the time, on average, those efforts end in a separation. We also know that some permanent marriages are failures as much as is a divorce. The spouses remain married, but in an unhealthy relationship.

Does this mean that we should feel no shame for a divorce? No.

The divorce reflects the failure of two spouses to accomplish a healthy and permanent marriage. They might have entered the marriage with obstacles that few if any people could have overcome. For example, substantial religious differences that shape the roles spouses should play in a marriage could be a problem with no solution. They might not have considered the potential effects of substantial differences in their interests in activities. However, a divorce is a public declaration that the spouses failed to have a successful marriage, and that might have included shameful behavior on the part of one or both of the spouses, especially towards the end of the marriage. Therefore, some shame is inevitable.

Sensible Practice:

Oddly and ironically, the path through shame is to experience shame publicly. This means publicly admitting to the failure. However, this also means admitting to the reality, not unhealthy shame. We acknowledge that we are ashamed, but what we are ashamed of is failing to shape our efforts to make the marriage work. If we behaved in a shameful manner, we also publicly acknowledge that. We might even be ashamed for being too naïve or hopeful and not considering the obstacles that we faced.

The way to process shame successfully is to feel it
and admit to shameful behavior (if it occurred), rather than hide
it behind a façade of blaming the other spouse.

By openly admitting to shameful behavior, shame passes away. By hiding shameful behavior, shame smoulders and prompts us to behave in a harmful away, such as lying to people, or worse yet, having children live in a fantasy world and hate the other parent.

3. Anger

Anger comes in two flavors. Not surprisingly, there is a great deal of literature addressing anger. The most advanced thinking and science recognizes that anger serves many functions, but basically it can be categorized into two groups:

1. Primary Anger and
2. Secondary (Defensive) Anger

When we are threatened or hurt, anger serves to mobilize
our resources, shoot adrenaline into our veins
and make us ready to defend ourselves
or to attack the threat.

Primary Anger overrides all of our other emotions because our other emotions might have little effect on our survival, whereas this type of anger directly affects our survival. Primary Anger overrides fear, shame and caution. Anger puts us in the here and now, because what we did yesterday, or what we plan to do tomorrow is irrelevant if our survival is threatened in the here and now. When someone almost causes an automobile accident, he or she gets angry and shouts, "*You could have killed someone,*" they are telling the truth. Worse yet, the person who could die is us.

It is not always our literal survival that is at stake. Sometimes it is the survival of important parts of our life. If we have been robbed, we are not threatened with death, but we are threatened with loss. If it can happen once, it can happen again, and what we have could be lost. If our spouse has an affair, we are threatened with the loss of our spouse, our marriage, money and time with our children. If our spouse develops a drinking problem or becomes addicted to gambling, we get angry. Our life is not threatened, but our lifestyle is. Even when someone is late picking us up, or a child is late coming home, the anger is because of the threat of loss (real or imagined). This is all Primary Anger.

The only thing wrong with Primary Anger
is when it is expressed without deliberation.

Deliberation is the thoughtful moment when we think through the consequences of future action. Punching a child in the face because he or she came home late is certainly not going to turn out well, so we need to think through how to address the issue effectively, considering our anger. It is important to remember that an important function of anger is that it mobilizes us to overcome hesitancy in addressing whatever or whoever made us angry. To not act, therefore, represses anger and this leads to all types of difficulties, including physical and psychological problems.

To express anger without deliberation
can be self-defeating and destructive.

Often in a divorce there is good reason to feel Primary Anger, and there is nothing wrong with that. Getting angry at a spouse for causing an accident by driving drunk is Primary Anger. Getting angry at a spouse for having an affair is Primary Anger. Interestingly, people who tell you to get over it are (inadvertently) advising you to do an unhealthy repression of Primary Anger, advice which is certainly neither helpful nor effective.

Deliberation is important so that the expression of the anger
is not self-defeating or destructive. It is important to take time
to think about how to express the anger
without causing more harm than good.

Secondary (Defensive) Anger is anger that is covering up feelings that are more difficult to deal with. It is easier to get angry at a spouse who we think is flirting, rather than deal with the real feeling of anxiety about being abandoned or insecurities. Flirting might be our interpretation of friendly behavior because we are insecure and fear that we might lose our spouse or that he or she might betray us.

Secondary Anger are difficult feelings to have and to process, and even admit that they exist. Anger coupled with blame covers up guilt and shame, as we have seen earlier. Anger can cover up feelings of helplessness. One form of domestic violence has its roots in feelings of helplessness.

In divorce, Secondary Anger is almost always self-defeating and destructive. An affair can ignite Primary Anger, but suspicion of an affair based on inference probably ignites Secondary Anger, when the core feeling is fear or insecurity. Anger about a waning affectionate relationship might reflect difficulty dealing with the sadness of the loss of that type of love in the marriage. Anger at the criticisms by the spouse likely reflects taking those personally, and worse yet, perhaps finding an element of truth in them. Anger toward a spouse who is very close to his or her extended family might reflect selfish difficulty sharing the spouse with others. These Secondary Angers are self-defeating because they do not address the core feelings undergirding the anger, and they often promote the very thing dreaded. Psychologists call this a self-fulfilling prophesy because when we are suspicious that something bad will happen, we inadvertently promote those bad things to happen.

Sensible Practice:

(1) The first step in overcoming anger as an obstacle in divorce is by far the most challenging. This step is to reflect on the anger and determine which is Primary Anger and which is the Secondary Anger. Be patient and take this step with rigorous honesty and courage. If in doubt, lean in the direction of classifying the anger as Secondary Anger.

(2) However, some angers can be both. For example, if a spouse had an affair, Primary Anger fits well, but there might also be Secondary Anger. An affair can trigger personal insecurity. This might mean believing that the spouse had an affair, because you were not good enough. It is also be an example of a difficulty being able to process what might be true cause of some of the anger directed at the spouse.

Here are practical Steps. Prepare a Primary Anger List and start there:

(1) Develop a Plan for the healthy expression of those angers. For example, you might propose to your spouse that you want to clear the air so that the two of you can start your divorce relationship with a clean slate. You propose that you each take ten minutes to air your anger while the other person listens, or you might propose that you both write letters venting your anger at one another. If your spouse is uncooperative, you can write an angry letter to your spouse, giving yourself the freedom to say anything that you want, but then send the letter to a friend, relative or even a therapist, and not to your ex-spouse.

Primary Anger needs to be expressed to someone,
or it festers and does all kinds of mischief with us.

(2) Once complete, prepare a **Secondary Anger List**. One by one, delve into the core feelings that the anger has been covering up. It might be guilt, shame or

your deep feelings of being a failure. Sadness from loss is likely an important feeling to address. You might also uncover some self-hatred, feeling like you deserved to be left by your spouse. Or, you might even discover an inflated sense of self-importance, feeling like it is impossible that someone would want to leave you.

This can be a painful exercise, but like cleaning out a wound, you are preparing yourself for healing those troubling feelings. It might help to do this with another person. Family is always a little tricky, but a trusted close friend can help. Sometimes, a counselor can help more effectively than a friend because the counselor can not only provide you with reassurance, which a friend might do, but also assist you dealing with your healing and overcoming your anger.

4. Trauma Triggers

After dealing with the challenges of guilt, shame and anger, resolving trauma triggers is easy—or at least easier. First, we must review another common aspect of being human. When we begin to interact with someone with whom we have not interacted for a while, we automatically regress to that last interaction. Relationships have a personality, just like people, and within the context of a relationship, we tend to behave as we typically behaved with that person in the past. If I meet a colleague, with whom we had a teasing relationship in the past, within seconds of being together, we are likely to begin teasing each other.[43]

> **When we interact with our spouse,**
> **even in our imagination,**
> **we have a natural tendency to regress to**
> **our part of that relationship personality.**

When that relationship included hurtful or frightening experiences, we might even have trauma reactions when in the presence of that person. This is anxiety-the anxiety that we might experience another hurtful or frightening experience.

---

[43] This is a neurological event, called Hebb's Law. When people have a strong emotional experience in a situation or with a particular person, two sets of neurons in the brain fire at the same time. The next time we are in that setting or with that person, the strong emotional experience fires in our brain, even if there is no reason for it. You get beat up at a certain street corner; the next time you are at that corner, you have the same feelings of getting beat up again.

There is a good deal of research and literature on the treatment of this type of anxiety. Most of those treatments involve what is called Desensitization. Desensitization is a form of getting used to something. If we fall off a high dive and do a belly flop, we are likely to be afraid the next time we stand on the high dive. However, if we dive five or ten times more, and it goes well, the anxiety diminishes or even disappears. If we are anxious around spiders, we can overcome that by desensitization, by pretending that we are holding spiders, or by actually holding spiders. When we discover that they are not dangerous, we might even get playful or exploratory with them, but our anxiety diminishes.

Sensible Practice:

When treating trauma trigger reactions, anxiety can be reduced by imagination, such as imagining interacting with our ex-spouse and even imagining them engaging in behaviors that were previously frightening. After practicing this imagination, when the anxiety is reduced to a manageable level, we can then interact with our ex-spouse in person, and by doing so, reduces the anxiety even more.

Of course, this practice should only be followed if it is actually safe to do so. As long as we are safe, the anxiety reduces, but if we are not safe, we might be exposing ourselves to further abuse. However, if we have also practiced not taking things personally and not inferring excessively, most of the time the ex-spouse is safe.

He or she can criticize us or make nasty comments, but if we do not take those personally, the ex-spouse will do no harm.

You can simply say, *"I'm sorry that you feel that way"*.

5. Distorted Perceptions

Distorted perceptions are tricks of the mind. Distorted perceptions come from incorrect inferences or from rewriting history in order to blame someone else. Both incorrect inferences and rewriting history are the result of what we tell ourselves is real, not what is actually real. If a person tells himself or herself that the spouse was staying late at work because she was having an affair, he is developing a perception that might be incorrect. If he believes it, he is forming a distorted perception and creating negative emotions. If he acts as if his spouse had an affair, when she did not, he is in for trouble. Remember, inferences are just guesses, and even when a person is pretty sure of the guess, it can be wrong.

Sensible Practice:

As a reminder, when presenting some of our earlier Sensible Practices (particularly when we addressed inferential thinking and negative beliefs about our spouse), we recommended the practice making a list of beliefs, examining on what foundations we developed those beliefs and seeking to prove that those beliefs are incorrect or at least incomplete.

**In a sense, the exercise is to assume that what you believe
is untrue and look for proof that this is correct.**

For example, if you think that because your spouse did not seem to love you at the end of the marriage, he or she probably never really loved you, you might sit and argue with yourself that the nice spouse who loved you was the real one, and that getting mean towards the end was in reaction to your getting mean, or simply that you both brought out the worst in each other.

As with the suspected affair, you might try to explain your spouse staying late at the office by imagining other inferences, like avoiding you was because you were so difficult to be around. Your spouse might have been struggling at work and frightened of getting fired, but embarrassed to tell you. If you can come up with several reasonable explanations, you may doubt that your initial inference was true.

The point is that if you can change your beliefs by challenging the inferential foundation and self-talk supporting those beliefs, you will behave in a healthier way and may overcome this obstacle.

6. Sadness of Loss

Loss is sad.

Everyone who goes through a divorce needs a really good cry. The scope of the loss will depend on the facts of the marriage, but it is always sad. The list of losses can be relatively short or incredibly long. Sadness is difficult to process alone. It is best processed with a friend or family member who will be emotionally supportive and not someone who will get angry at your ex-spouse or distract you with euphemisms and unhelpful advice, like "*It will get better*" or "*Give it time*".

Sadness is like a pool of water where you just need to dive in.

Sensible Practice:

Exploring sadness related to one event can often trigger sadness about other life events. When that happens, it can be wise to take breaks.

(1) Start by listing the losses involved in the divorce. This can include lost relationships with friends and in-laws. It will likely be helpful to explore the losses associated with your spouse. This could include remembering past events, like the birth of a child or the day that you decided to marry. Relive those days in your imagination and think about the feelings and hopes that you have lost when you took the marriage for granted or when the two of you began to detest each other.

What is sad is that those feelings were as real as the negative feelings that you might have at the time of a divorce, both for you and for your spouse. Those were enormous losses. Explore the lost hopes that you had for the marriage, and if there are children, the lost hopes you had for the type of family you wanted your children to have. These lists might trigger other memories of losses that had nothing to do with the marriage or the divorce.

(2) **Process them**. Processing loss involves reliving experiences and allowing yourself to feel the sadness. The only path is through the sadness.

Have a friend or family member ask you questions about other possible losses associated with the divorce. How much money did you lose, and did that mean a loss of financial security? How will you deal with the loss of time with the children? Did you lose sentimental objects in the home? What dreams did you have earlier in the marriage that are now lost? Have a good cry. While daunting, the sadness of loss can be overcome by going through it, not avoiding it.

A normal reaction to sadness is to discover things that could have been done differently and might have led to a different ending. This can not only lead to a feeling of guilt, if those potential actions are things that you could have done or not done, but also, it can lead to anger at a spouse who could have made different choices.

**Going through those feelings is part of processing the sadness
because the permanence of the past is part of what is sad.
People do not usually get do-overs.**

Summary: The Defensive Emotions of anger and blame lead to arrested emotional development. In plain speak, people get stuck in anger and blame in a way where the rest of their lives are shaped by it. Both Ken and Allan have seen cases in which the organizing principle in a second marriage is badmouthing the prior spouses. That is the dominant emotional connection between the two new spouses, not love. They thrive on being better than the first spouses and live that narrow, shallow life.

However, it takes courage to face the real feelings involved in a divorce, especially sadness. As a famous author once said: true sadness leaves a hole in your heart that never heals. You come to live with it, but your new life is not dominated by it. You become emotionally available to move on and even love again. Any leftover negative feelings about an ex-spouse and the divorce are balanced with fond memories and clear thinking.

Nature abhors a vacuum! As you resolve challenging feelings, they only truly recede into the past when replaced. They must be replaced with feelings that are the opposite of the negative feelings: One word to remember: **Kindness!**

Part Two: Sensible Solutions for Practicing Kindness

The practice of kindness begins with being kind to yourself.

This sounds a bit trite, but it is essential to the practice of being kind towards others, especially to your ex-spouse. Up to this point in the book, we have given a number of Sensible Practice exercises. Some might have been challenging, but here you are.

Hopefully you have made a commitment to engaging in a Sensible Divorce, and you must appreciate that about yourself. If you have worked hard to overcome the applicable six challenging feelings (e.g., emotions) presented above, you have been courageous and strong. Overcoming those obstacles is not a one-time task. We face those obstacles in many different aspects of our lives and are processing those emotions constantly. Developing an ability to process these feelings well will be a great benefit to you.

Now we switch gears and look at being kind to your ex-spouse. Kindness does not always equate with 'nice'.

We are being kind to our children when we demand that they do chores, study for school, practice their sports, learn to work out conflicts with their siblings and so on. Better preparing our children for their adult lives is an act of kindness, even when we are not being nice.

We are being kind to ourselves when we make demands on ourselves to do things that will improve our lives. It is an act of kindness to ourselves to demand that we walk in the morning, even on days when we do not feel like it. It is an act of kindness to demand that we share information with our CPP about the children, even when he or she does not do the same for us. It is an act of kindness to ourselves to be proud that we are behaving in a socially mature manner towards our ex-spouse, and modelling that for our children, regardless of how he or she behaves.

Kindness does not always equate with being passive or permissive.

It is an act of kindness to be assertive and let others know honestly what you think and feel, even when that includes ruffling some feathers. As we will see, this includes being assertive with your CPP, but doing so in a kind manner.

When we set limits on others and establish boundaries between ourselves and others, we are behaving in a kind manner. Doing so facilitates healthier relationships. We also set limits on ourselves. We limit what we say or do to our CPP and do not allow ourselves to engage in behavior that hurts him or her. We treat our spouse's new mate with courtesy, regardless of how he or she acts with us. We make polite requests to be treated with courtesy.

When we learn not to take the comments and behavior of others personally, we see their comments and behavior as expressions of who the other person is and not about us. Often this informs us that the other person is suffering, and the kind internal response should be one of empathic compassion. Our ex-spouse is not feeling good inside when he or she makes a hateful comment about us or accuses us of something that is not true. We should not take it personally, and the experience of our ex-spouse should make us sad, not angry.

Kindness means being honest, but in a kind way.

We redefine our divorce, in a way that is not only kind to ourselves and our spouse, but also is honest to ourselves (and others). Here are some examples:

- *"We never worked out a way to resolve our disagreements, and it just wore us down."*
- *"We got so side-tracked with children, money, work and the daily stuff that we did not nurture the garden of our relationship very well."*
- *"We had very different interests, and over time, and we just lost our connection with one another. I found someone with similar interests, and he/she looked too good to pass up. However, it was a mistake to end the marriage that way, and I am sorry that I did."*
- *"We both have a lot of good qualities, but in the end, we only brought out the worst in each other. It was just too hurtful to continue."*

We do not blame our ex-spouse, which is unkind, but also we do not blame ourselves. Acknowledging mistakes is not the same as blaming. It is kind to set limits and boundaries on others and on ourselves, make demands of others and of ourselves, and assert our thoughts and feelings. Kindness does not necessarily mean that we are always nice. However, it does mean that we are always courteous.

Is it ever kind to be a little dishonest? It can be. We might pretend to enjoy our in-laws more than we actually do, as an act of kindness toward our spouse or our children. We might honor our child's choice of mate, even when we might not particularly like him or her, keeping our thoughts about him or her to ourselves. While we concede that this is a form of dishonesty by omission, being courteous to our spouse's new mate is an acceptable and understandable form of dishonesty, under the circumstances. Sometimes, we can also be a little dishonest with our children. Our responsibility to teach them well often trumps saying what we really think at times.

Is it ever kind to be a little dishonest with a ex-spouse?
The answer is the same as above.

Being empathic and compassionate sometimes trumps being fully honest. If our ex-spouse asks an opinion about his or her new mate, we are honest, but might withhold some information out of empathic concern. We might say something like, "*I worry that you are moving too fast, but only you can judge whether he or she is the right person for you.*"

Summary: The practice of kindness begins with being kind to yourself and redefining your life in a kind way, including your mistakes and failures. Kindness not only means being courteous, but also means making demands, being assertive, generally being honest and setting limits and boundaries in a kind way. Kindness is undergirded by empathic compassion for yourself and for others, including your ex-spouse. Two words to remember: **Be kind!**

Chapter 12

Making Divorce Vows and Rehearsing Sensible Responses to Your CPP[44]

Part One: Making Divorce Vows

When people marry, they make promises to one another. Although they might not be able to keep all of those promises, they intend to try. People want their soon-to-be spouse to know their intent. As marriage has become more egalitarian in our culture, an increasing number of grooms and brides write their own vows, rather than simply reiterating the prescribed vows that the person officiating offers with a, "*Repeat after me…*"

Those who are wedding make the promises personal and meaningful because they already know a great deal about each other. When a bride promises to laugh at the groom's stupid jokes, she is promising to be a compassionate mate in a way that he understands.

---

[44] We will be using your CPP (Co-Parenting partner) for simplicity and because most post-divorce interaction is between CPPs. However, vows can be simple for spouses when there are no children.

When a groom promises to *"Take you and your dog to be…"*, she knows he is promising to honor her other relationships in life. It is an important way to start a marriage with a clear understanding of one another's intent.

**One important step on the pathway to a Sensible Divorce
is to make a list of "Divorce Vows," namely promises to your CPP.
Doing so creates a vision based on long-term goals.**

Would you want a vow to be: *"When I write emails to you, I will make them long and mostly about criticisms of you"* or *"When I see you at the children's events, I promise to sit as far away as I can and ignore you?"* When people look at choices like this, they see the misery that they could create for themselves, their children and even their CPP. Compare the above vows to, *"When I write emails to you, I will be respectful, to the point and informative"* or *"When we are children's events together, I will greet you and whoever you are with and interact with you enough to make the event go smoothly for everyone involved."*

Spend time on these Vows and make certain you are thorough. You are in essence writing a script for yourself in the divorce. The clearer your vision will be in the divorce, the easier and more effective your effort will be to keep those promises. Think through all of the future experiences that you are likely to have and make a vow. For example, what if your child invited your CPP into your house to look at the new paint in her room? Make a vow on how you would handle that.

Warning! It might be easy to envision divorce vows as an indirect way to change the way that your CPP interacts with you. If you think this, however, you are in danger of making a major mistake. You have absolutely no control over your CPP. You only have control over yourself. Your CPP might be overcome with wonder, admiration and gratitude for any changes that you make, but it is also possible that your CPP might just keep doing what he or she has been doing all along. Now you have fair warning.

**The goal of this approach is for YOU to step out of a toxic dance
with your CPP, regardless of what
he or she says or does not say,
or what he or she does or does not do.**

At the same time, if one spouse begins to behave in a sensible manner, pressure is put on the other spouse to do the same. There is no reinforcement for behaving poorly. No one likes dancing a toxic dance alone. Your spouse might actually want out of the toxic dance as much as you do. When you show a pathway, he or she might be very interested in following your lead. People want to be happy and not to suffer. A divorce might hold the promise of more happiness and less suffering, but that does not happen by itself. It takes a Plan, such as recommended in this book.

> **When your CPP sees the changes in your behavior,**
> **he or she might be very interested in what those changes are,**
> **why you have changed and how he or she can join you.**

You might hope that your changes lead to changes in your CPP's behavior, and frankly, your authors hope for the same thing. However, seeing that as a goal and having that as a motive is likely to be very disappointing. It is best to assume that your CPP might be willing to continue to dance that toxic dance alone and then plan accordingly.

Sensible Exercise: Make your Divorce Vows, including some of the lessons in this book. I....

- **Make a vow** never to take what your spouse says or does personally, but always listen for useful information.
- **Make a vow** to dismiss out of hand highly unlikely inferences and to check out inferences that might or might not be accurate.
- **Make a vow** to practice kindness with yourself and your CPP. As part of your vow to practice kindness, make a vow to treat your CPP and anyone associated with him or her with courtesy. Flesh out what you mean by courtesy. For example, being courteous at a public event for your children might include smiling and greeting your CPP, if he or she is close by, or waving if not close by, even if he or she does not smile or waive at you.
- **Make a vow** to be completely honest with your CPP, with the exception of when honesty is trumped by empathic compassion. It might mean introducing yourself to your CPP's significant other and making yourself available if he or she has questions about the children.

- **Make a vow** to support your CPP to the children and never take sides with a complaining child against the other parent, even when you agree with the complaint.

In this Sensible Exercise, visualize the ways in which you and your CPP will interact in the future. Will there be telephone calls about the children? Will you have to make decisions about the children? Those might include medical decisions, decisions about school and decisions about extra-curricular activities. In addition, I … (make vows for those circumstances).

- **Make a vow** for how you will behave during the process, even if your CPP disagrees.
- **Make a vow** to think about ways in which you should interact with your CPP, but currently do not.
- **Make a vow** on how you will attempt to expand your interaction with your CPP, to include those ways to interact.
- **Make a vow** that your future requests made to your CPP will always be made politely.

Once your List of Vows is complete, it is time to decide whether or when to share them with your CPP. The vows are your commitment to yourself. In fact, you do not have to share the vows in order to keep your promises. However, think through whether there might be some value in sharing them. A possibility is sharing a very short version. You can let your CPP know that it is your intent to change the way that you interact with him or her, including to be more courteous, without going into the details. Or you could share your broader intent and the full list of vows. Or you could ask if your CPP wants to learn more, see a copy of them, have you summarize them, provide a sample, etc. You get the idea.

If you share the vows, in any form, with your CPP, be prepared for an invitation back into the toxic dance. Your CPP might make some snide comment about you or make a sceptical remark about your never keeping your promises.

**Be prepared and do not accept the invitation
back into that dark movie/toxic dance.**

Rehearse and practice some kind/polite/courteous responses and have them ready at hand. For example, if he or she says, "*That'll be the day*," you might respond, "*I understand that you are skeptical and only time will tell*". Recognize too, and perhaps mention to your CPP, that you might not be perfect in breaking bad habits, but that you expect with time you will be able to keep most of your vows most of the time.

If your CPP is on board with making changes to have a Sensible Divorce, you might suggest that he or she also make a list of vows and that the two of you share those with one another. New ideas might come up in such a discussion. Some of the earlier Sensible Exercises, such as apologizing and making amends, might have already included your spouse. Sharing your vows might put that in context for him or her, and he or she might benefit from knowing your full intent.

Be Realistic: No one is perfect. When people marry, they might have unrealistically high expectations of what it will be like. A divorce relationship might suggest the same unrealistic expectations- that it will always be great. That is not how relationships work. We mentioned earlier that healthy marriages often have as many disagreements and ups and downs as a marriage that ends in divorce. People have legitimate disagreements about important matters. There is no way around that.

The difference between a Sensible Divorce and a Messy Divorce is not that there are fewer disagreements. The difference is how those disagreements are handled.

Provide for Disagreement Resolution: If you make Divorce Vows, include how you will handle disagreements with your CPP. In healthy relationships, people approach disagreements with the following general Plan (modified to fit the circumstances):

1. The focus stays on the disagreement, not attacks on the person with whom you disagree.
2. Both parties gather information from one another first, rather than trying to win the disagreement. The information includes the goals for the different positions.
3. Agree to keep it clean: be sure you do not escalate to name-calling or berating each other.

4. Look for Win-Win solutions—a way to accomplish as much as can be accomplished for both people. Ask friends and family for ideas or a fresh way of looking at the disagreement.

5. If either spouse steps out of line (e.g., calling an inappropriate name), find a way to recover quickly (e.g., an apology, coupled with forgive and forget).

6. If the parties cannot resolve the disagreement, and someone has to give in, the person giving in proposes something to make up for giving in. In a sense, the person losing gets something in return of equal or greater value. Reciprocity is important.

Summary: In Part I of this Chapter, we used the exercise of making Vows for your divorce relationship as a means of clarifying your intent and to flesh out the vision of your behavior toward your ex-spouse, during and after the divorce.

We have alerted you to the danger of expecting your ex-spouse to change as a result of you changing. You do not have that control. You can invite your ex-spouse into a healthier relationship, but he or she has the option to reject your invitation. You need to focus on making and keeping your vows for your sake, and if you have children, for their sake. One sensible parent is better than none.

Finally, we have encouraged you to be realistic, and if you make Divorce Vows, include how you will handle disagreements with your CPP. Your spouse will always be able to push your buttons and arouse feelings and emotions in you. Mastering yourself is the goal and your task. You will have moments when you regress to old behaviors and make mistakes. Recognize your mistakes and apologize for them, independent of how your spouse reacts to your apology. All these are steps in the Plan for a Sensible Divorce.

Part Two: Rehearsing Sensible Responses to Your CPP

A sad reality when marriages move towards divorce is that criticisms have usually narrowed down to a handful and become boringly predictable, even though still hurtful and frustrating. The predictability, however, is helpful once divorced.

Most divorced people can predict the most likely future criticisms.
This provides the opportunity to rehearse sensible responses.
Rehearsing undercuts mistakes.

When someone applies for a job, a coach will have the applicant rehearse responses to predictable questions. In a Sensible Divorce, people predict situations that are likely to be emotional and rehearse responses to keep things sensible.

Be assertive, not controlling: Your authors are not advocating passivity, but are advocating setting boundaries by asserting yourself. An act of kindness is making the communication loop very clear, and this is accomplished by being assertive. Assertiveness is different from fighting back. Assertiveness completes a feedback loop from which we all have the opportunity to learn, even from your CPP.

Look at the following Examples:

"You're late."
"Oh, like you are always on time!" [Fighting back]

"You're late."
"You're right, I am sorry." [Assertion]

"You're late."
"I had no control over that." [Assertion]

"You're late."
"You are right, and it will be difficult always to be on time every time. Let's be kind to one another and have an intention to be on time, but give each other plus or minus ten minutes." [Assertion and problem solving]

"How typical, you always want to be in control."
"How immature! You act like a teenager, and like I'm your mother. Well, no more." [Fighting back]

"How typical, you always want to be in control."
"I am sorry that you did not like my suggestion. It was made with good intentions." [Assertion]

"How typical, you always want to be in control."

"I will think about that. I do not want to be a person always trying to control things." [Assertion]

"How typical, you always want to be in control."
"I am sorry that you see me that way." [Assertion and not taking the comment personally]

Sensible Exercise: Think about situations that are likely and predictable in the future. For example, assume a new boyfriend or girlfriend shows up at a child's event with your CPP. Rehearse a sensible response. Think about the types of statements, or behavior (e.g., he/she rolls her eyes), that typically trigger you. Write them down. Think through assertive, honest responses, for each item on the list. Now, act them out: pretend that your CPP is there and has said or done those things, and out loud, give your responses.

Rehearsing like this is a way of learning. Hearing yourself improves the likelihood that you will be able to remember and repeat. Rehearsing also gives you a chance to hear out loud what you would like to say and change it for the better. Rehearsing responses out loud prepares you to break habits and resist the invitation to the toxic dance. Remember it is assertion, not control, you are seeking.

**A key to behaving in a sensible manner in relationships
involves setting clear and sensible boundaries.**

Setting Boundaries. We all have a better ability in relationships if we feel safe. When we do not feel safe, we are inclined to react with the primitive part of our brains, rather than our thinking brains. The primitive parts of our brain want to attack the threat or run from it, neither of which is particularly useful in most circumstances. The primitive parts of our brain also lead people to be very picky about small things. Setting boundaries in relationships leads to feeling safe, so that we can be deliberate in our responses and interactions with others, and keeping small things in perspective. This is the goal. For example, if your CPP yells at you, set a boundary, *"I will always listen to you when you keep your voice down and are courteous, but will never listen when you yell."*

**In a Messy Divorce, boundaries are often lacking
for both spouses, generally leading to the emotionally based
responses of attacking one another or
going to great lengths to avoid one another.**

CPPs end up in conflict over relatively minor inconsequential details. In other words, ex-spouses are operating in the wrong part of their brain. Most ex-spouses are at least hesitant to interact with one another. The reason is that they do not feel it will be safe to do so.

You might have immediately dismissed some of our suggestions because you thought of interacting with your spouse as abhorrent and to be avoided. You might anticipate hurt, anger and perhaps even more sadness. Setting boundaries is how we make relationships feel and be safer.

However, setting boundaries in a conflictual relationship often implies to people that they can assert a boundary and the other person will respect that boundary. However, the other person might not respect that boundary. If we are at a party and someone is standing closer to us than we feel comfortable with, we can say, *"Would you please not stand so close?"* If the person backs up a bit, we have successfully set a boundary, but only because the other person respected our boundary. What if the other person does not back up? We recognize immediately that we are not dealing with a cooperative person and need to take a different tack. The easiest response: We can turn and walk away.

In messy divorces, people are often uncooperative with one another's boundaries. Therefore, simply asserting a boundary might be ineffective, and a different strategy is required. The temptation is to try to control the other person, and so we are tempted to escalate in our efforts to get cooperation with our boundaries. This often is ineffective, and we end up attacking or running. We are again operating in the wrong part of our brain.

A different and safer strategy is to set boundaries in a manner that does not require the cooperation of the ex-spouse. Let us give some examples in order to clarify. Assume that CPPs escalate into arguments if they talk on the telephone or in person. Or, one of the CPPs refuses to talk in person or on the telephone. Assume that at some point, that one or both soon discover that they need to communicate information in some way, so they begin to email one another. However, they soon discover that they escalate to arguments in their emails, spending way too much time reading offensive emails from the other ex-spouse and writing lengthy defensive and attacking responses.

Multiple and/or lengthy emails are, in essence, doing the toxic dance remotely.

To set a boundary, imagine that you propose that the emails remain focused solely on information about the children and that both of you refrain from criticisms and denigrating comments. Assume further that the other spouse responds with an email full of criticisms and denigrating comments. You set a boundary, but the other did not cooperate or respect the boundary. Now, what to do?

1. The first step is recognizing that you have no control over the decisions of others and remembering that you have complete control of your decisions. You can control what you choose to read and write.

You can set a boundary, by only reading an email (or parts of it) and only responding to emails (or parts of it) that contain information about the children.

2. Of course, the next step is to let your ex-spouse know about the boundary you just set. One might write an email to the ex-spouse saying something like: *'From here on, I will start reading your emails, and if the email only contains information about the children, I will keep reading. If I come to a criticism of me or a denigrating comment about me, I will stop reading or ignore the rest of the email. Do not assume, therefore, that any information not about the children will be read by me. In fact, assume just the opposite. If there is more information about the children later in the email, I will not have read it because I stopped at the criticism. In addition, I will not respond to any questions or comments that do not relate to the children.'*

From that point on, the final step is that you must follow through with this Plan. The boundary is set: only email information about the children will be read.

Note: No matter what your CPP does. The boundary does not require any cooperation.

Now let's take the same problem, but assume that rather than speaking directly or sending emails, your CPP begins to send both useful information and criticisms through the children.

The first step might be to assert to your spouse that it is harmful to send information and criticisms through the children and offer an alternative way of communicating. However, what do you do if your CPP continues to behave in this destructive manner? The temptation is to do the same and send messages back through the children, but this only compounds the problem, at least for the children.

1. Again, the first step is always to focus on where you have control and where you do not. You have control of yourself and do not have control of your CPP. Control of yourself includes how you interact with your children, including when they are confronted with a life problem. In fact, this is the point.

   When our children bring us a life problem, if we focus on our job as parents, we realize that we can teach our children effective strategies for dealing with problematic situations.

2. In this situation, you have an opportunity to teach critical thinking, which means that you are not influenced by gossip, but always measure gossip by your direct experiences. In a sense, your CPP is gossiping about you to your children. You might get upset and be tempted to try to control the other parent and get them to stop doing that.

Critical thinking. You need to remind yourself that you do not have control of your CPP, so do what you can to teach your child about this skill. You can teach your child that when the other parent says negative things about you, the child should think about whether or not he or she agrees with the comment. If he or she agrees with the comment, it should be brought up with you so that you can talk to the child about it. If the child disagrees, then the comment can be dismissed as gossip. If the child is older, you might even include that they can tell the person who is gossiping that they do not like to talk about people behind their back.

Let us give an example to illustrate this point. Assume that your child comes to you and says, "*Dad said he wants to take us to the circus next weekend, but that you won't let us go because it is not his weekend.*" The temptation is to confront the other parent or even worse, make a denigrating comment about the dad to the child. Instead, you should focus on what life lesson you can teach your child and take a different strategy.

We preface this with an important point. You are always wrong to criticize or denigrate the other parent to your child. However, giving facts is not criticism or denigration. It is very helpful to give children facts.

**Parents attempting to protect their children
from being caught in the middle of parental conflict
often believe that this means not giving factual information.
However, factual information is very helpful to children
in order to build their critical thinking.
Critical thinking is the escape route for children
with conflictual parents**.

When people do not give children factual information, they might come to believe things that are not true, which hinders the development of critical thinking. It is a shame that teaching life lessons is required because of the other parent's behavior, but that does not change the fact that this is a parental task.

In our Circus Example above, the task is to give factual information in a way that is not critical of the other parent but teaches an important life lesson. The response to the child might be, "*Your dad seems to have jumped to a conclusion that is not true. If he had asked to take you to the circus next weekend, and we had no plans, I would say yes. It is a shame that he did not ask.*" Notice that this is just factual information.

**To be effective, however, in teaching critical thinking
to children, people must have a reputation
with their children of always being honest.**

They must always know that if they hear something, they can ask at least one of their parents and always get the facts. To take our Circus Example one more step, assume that your child comes back from the other parent next time and says, *"Dad said he did ask to take us to the circus, and you said no."* The response must be honest, factual and not critical of the other parent. For example, the response might be, *"He asked last year, and I did say no because we had plans that I could not change. He did not ask this year. Maybe he thought I would say no again."* Or the response might be, *"Perhaps he asked in an email that I did not read. I told your dad that if I am reading an email, and he says mean things to me, I am going to stop reading. So maybe later in his email he asked, but I did not see it, and therefore I did not respond. He might have thought that meant I was saying no."*

The hesitation to give children factual information about the other parent is often because of good intentions. People do not want their children to think poorly of the other parent. However, critical thinking is best learned when they have information about reality.

Let's take one final look at the Circus Example. Assume the first time the child brings it up, you had refused the request for no good reason. Now the honest response to the child might be, *"You know, your dad has a right to be upset, and so do you. When he asked, I got angry for no good reason and said no. I apologize to you for that, and I will apologize to your father. I will also let him know that, if there is still time to arrange taking you to the circus, that is fine with me."* Again, you have taught your child useful life lessons.

Here, you might be hesitant to give factual information because you do not want your child to think poorly of you, but the parental task is not to manipulate your image or the image of the other parent. It is to teach life lessons and provide factual information. In this last example, you are teaching your child that sometimes you make impulsive emotionally based decisions and doing so is a mistake. When people have made that mistake, they should admit it, apologize and see if they can salvage the situation.

**The critical lesson of this section of the chapter
is to learn to set boundaries by focusing
on what you have control over and what you do not.**

If your spouse is not cooperative and respectful of your boundaries, you need to take a strategy that is not dependent on cooperation. Children often find themselves caught in the middle of conflictual parents in a messy divorce, but people have complete control of how they address this with their children. As long as they have the reputation of being reliably honest without criticisms of the other parent, they can teach their children helpful life lessons that they can apply in their own lives.

One additional and final step to complete the information loop: The Open Information System. In order to complete the loop, you have one more step to take. You need to provide information to your CPP. The reason for this is a little theoretical, but important to understand. In an Open Information System, everyone in the system has the same information, and that is accomplished with communication. The reason this is important is because open information systems are self-correcting. When some people have some information and others have different information, there is inevitable conflict. This is a Closed Information System. Whether or not your CPP provides you with important information is out of your control, but you do have control over whether you provide your CPP with information.

Again, in our Circus example, you might write an email: "*Sarah told me that you wanted to take them to the circus next weekend, and that I would not let you because it is not your weekend. I told her that you seem to have jumped to a negative conclusion about me. Had you asked, I would have said yes, because we do not have any plans…*" This is polite and useful information without any criticisms, without any attempt to control or make the other parent feel bad. It gives the other parent a chance to provide the child with a corrective experience, but even if the other parent does not do this, the other parent might at least be more reluctant to make similar comments in the future.

Or, in the last example, the email might say, "*Sarah mentioned that you wanted to take them to the circus and that I said no. I apologized to her, and I apologize to you. For some reason it upset me, and I made a mistake. Is it too late to take them? If you can make the arrangements, they can go to the Circus with you.*"

Summary: Here as elsewhere in this book, the lesson is that no matter what your spouse or spouse does or does not do, you can behave in a sensible manner and not be stuck in a toxic dance. It just takes some creative thinking and a focus on yourself and not on your spouse. You might be skeptical because of the bad experiences you have had with your ex-spouse. However, we can tell you from direct experience that situations like that can be turned around, often because one of the spouses invites the other to a new and sensible dance. Model social maturity to your children.

Our bottom line regarding this Chapter:
Make Divorce Vows and rehearse sensible responses to your CPP!

Part IV
Developing a Sensible (And Effective) Approach to the Legal and Planning Tasks of a Divorce[45]

"Taking the path less travelled..." (Buddhist advice)

---

[45] Part IV of the book is for spouses who have not prepared or submitted a Marital Settlement Agreement to the Court. If the reader has completed a divorce and has Court Orders in place, this Part might be interesting, and perhaps useful, but might not directly apply to your situation, unless there are post-Judgment Motions pending or contemplated.

Chapter 13
Getting the Lay of the (Legal) Landscape Goal Based Planning and the Attorney-Client Initial Interview

The Legal Planning Tasks:
The Goal Based Planning Way

Introduction to the legal aspects of marriage and divorce. A marriage (when there are children) has five important areas of legal responsibility, to which certain laws apply.

Two parts apply to the financial aspects of the marriage:

1. Property and Debt
2. Spousal Support

Three parts apply to the care of the children of the marriage:

1. Custody (Decision-making)
2. Co-parenting Time Schedule (Daily Responsibility for Children)
3. Child Support (Financial Care)

At Marriage: We do not typically think about the legal aspects of a marriage, although most of us are aware of some of those laws. For example, in some States, one spouse cannot take out a loan or even a credit card without the signature of the other spouse. In addition, while married, we are financially liable for our children. Some of this is not by choice, such as when our child causes damage and we have to pay for the repair. We are also legally responsible for the daily care of our children, and if we fail to take this responsibility, our children can be removed from our care. In other words, the State has an interest in the management of the financial lives of spouses and in the care of children. Those laws coincide with values and goals of spouses, so they are not usually considered, unless there is a substantial breach.

At Divorce: Similarly, the State has an interest in the distribution of property, debt and income and the care of children when people are divorcing. Divorcing spouses must submit to the Court their plans for these identical areas of responsibility. This is often called a Marital Settlement Agreement ('MSA').

If the spouses fail to develop their own plan and/or disagree about certain aspects of the legal tasks, the divorce will include a contested trial, where evidence is offered and the judge makes the final decisions about any one or all of the five areas mentioned above, where needed.

The MSA. As introduced above, the MSA sets forth a Plan to address the following, summarized below:

FIVE MAJOR LEGAL ASPECTS OF A DIVORCE

1. Property and Debt
2. Spousal Support
3. Custody (Decision-making)
4. Co-parenting Time Schedule (Daily Responsibility for Children)
5. Child Support (Financial Care)

At the outset, and most important, a new Mindset is required
when developing a sensible (and effective) approach
to the legal aspects of a divorce.

Let's begin by setting the stage regarding this new Mindset:
When making decisions about the legal tasks,
rather than seeing those as goals,
we recommend you see them as tools to reach long-term goals.

The legal system is invested in the distribution of property, income and the children, where the legal tasks focus on distribution. However, for spouses, when preparing the MSA, the focus should be a goal-based planning process- not a focus on the distribution. The reason for this is that the distribution as conceived in law is a Zero Sum Game, where anything one spouse gets is at the cost of the other spouse. In other words, law changes the Non-zero Sum games of co-parenting and financial planning into Zero Sum Games of distribution.

We have discussed this earlier in the book, where the divorcing spouses can achieve a 'sensible divorce', with optimal outcomes for both spouses, by following our Four Step Goal Based Planning Model first introduced in Chapter 4.

For lawyers and judges, the case is generally finished on the day of the final Judgment of Divorce. However, spouses walk out of the courtroom with lives to lead and futures to experience, particularly if there are children involved. Their divorce does not end that day; it starts that day.

Worse yet, what might appear as an advantageous outcome
on a legal task at the time of the divorce,
might actually be an obstacle to reaching long-term goals.

Because the court system is essentially set up to resolve disputes, lawyers and judges often think of divorcing spouses as in a dispute. However, your authors submit that the legal outcomes, meaning the agreements and the Court orders effective at the time of the divorce are best viewed as the beginning of the Plan to reach long-term goals, not the end of the divorce process.

Sensible spouses should resist the temptation to view themselves as in a dispute, competing for limited financial resources or time with their children. The sensible approach regarding the legal tasks is to plan to reach shared long-term goals. Only when there is a plan to reach those goals are the legal outcomes designed as the first step in the plan.

Shared goals. Sensible spouses do not necessarily have a dispute with regard to the long-term outcomes for their children or even the financial outcomes for each other. They usually want the same type of positive outcome for their children. Most divorcing spouses also have the goal of both doing reasonably well financially down the road, not only because it is the right thing, but perhaps more importantly, it will be good for the children. The sensible approach to the legal tasks, therefore, is to plan in order to reach those shared goals, rather than compete in an artificial dispute over legal outcomes.

Goal Based Planning. The initial attorney-client meeting is critically important.[46] Let us give a simple example of how the legal system can initially side-track divorcing spouses and create artificial disputes. When spouses initially meet with their attorneys, the attorneys will generally explain the legal outcomes that must be reached and ask what their client's initial position is on each of those legal outcomes. Because the process started with a focus on positions, unless both spouses happen to have identical positions, the attorneys have inadvertently created a dispute. Each client and his and her attorney are now engaged in a battle, to see which spouse's positions will prevail.

In Goal Based Planning, the place to start is to focus on the long-term goals of both spouses.

Many experienced attorneys might begin by asking questions about their client's long-term goals, beyond the legal outcomes. However, it is rare for these same attorneys to ask their clients about the long-term goals of their spouse. They will likely take positions on legal outcomes without this important information.

---

[46] Toward the end of this chapter, we provided some sample goal-based planning questions to be used at the initial Attorney-Client Interview.

We recommend that this critically important practice change.
Learning about both parties' long-term goals grows the pie
for both of them.
Read on!

It might be up to the spouse to slow an attorney down and not consider legal outcomes until a comprehensive plan to reach the long-term goals of both parties is complete. It is only at that point that the legal outcomes that will give the long term plan a good start can be designed.

There are two major advantages to start by learning about <u>both</u> spouse's long-term goals <u>before</u> even thinking about the legal outcomes:

1. First, unnecessary and artificial disputes can be avoided.
2. Second, substantial research has determined that if the focus is on both spouses' goals, the planning process increases the value of the settlement for both spouses, including the attorney's own client. In other words, each attorney is increasing the size of the piece of the pie for his or her own client by learning about and developing a Plan to help **both** clients reach long-term goals.

This second point is not obvious. Because attorneys, and often clients coming into the legal system, assume that the legal process is a competition over limited resources, whether that be money or time with children (or both), they put on the mantle of selfishly attempting to prevail on what appear to be favorable legal outcomes.

The goals and outcomes for the other spouse are irrelevant in such a process, because there is an assumption that the other spouse and attorney will be putting on the same mantle. However, research disabuses us of those underlying assumptions and proves that the best way to optimize or maximize outcomes for both clients is to grow the pie first, by focusing on the long-term goals of both clients, so that each piece is bigger.[47]

---

[47] For readers who are curious about this point, we refer you to the contributions of John Nash (*A Beautiful Mind*), who is best known for his concept of the Nash Equilibrium but who probably had much more impact with his concept that negotiations turn out best for both parties to the negotiations, if before

We also remind the reader of the Traps of the legal system (Chapter 10 of our book), an important one being turning the Non-zero Sum Games of financial planning and raising children into the Zero Sum Games of distributing property, income, responsibility for and time with children.

The antidote is to resist the Zero Sum Games
and engage in financial planning and
planning how best to raise your children.

An example of dividing the cake and a discussion of sharing goals. Let us look at a simple experiment, which has actually been carried out in real life. Two people are shown a marbled cake, with some chocolate and some vanilla. One person is given the assignment of cutting the cake, and the other person gets to choose the first piece. The assumption is that both people will want the biggest piece. Therefore, the only solution appears to be for the first person to cut the cake as close to equal as possible, making the choice of piece of cake irrelevant. Both people get one-half of the cake.

However, assume that before cutting, the people discuss their goals. One says that she loves cake and would like a big piece. The other says that she loves chocolate cake and is not real fond of vanilla cake. She also adds that she does not want a particularly big piece because she likes to keep her weight down. The person cutting the cake then notices that one end of the cake has more marbled chocolate than vanilla. Consequently, the person cutting the cake cuts a smaller piece on the end with more chocolate, and the other person chooses that piece. By discussing goals, our subjects have enhanced the value of each piece of cake, even though it included an uneven division. In this case, they grew the cake to reach goals.

The Co-parenting Time Schedule:
The Goal Based Planning Way

---

competing, they cooperate to grow the size of the pie. A good deal of subsequent research has confirmed his point, including research on attorneys who are effective or ineffective negotiators. (For example, Andrea Kopfer who published *Shattering Myths: Empirical Evidence on the Effectiveness of Negotiation Style).*

A detailed example of dividing the holiday time and a discussion of sharing goals. A discussion on how to 'divide' holiday time with children can work in much the same way. For example, rather than simply alternating years for who gets Thanksgiving and the rest of the holidays, imagine a discussion with regard to the goals of both spouses with regard to the eleven Thanksgivings (assuming the youngest child is 7 years old.) left before their children become adults. They share the goal of the children having really memorable Thanksgivings and the hope that when the children are adults, they will continue to want to spend holiday time with their parents and with extended family when possible. One parent might say that he or she would like to preserve the family tradition of the children having Thanksgiving dinner with his/her extended family, all of whom live in the area. Up to this point, that is what they have done.

Assume the other parent says that he or she agrees that tradition means a lot to the children, but would like at least once or twice to fly to the area where his or her extended family lives and have Thanksgiving with them. He or she also adds that he or she would at least like to see the children sometime over the Thanksgiving break from school every year. One of the attorneys asks if the client's extended family would be okay with the client coming to the traditional dinner. The soon-to-be ex-spouse says, '*Wouldn't that be cool*'. The client says that some of his family is angry at her for initiating the divorce, but they always liked her before. To their credit, these parties entered into a goal planning dialog.

As the reader can see, by discussing goals,
the spouses are setting the stage for an optimal way
to celebrate Thanksgivings.

Trying to make everything equal became irrelevant to providing the children with optimal Thanksgivings. The final Plan might also include how to repair the damage between the wife and the husband's extended family All this is part of a long-term goal: preserve an important tradition, provide the wife with a couple of options to spend Thanksgiving with her extended family over the next 11 years, and perhaps have both the children's father and mother at a Thanksgiving dinner together when with his family.

This same approach can be applied to every holiday, that is, with the long-term goal of having the best holidays possible, given the circumstances. The planning is done together, and the long-term goals of both parents receive equal consideration.[48]

This approach requires patience on the part of the attorneys and the clients. If the question in the first meeting was simply whether the client wants one-half of all holidays, the wife might say, 'Of course', and the husband might say he wants them all, so the children can continue to go to his family's celebration. This results in a dispute that minimizes the outcome for both clients.

This might seem like 'pie in the sky', because there is often so much hurt, anger and sadness at the time of a divorce that a discussion about goals might seem impossible. First, your authors have witnessed discussions like this, so they are not always impossible. Second, what if one spouse is sensible and focuses first on goals, even though the other spouse is bitter and insensible? A meaningful dialog is possible, though not always. Because Goal Based Planning is always possible, it is beneficial to begin with goals, not positions.

Perhaps surprisingly, there is another advantage of working with attorneys. because they are less emotional about the planning. In addition, they can keep their clients focused on long-term goals.

For example, assume the husband wants to be sensible, but his wife is bitter. Although she initiated the divorce, she blames him for her decision to assuage her guilt and sadness. She is not being sensible. Being sensible, he tells his attorney that his goal for Thanksgivings is for the children to have memorable

---

[48] Research identifies this type of inductive decision-making (planning each holiday based on facts) is superior to deductive decision making (splitting all the holidays equally). In economic research, this is defined as "incremental decision-making."

experiences and to spend at least some holiday time with each parent, with the hope that the children will continue to spend holiday time with each of them after they are adults.

The discussion with his attorney includes information about his family tradition (where her extended family lives) and includes information about the rift with his extended family and the wife (because she initiated the divorce).

One can see that this is a discussion about Thanksgiving,
and not about any position on the legal outcome.

The attorney can speak with the other attorney to find out about the wife's goals. Unanswered questions can go back to the wife by her attorney, and although the spouses are not speaking to one another, in a round-about way, they are having the same discussion as earlier, but through their attorneys, possibly with the same outcome on the legal issue.

This is a win-win.
However, in some cases, attempts to
secure an uncooperative spouse into a
Goal Based Planning process will fail.

Proposal for a less than optimal outcome in lieu of a toxic dance. In our example, imagine that no matter what the husband and attorneys do, the wife insists that one-half of all the Thanksgivings with the children are spent at her residence.

She is insisting on the toxic dance in a messy divorce, resulting in a diminished value regarding the legal outcomes for both spouses and the children. The best the husband can do is to refuse to do the toxic dance and focus on goals for himself and the children.

In lieu of the toxic dance, under the circumstances, it would be sensible for him to propose that the children spend most Thanksgivings with him, but that she has the option of having the children for two Thanksgiving breaks to travel to see her family and that she has every Thanksgiving weekend with the children to celebrate.

Note: We admit that a less than optimal agreement on Thanksgiving is not the end of the world. However, let's look at a more serious issue.

Another Example. Divorcing spouses have a two-year old son. What type of parenting time schedule a two-year-old should have, is very controversial, even among respected researchers and experts. This is because of the immense risks of attachment problems for a two-year-old.

Children with damaged attachments spend the rest of their lives suffering, at best mildly in failing relationships, and at worst, as criminals or at high risk for suicide.

Experts who want the child to attach to both parents are right, and the implication is that a two-year-old should spend time with both parents. However, experts who want the child to have at least one secure attachment to a parent, rather than two insecure attachments are also right, when they say that the child should live mostly with one parent. It sounds like a problem with no solution.

However, this is only true if the focus is on the legal task of deciding parenting time with the child. If the focus is on the child developing secure attachments to both parents, a plan can be developed, and once developed, a legal outcome can be designed for the court.[49]

The Financial Plan:
The Goal Based Planning Way

---

[49] Typically, this requires a developmental psychologist to participate in the planning because the plan will be complicated.

The same focus on financial goal-based planning, rather than distribution, is likely to optimize outcomes for both spouses. The questions are not about who gets the house and how much support is a judge likely to order. The questions are about the long-term financial goals of each of the parties, and how their current property and future income can be used to reach those goals. Rather than the husband getting the house, the plan might be to put the house into a trust, to be sold at a date certain in the future, to pay for college for two children.

SAMPLE FINANCIAL AND CHILD-RELATED
GOAL BASED PLANNING QUESTIONS
FOR THE ATTORNEY-CLIENT INITIAL INTERVIEW.[50]

Instead of asking questions about legal outcomes, the questions should be about goals:

- What financial condition would you like to be in 5 to 10 years?
- How about your spouse?
- What is your thinking about retirement- yours and your spouse?
- What kind of work would you like to be doing?
- What are your goals for your children?
- What are your spouse's goals for the children?
- What are some of your goals for your children regarding holiday time? How about the goals of your spouse?
- Is academic success of the children important to you? How about your spouse?
- Is owning a residence important to you? How about your spouse?
- What would you like your children's experience be like now that their parents will be living separately?
- What types of relationships would you like your children to have with each of their parents?
- In the long-term, what kind of relationship would you like to have with your ex-spouse?

---

[50] Many attorneys ask clients about their goals, but not often about their spouse's goals. Many attorneys may ask about the positions the other spouse is taking on legal outcomes, but not about his or her goals. In order to have an MSA be a good Plan, the goals of both spouses should be addressed.

These questions will have financial implications. Some legal outcomes might help reach long-term goals, but some might be obstacles. If the focus is on legal outcomes, instead of goals, there is a temptation to make emotional decisions or let greed or other problematic emotions dictate a position.

For example, one spouse might be a higher earner and not want to pay spousal support. This might be an emotional decision, or it might be selfish greed. However, paying spousal support might be a better way for both spouses to reach important financial goals. Likewise, dividing children's time can be very emotional. Both parents might be tempted to compete for every single minute, when a schedule for the children, entirely different from what either of them want, might be the best way for both parents to reach goals they have for themselves and their children. It might also be emotional to distribute marital property, even when the focus is on being 'fair', when an 'unfair' division might actually better help both spouses reach long-term goals.

A new Mindset is needed to have a sensible approach regarding the legal tasks of the divorce, identifying long-term goals and then designing the legal outcomes to give both spouses their best chance of achieving those goals.

Research in an area of mathematics makes clear that the best outcomes for two people in negotiations occur when they cooperate to achieve the goals of both parties. In a sense, they grow the pie before splitting it, so that they both get more than one-half.[51]

Attorneys often ask his or her client about their goals, but not about the other spouse's goals. The most effective bargaining process is one that starts with getting the goals of both spouses on the table. We have illustrated this in our earlier discussion about Thanksgiving and will continue to illustrate it regarding other legal outcomes as we get into specifics. For now, we are introducing a new Mindset that sensible negotiations require.

It is important that the attorneys know and understand (and hopefully incorporate) this new mindset as one of their important Practice Tools.

---

[51] For mathematics buffs, or if you are curious, the actual results of Game Theory research suggest that by cooperating, parties can grow the pie to 146% of the objective value on the table, instead of 100%. That is an extra 46% to share!

In a Sensible Divorce,
the attorneys' job is to help plan for long-term goals,
and not compete for his or her client's position
on each and every legal outcome.

However, for attorneys to do their jobs, clients
also need to keep their focus on goals
and avoid the traps of the traditional family law system.

Chapter 14

Four Step Goal Based Planning Template for Making Decisions Regarding the Legal and Planning Tasks[52]

FOUR STEP GOAL BASED PLANNING TEMPLATE FOR MAKING DECISIONS REGARDING THE LEGAL AND PLANNING TASKS[53]

In this Chapter, we introduce our Template for making collaborative decisions in a goal-based Plan, where the focus is on reaching long-term financial **and** children-related goals for the family, taking into account the realities in the current situation.

---

[52] See Chapter 4, where our Four Steps are introduced. See also the following Chapters where we address the tasks in planning regarding the children (Chapter 15) and the tasks in planning the financial issues (Chapters 16 and 17).

[53] As you may have suspected by now, the applicable Planning Tasks and our Four Planning Steps Template for Custody, Co-parenting and Financial Plans are basically identical.

As a reminder, the Four Steps are the following:

Step One: Describe in detail the current situation.

Step Two: List each spouse's long-term goals, specific to the decisions being made.

Step Three: Plan the steps for reaching long-term goals.

Step Four: List the obstacles and steps to overcome them and create a Plan.

Applying the Four Steps in our Template is slightly different depending on the legal or planning task being addressed, but this is the basic process and procedure throughout. We will be repeating the Template as we go through each of the tasks, illustrating the slight differences in application, but if you have these Four Steps in mind, you will be able to apply them well.

Because our focus is on planning, not litigating,
we break down the legal and planning tasks
slightly differently.

Brief Overview: Legal Tasks 101

1. **The child-related legal tasks** involve reaching agreements regarding the following:
   (a) child-related decisions (our **Custody Plan**) and
   (b) taking care of the children on a daily basis (our **Custody Plan** and our **Co-parenting Time Schedule Plan**).
2. **The financial-related legal tasks** involve reaching agreements regarding the following:
   (a) distributing marital and non-marital property and allocating debt
   (b) sharing future income regarding spousal support and child support (our **Financial Plan**).

Because the primary focus in the legal system is on the legal tasks, many if not most jurisdictions have child support formulas or guidelines based on the parenting time schedule. There is some foundation for this thinking. Child support is linked to the parenting time schedule where the guidelines often help flesh out the costs of having children in the home. Planning for the support of the children is part of the larger picture of the financial lives of the parents. Because of this, it fits into planning all forms of income-sharing.

Unfortunately, many parents and attorneys link the child support to the parenting time schedule and confound the decisions about that schedule as a result. However, when engaging in Goal Based Planning, planning child support is separate from the parenting time schedule, where the schedule is simply one of the factors important in that planning. The schedule might suggest a baseline expense, depending on where the children are when they are incurring expenses. In Goal Based Planning, expenses should be based on the goals of the parents for the financial support of their children, and not based solely on the schedule.

**Caveat: Linking child support to a parenting time schedule
is one of the traps of the family law system.
Don't fall into that trap.**

Now: Get Ready to Multitask!

The only way to accomplish a sensible and effective Marital Settlement Agreement (MSA) is to multi-task.

**This means working within the law
and (simultaneously) accomplishing a goal-based Family Plan,
which includes all of the financial, custody
and co-parenting relationship issues.**

Therefore, we strongly recommend that spouses use our Four Step Goal Based Planning Template for a successful co-parenting relationship at the same time they are planning the financial specifics of their MSA. When an agreement is reached regarding all issues (i.e., the Custody Plan, the Co-parenting Schedule Plan **and** the Financial Plan) these terms will be set forth in the MSA, and submitted to the Court to get a divorce.

**While the legal tasks are not particularly important in the long run,
agreements on the legal tasks are legally required.**

To underscore this, most amicable spouses pay little attention to the legal tasks, because they plan to have an amicable co-parenting relationship that is flexible, where they do not strictly follow the schedule submitted to the court in an MSA.

Even in the 60% of divorcing spouses with children with less than amicable divorces, they rarely follow the schedule in their MSA over the long-term. Only about a third of divorcing parents are following the court-ordered schedule two years following the divorce. This is because life is not static, especially with children. Circumstances change. Even work schedules of parents change. As a result, parenting time schedules change.

There is very little research on whether or not divorced people follow the financial tasks as outlined in their MSA after the divorce, but it is very likely that changing circumstances also affect those agreements, especially support agreements.

The law usually requires that people file motions for modifications with regard to support issues, but we have little research on whether or not people do, especially people in amicable post-divorce arrangements.

To repeat and summarize our point:
You must multi-task and address the Custody Plan,
the Co-parenting Time Schedule Plan,
as well as the Financial Plan.

GOAL BASED PLANNING.[54]

If you went to a financial planner, the planner would focus on the details about you and your life. This might seem very personal, but the planner has a Template- an approach that he or she takes with every new client. Without a Template, the planner would never know where to start or how to proceed. The same is true for having a 'sensible approach' to making decisions in a divorce.

This is why our book is titled *Planning a Sensible Divorce.*

---

[54] Goal Based Planning is initially introduced in Chapter 4. It is critical that goal-based planning start at the time of the Initial Client Interview (Chapter 13).

> Again, we refer you to our Four Step Goal Based Planning Template for Making Collaborative Decisions.[55]

We also believe it is important at this juncture to define '**Family Plan,**'[56] which describes a Plan that encompasses all three of the Plans presented in our book:

(1) **Custody Plan**
(2) **Co-parenting Time Schedule**[57]
(3) **Financial Plan**

In this Chapter, we also introduce this Template for Making Collaborative Decisions in a goal-based Plan, where the focus is on reaching long-term financial **and** child-related goals for the family, considering the current realities.

Because our focus is on planning for the family, not litigating, we break down and treat the Legal Tasks and Planning Pasks differently.

[Please read on, where this is summarized in an outline format below!]

---

[55] In Chapter 6, we introduce our Four Steps for Making Collaborative Decisions based on goal-based Planning.

[56] See also the following Chapters, where we present three different Plans as part of goal-based planning divorce process, all encompassed under one name- our **Family Plan:** (1) Custody Plan (Chapter 15), (2) Co-parenting Schedule Plan (Chapter 16), and (3) Financial Plan (Chapters 17 and 18).

[57] The co-parenting **tasks** added in this book for the Co-parenting Time Schedule Plan are usually not required by law, although research indicates that those tasks are substantially more important to outcomes for children when compared to the Co-parenting Time Schedule per se. Our book attempts to address this information gap.

I. LEGAL TASKS.

1. Children Legal Tasks:

a.   **Custody Plan:** This Plan determines the type of legal custody that will be in effect, specifically, whether major decisions will be made jointly by both parents, solely by one parent or some hybrid version. This is the subject of Chapter 15. The list of major decisions about the minor children are usually enumerated in the applicable State statutes law and various Appellate Court decisions. However, in a sensible divorce, parents can modify the list present in law, usually adding other decisions that will help the family run smoothly.

b.   **Co-parenting Time Schedule Plan:** This Plan determines what type of parenting time schedule will be in effect for the minor. children- specifically, which parent will be principally responsible for the children at various times of the day and night. We call this our Co-parenting Time Schedule Plan. This is the subject of Chapter 16.[58]

---

[58] As mentioned above, sensible parents make many parenting decisions about children that are not enumerated in law. The co-parenting decisions grounded in law are a list of decisions that are joint, sole or some hybrid decisions. That's basically it. Of course, these should be included in the MSA. However, and in addition, in many (perhaps most) cases, it may be prudent to prepare a more extensive list of likely (legal) decisions in the future and include them in the MSA. Those too need to be designated as joint, sole or some hybrid decisions.

2. **Financial Plan:** This Plan has two component parts, which sets forth the distribution of assets and debts and allocates income between the parties. We call it our **Financial Plan:**
    a. Distributing marital and non-marital assets and allocating debt
    b. Sharing future income
        i. Spousal support
        ii. Child support

II. PLANNING TASKS

Note: The Planning Tasks enumerated below, are separate and distinct from the Legal Tasks presented above, and as a general rule, much more important.

1. **Child-related Planning Tasks:**
    a. Setting forth the actual parenting time schedule
    b. Having rules and procedures for information-sharing about the children
    c. Establishing rules and procedures for flexibility in the parenting time schedule and access of parents to children and children to parents
    d. Designing child-focused transitions
    e. Coordinating parenting across homes
    f. Having a more extensive list, beyond those prescribed in law, with rules and procedures, for making joint parenting decisions about the children.

    Note: The above child-related goal-based **planning tasks** focus is on PLANNING TASKS and not on DISTRIBUTION TASKS (meaning the legal tasks). This focus will likely optimize long-term outcomes for the children!

2. **Financial-related Planning Tasks:**
    a. Plan a budget, including child-related expenses
    b. Plan for paying down debt, using income and property

c. Plan savings for future retirement of both spouses

d. Plan for owning/renting homes that accommodate the children

e. Plan the distribution of property to facilitate these plans

f. Plan the distribution of future income to facilitate these plans, including, if needed, increasing total family income. (Income-sharing is often required but should not be seen as a burden to the payer and a boon the receiver. In our Model, income-sharing is seen as a tool for reaching the goals of both spouses!)

Note: Like child-related goal-based planning tasks above, financial-related goal-based planning, does not focus on distribution. The questions are not about who gets the house or how much support a judge is likely to order. The questions are about the long-term financial goals of each of the parties, and how their current property and future income can be used to reach those goals. This approach is also likely to optimize outcomes for both spouses!

An Example: Assume that the divorcing spouses own a vacation cabin and both want to receive the cabin in the property division. As a legal task, this establishes a conflict of interest. One of the spouses has to give in or the issue must be resolved through litigation. However, using our Four Step Planning Template and approach, they discover similar long-term goals: Using the cabin on weekends and vacations with the children, with the children to own the property eventually, when they are adults.

They therefore agree:

- Place the property in a trust for the minor children, naming themselves as Co-Trustees and the children as the beneficiaries.
- Develop a procedure for scheduling between themselves for use with the children.
- Place the cabin available for rental and pay a cleaning service out of the proceeds.
- Deposit rental proceeds in an account held by the trust.
- Use rental proceeds for maintenance and taxes.

To Lawyer Up or Not to Lawyer Up—This is another important question to ask when applying our Four Step Goal Based Planning Template for making decisions regarding the Legal and Planning Tasks

Spouses about to divorce, especially those with limited resources and a relatively uncomplicated financial picture, usually have opinions and/or fears about divorce lawyers. If they have a relatively amicable parting, they might seek do-it-yourself options or meet with a mediator as unrepresented clients. If they have a good deal of conflict with one another, more resources and a more complicated financial picture, they might choose to hire attorneys, anticipating a battle and wanting an experienced battler. However, most of these opinions and/or fears are unwarranted.

Most divorce lawyers are knowledgeable about the long-term implications of divorce agreements, but most important, many divorce lawyers have been trapped by their legal training and experience and have (inadvertently) fallen for the Ten Traps in the Traditional Legal System (see Chapter 8). However, if spouses are clear that they want to make good (meaning effective) Custody and Co-parenting Time Plans (see Chapter 15) and Financial Plans (see Chapters 16 and 17) to reach long-term family goals, lawyers can be invaluable in reaching those goals! Consider the following:

1. Lawyers are wordsmiths who can draft agreements in a Marital Settlement Agreement to accomplish the goals of the clients.
2. Lawyers are trained problem-solvers, able to explore options most spouses might not even think about or know exist.
3. Lawyers are usually trained in factors that are important for children of divorce and have seen creative solutions from prior cases that are beneficial to divorcing parents.
4. Lawyers are also trained in financial planning, tax implications and legal alternatives to simple distribution that, again, spouses might not be aware of or know exist.
5. Lawyers are familiar not only with the steps in a legal divorce but also with the other people in the system who will be involved.

6. Lawyers can help manage the emotions of the spouses, that can derail the process, and keep the focus on problem-solving and planning to meet goals.

7. Lawyers can recognize when one of both of the spouses have special needs. They are usually familiar with local programs (e.g., for an alcohol problem) and providers (e.g., for a counselor to help with unmanageable sadness) who can help. They also usually know mental health providers that can educate parents on the long-term needs of children with divorced parents.

Many divorcing spouses anticipate that hiring attorneys will be expensive. This too is a distorted image. Divorce lawyers usually do have a high per-hour fee, but that only becomes excessively expensive in highly litigious cases, where there are many time demands made of the lawyers, especially if the case goes to trial.

Let us try another analogy. Financial planners are expensive, but are they really? If you were to retire with $500,000 in net worth without a financial planner, but paid $4,000 or $10,000 to a financial planner and retired with $900,000, would you have regretted the cost?

However, hiring an attorney is not without risk. Some attorneys have personal problems. Your authors know one divorce attorney, for example, who sees himself as the little guy, with a mission in life is to beat the big guys (successful attorneys). Other attorneys hope for potential new clients with a conflict-oriented expectation, who can add to existing conflict with power struggles with the other lawyer. However, most attorneys are very sensible professionals, and if a client has a sensible approach to a divorce (or will take advice to pursue a sensible divorce), the lawyer can be a great help.

Most important: Your authors strongly recommend that the client start with a very clear directive to the attorney, such as:

"I want you to help me come up with a plan to meet the long-term financial and parenting goals for me and my spouse."

In fact, when a client does this, most divorce lawyers will be delighted and work hard to reach that objective.

So, our answer to the question posed above is a simple one:
If you want a sensible divorce, you should
be clear with your lawyer
as to why you are hiring him or her.
This means,
LAWYER UP!

Summary: Our point in this Chapter is that at the time of the divorce, the focus should be on a goal-based Plan to reach long-term goals **and** simultaneously with an attorney to craft the legal tasks in the best way possible to implement the Plan.

This is the approach that we will take in the next four chapters. In Chapters 15 and 16, we address two child-related legal tasks. In Chapters 17 and 18, we address the two financial legal tasks.

With regard to the child-related tasks, it may be prudent to multitask and work simultaneously on two documents: the MSA **and** a Co-Parenting Agreement.[59]

In other words, we are suggesting more multi-tasking, at least with regard to children's issues, but also possibly with regard to some financial steps regarding child support, which will be part of the Financial Plan. Divorce lawyers can be a great help in putting together the needed agreements in a way to be approved by the Court and have a Sensible Divorce.

This Chapter is key in our book, because it provides the
bridge between accomplishing the necessary *legal tasks*
and the necessary *planning tasks* in a divorce, primarily focusing
on reaching family's long-term child-related and financial goals. While
the planning tasks are the most important,
the legal tasks are necessary for getting a divorce.

When there are minor children, as we have pointed out, the primary task of the parents is to plan for their futures, and the primary task of the attorneys is to

---

[59] We remind the reader than your authors have produced a Co-Parenting Training Workbook, available from www.unhookedmedia.com which can be the working document for the Family Plan.

facilitate the plans of the parents, while at the same time meeting the standards of the law and the Court.

This means that in the settlement negotiations, spouses and attorneys are multi-tasking, focusing on both the legal tasks and the family planning tasks. As we have pointed out, attorneys can provide invaluable help with both sets of tasks. They not only have special knowledge about the law, but also have knowledge about the implications of choices made and can help keep the parties on task when problematic emotions threaten to be disruptive.

Chapter 15
Custody Plan
and the Legal and Planning Tasks

A Sensible Approach—Developing a Custody Plan

Remember there are two basic **legal** tasks regarding the daily care of the children, organized as set forth below:[60] The next several chapters will contain some, perhaps, unfamiliar language, which we will call 'legaleze'. Spouses do best when they understand some basic legal terminology.

1. **Custody Plan:** Determining what type of legal custody to have—specifically, what major decisions constitute legal custody in your family and whether those decisions will be made jointly by both parents, solely by one parent or some hybrid version. We call this the Custody Plan (also called the 'Legal Custody Plan'), meaning the list of decisions that are joint, sole or some hybrid. This will be the subject of this Chapter.

---

[60] Jurisdictions, usually counties and states, have various names for these two tasks. We have choses names that we hope will be clearest with regard to what they mean.

2. **Co-parenting Time Schedule Plan:** Determining what type of parenting time schedule you will have for your children—specifically, which parent will be principally responsible for the children at various times of the day and night. We also include our Co-parenting Tasks Plan. This will be the subject of Chapter 16.

Before proceeding any further, in addition to the two Plans mentioned and defined at the beginning of the Chapter, we remind you and will define one additional Plan- our 'Family Plan'. What is it, and what does it mean?

**As previously mentioned,
our 'Family Plan' is an all-encompassing term[61],
which describes a Plan with multiple tracks:
custody, co-parenting and finances.**

**We also refer you to our
Five Tasks and Rules for Successful Co-parenting (see Chapter 7).[62] [63]**

To begin, we will address the Custody Plan, before addressing the Co-parenting Time Schedule Plan in Chapter 16. As previously stated, sensible parents make many parenting decisions about children that are not specifically enumerated in law, in addition to those decisions to be made joint, solely by one parent or some hybrid arrangement. At a minimum, these decisions should be included in the MSA.

However, your authors strongly recommend that there be an additional listing of decisions likely required in the future. Those too need to be designated as joint, sole or some hybrid decisions. Joint means that both parents must be

---

[61] While we do not use the term "Family Plan" very often in our book, it is a good term to use because it is very broad and includes all of the other plans for the children and the family- e.g., Custody Plan, Co-parenting Time Sharing Plan, Financial Plan, etc.

[62] There is also a financial component related to the daily care of the children, which we will introduce in Chapter 16 and address in more detail in Chapter 17.

[63] A separate self-standing Co-parenting Agreement may not be a required submission to the Court, as terms of the co-parenting agreement may be included in the MSA. Each case is different. This is another way that lawyers can provide helpful advice.

involved in the decision, where both parents have equal legal authority. Sole means that one parent has the sole authority to make the decision. Hybrids can involve a number of combinations, such as:

1. Parent A has the final decision-making authority, but only after getting input from Parent B.
2. Parent A has the authority to make the decision but must inform Parent B.
3. Both parents have equal authority, but in the case of an unresolved disagreement, there is a designated decision-maker. This could be one of the parents or it could be a relevant expert (e.g., doctor, coach, etc.).

A Custody Plan (i.e., dealing with decision-making) is different from the legal custody requirements in the law in at least three important respects:

1. The list of decisions in the MSA should be much more extensive, including predictable situations. For example, the law might not list deciding bedtimes or how much screen time is healthy, but sensible parents discuss these and make decisions.
2. The procedures for sharing information should be set forth, so that future decisions are effective.
3. The rules and procedures for how joint decisions will be made should be specific.[64]

Before addressing the decisions to be made about custody, a residential plan and child support, we re-introduce the use of Bounded Rationality as an adjunct to the more scientific decision-making model which we feature below.

DECISION-MAKING:
BOUNDED RATIONALITY VS. SCIENTIFIC METHOD PLUS
A CONVERGENCE OF EXPECTATIONS ON SOLUTIONS

As previously discussed, there are two ways that people make decisions: the Scientific Method and Bounded Rationality.

---

[64] For example, in our Co-Parenting Training Workbook, available at www.unhookedmedia.com, we introduce an evidence-based procedure: our Six Step decision-making Model.

1. **Bounded Rationality** recognizes that spouses, in their conscious and unconscious minds, have a font of important information that the attorneys do not have, which must be allowed to surface during the negotiations.
2. The **Scientific Method** involves making a list of options available, looking at the pros and cons of each option and then picking the option that has the best balance of pros and cons.

As useful as the Scientific approach can be in some situations, most people do not make life decisions this way. Bounded Rationality involves the way most people make life decisions. This is because people have an enormous amount of information stored in their brains, some of which they might not even be aware of when bargaining.

3. When people are in a situation where they can share information, and are bargaining, something occurs that is magical. It is called **a Convergence of Expectations on Solutions**- some of which are creative and some of which surface as a complete surprise to everyone involved.

Ideas that seem to come out of nowhere are actually Bounded Rationality at work, and this works best when the spouses are together making the Plan. Four-way meetings[65] with two lawyers and two clients are the best way to do this, because this includes the Bounded Rationality of four people with very different skills and experience.[66]

Although more cumbersome, if spouses cannot tolerate being in the same room at the same time, this can be accomplished in shuttle negotiations, with each lawyer and his or her client in a separate room, but with the attorneys 'shuttling' to each other's rooms or even a third room and talking.

Taking days by meeting with clients in offices, and then scheduling attorney-attorney meetings, greatly disrupts the process of a Convergence of Expectations, which depends heavily on information and ideas spontaneously popping up. For example, a mother might say, "*I think you (the father) should*

---

[65]We understand that there are situations where Four-way meetings would be inappropriate and/or ineffective.

[66] Using a skilled mediator is another alternative.

handle extracurricular activities for the children. You are just better at that kind of thing."

However, keep in mind that Bounded Rationality can also be impulsive and not consider all of the factors involved. The Scientific Method is helpful in this way.

We always start with our Four Step Goal Based Planning Template for Making Collaborative Decisions.

A quick reminder regarding this Template:

Step One: Describe in detail the current situation.
Step Two: List each spouse's long-term goals, specific to the decisions being made.
Step Three: Plan the steps for reaching long-term goals.
Step Four: List the obstacles and steps to overcome them and create a Plan.

Step One: Describe in Detail the Current Situation.

There are five parts to fleshing out the current situation as applies to custody: (1) listing the major decisions required by law, (2) making a list of what have been major decisions in the family historically, (3) anticipating likely major decisions in the future, (4) deciding how major decisions were made that include both parents, including any difficulties making mutual parenting decisions, and (5) deciding what information-sharing accompanied the decision-making in the family in the past.

A List of Major Decisions: What are the major decisions listed in the law in your jurisdiction? Most if not all jurisdictions have a list in the law of what constitutes a 'major decision' in regard to legal custody.

Because you are making a Plan, not a legal outcome, add to the major decisions defined by law, meaning other decisions that will be best made with input from both parents. For example, most jurisdictions list 'Choice of School' as a major decision. However, you might include any special programming within the school, such as an accelerated class. If parents want additional decisions enforceable by law, they can add these decisions to the list of major decisions in the MSA. However, many if not most parenting decisions in a sensible divorce can simply be listed for the parents' use and may not need to be in the MSA.[67]

We remind you of the **Five Tasks and Rules for Successful Co-parenting After the Divorce,** which were presented in Chapters 7 and 9:

1. Sharing information
2. Having access and flexibility in the parenting time schedule
3. Planning child-focused transitions
4. Coordinating homes to be organized as similar as possible
5. Making decisions, solving problems and taking action

These tasks suggest that many parenting decisions that should be made at the time of a divorce are repeatedly remade as circumstances change. For example, coordinating homes to be similar will involve decisions at the time of the divorce about chores, rules, incentives and consequences, routines (e.g., bedtimes), homework routines and so on.

However, as children get older, those decisions need to be changed: some eliminated and some added. For example, decisions about a 16-year-old driving might be added when a child is getting to that age. Making rules and routines for transitions might also need to change with circumstances (e.g., when a child is old enough to ride a bike from home to home).

Joint decisions are generally the best decisions, so, err on the side of listing decisions when you are not certain if they need to be joint and work through that list during the MSA negotiations.

How have the listed decisions been made in the past? It is important to review how decisions have been made in the past. This is particularly true if there has been difficulty making joint decisions when there was a disagreement.

This could be an important obstacle regarding a Family Plan to reach family goals because it is very likely that joint decisions (and parenting time/schedule conflicts) when parents disagree will come up many times in the future.

---

[67] However, in cases when there is low trust, there is always a risk when the list is not inclusive, because it is not enforceable in a court of law. Thus, some decisions might be helpful and included in the MSA to keep parents on a sensible track. Your lawyer can advise you accordingly.

Remember, conflict is not inevitable. Conflict only arises when people fail to resolve disagreements.

The final step in fleshing out the current situation is to focus on how well informed you have kept one another about major decisions in the past and up to the present time. This is important because living in the same residence, you might have taken for granted the information-sharing process, because you were both there. A mother might casually mention that she was going to give permission for an activity at school and because the father was in the room, he could agree or disagree on the spot. Going forward, you will face the logistical challenge of operating an information-sharing and decision-making process when you live in separate residences.

For example, assume that one parent takes a child to put in a pierced earing and comes home, the other parent sees it, and gets angry. Had they discussed at what age pierced ears are acceptable, there would not have been a problem. This might sound petty, but parenting instincts can blow up into heated conflicts if the parents have not designed a plan for making these types of decisions and sharing information about them.

Step Two: List Each Spouse's Long-term Goals, Specific to the Decisions Being Made.

Begin to list what you are each trying to accomplish in the long run for the child, along with all available choices. This must be for each decision being addressed. A successful Plan is built inductively, building a whole Plan by adding together all of the individual decisions. For example, the parents might agree to the following:

"Both parents recognize that for our child to have a good experience participating in extracurricular activities, it should include input from our child, with the long-term goal of our child developing skills and friendships through those activities, and perhaps taking some of those activities into adulthood."

A Plan will be partly shaped by this goal. If the goal is for the child to have a good visible appearance by the time he or she reaches adulthood, then the Plan might include dental care, such as braces. Some goals are obvious, such as reaching adulthood in good health. Others might not be so obvious. Be prepared to run into disagreements in this Step, but do not get side-tracked trying to resolve those disagreements at this early stage.

As the you surface these goals, you might be tempted to argue about whose goals are more valuable, but this is not the time for that discussion. Here, you are simply surfacing long-term goals, and it is normal at this Step that some of those might appear to clash. The time to address this is in Steps 3 and 4 of our Four Step Template, but not here.

Continue to develop a clear vision of the future for your children based on your long-term goals for them. For example, if you want independent self-directed children, this might have to be included when making major decisions about their lives. In that way, the parents can teach them how and what to consider when making decisions.

All this could be an important when making a Plan in Step 4 (Creating a Plan). When you have a clear and thorough vision of that future, go on to Step 3 (Listing the Steps to Accomplish Goals), but also be open to discovering more goals as you go through Step 3 (Listing the Steps to Accomplish Goals) and Step 4 (Creating a Plan).

Step Three: Plan the Steps for Reaching Long-term Goals

At this point, you have fleshed out the current situation. You made a list of decisions that you consider major and should go into the MSA and a list of potential parenting decisions that will be part of the co-parenting relationship. You have also developed a vision of the long-term outcome for the children based on the long-term goals of both parents for the children. As a result, you have a picture of the starting point and a picture of the destination. In addition, you will develop a list of obstacles and steps to overcome them in Step Four. It is now time to develop a Plan that includes steps to take to reach your goals.

Listing the steps to take to reaching long-term goals with regard to the legal custody of children is particularly challenging, because it relies on an honest self-reflection and honest feedback to one another. Keep in mind that the purpose of this exercise is to reach long-term goals, not start arguments or make unnecessary criticisms of one another. This might make the task a little easier. However, taking a frank look at yourself, with the help of your spouse, can be emotionally challenging.

Some steps to accomplish goals might reflect a lack of information. For example, both parents might have the goal of the child having academic success, that is, doing as well as possible given who the child. However, neither parent might really know how to achieve this. Just telling a child to do his or her best will not accomplish the goal. The Plan might have to include a method for getting additional information needed in order to accomplish a goal. In the education example, it could be important to speak to experts about the skills needed for academic success. In the extracurricular activity example, the financial implications of various activities could be important. If you are not particularly well-off financially, this could be an important factor in making a Plan. A good question to ask is, "*What additional information do we need in order to make a good Plan.*"

A touchy set of decisions will be needed if either or both of the parents have new romantic relationships. i.e., how and when to introduce the children to the new potential partner, and if it is a serious relationship (e.g., a possible second marriage), what role the stepparent will play in relation to the children. However, many problems can be avoided by proactively making these decisions jointly before they are actually faced.

The best way to build a Plan that accomplishes goals is to do so inductively, not deductively. Therefore, one does not start saying, "*I want joint legal custody with every major decision.*" This might seem fair, and might even be a presumption in the law, but it is backwards to have a Plan that is constructed deductively. In almost all cases, such a Plan will fail to achieve the parent's intended goals.

The process of building a Plan inductively is a simple one: take the list of proposed decisions, start with one and then design a Plan for that decision. For example, let us assume that choice of school is on the list, as is the case in most jurisdictions. Flesh out what that means. Does it include choice of pre-school programs? Does it include any extracurricular activities associated with school, such as participation in elective academic activities; and so on? In this case, 'choice of school' needs further defining so that there is less of a chance of a misunderstanding later. Once there is a list of decisions, begin to design Steps in the Plan.

SIX STEPS FOR DECISION-MAKING

Step 1: Should this decision be made jointly, made by one parent with input from the other parent, or be the sole responsibility of just one parent?

Step 2: If sole, what rules and procedures need to be in place to make sure the other parent is alerted to what was decided. E.g., Assume decisions about religious training at a church is decided to be the sole responsibility of the parent who is most involved with that church. The agreement might be that the parent making the decision informs the other parent of the decision within a week, by email.

Step 2 cont'd: If one parent makes the decision, but with input from the other parent, what rules and procedures need to be in place? E.g., Assume one parent is a teacher and is the designated decision-maker regarding educational programming, but with input from the other parent before a decision is made. The rule might be that a telephone appointment is made, the decision is discussed and, if requested, the other parent can get more information and further discuss the decision. Then the teacher could make the final decision, if the parents cannot agree.

Step 2 cont'd: If a decision on the list requires that it be joint, whichever parent becomes aware of the decision makes an appointment with the other parent, before investigating the options. At the appointment, the two parents decide what information they need, how to get it and what the options are. After they get the information, they discuss the options and decide on one.

Step 3: Because of a history of having difficulty resolving disagreements (Obstacle), if the agreement is that the decision on the list should be joint, the parents focus on the **Ten Disagreement Resolution ('DR') Skills** (Chapter 6). We recommend you learn and practice them.

Step 4: Design information-sharing procedures. Critical to effective decision-making is both parents having the same body of information. This is accomplished with separated parents by having four procedures with rules:

1. General information-sharing. In most cases, this involves a once a week meeting or telephone call, having a list of the information wanted and needed, with each parent sharing everything that they know about the information on the list.

2. Information that a parent has about the children when transitioning to the other parent that will help the other parent. Could be by texts, a brief conversation at the transition, or a phone call.

3. Emergency information that cannot wait until the weekly sharing. A method of sharing needs to be designed.

4. Making sure that both parents get copies of all of the paperwork (e.g., soccer schedule).

Step 5: Apply the **Four Step Goal Based Planning Template** related to the decision. Then move on to the next decision on the list and follow these steps, until all of the decisions on the list have agreements.

Step 6: If the decision is on the list of those that must be in the MSA, craft the agreement terms (hopefully with attorney assistance) and apply the appropriate wording in the MSA, so it is part of the Family Plan.

**This approach may sound lengthy and tedious,
and is likely so, especially for parents who are extremely unhappy
with each other and sad about what they are going through.
However, it is definitely worth it.**

The temptation is to get everything over with as quickly as possible with the fantasy that the pain will stop by doing so. Remember, time does not heal all wounds; proactive planning heals wounds.

Step Four: List the Obstacles and Steps to Overcome Them and Create a Plan.

The biggest obstacle in most situations is acknowledging that the method of resolving disagreements did not work well during the marriage. The bad news is that people, like in our Tibetan tale, tend to keep doing the same thing over and over, even when it does not work. Some divorcing spouses will be tempted to continue to use ineffective decision-making approaches to child-related decisions. The good news is that decision-making procedures have been heavily studied in research, and effective procedures are well known and easily learned. That is, the skills are easily learned, but it takes a good deal of practice to break the emotional habits of a history of ineffective approaches. A basketball player might practice making four shots for hours. Why? Because Skills are accomplished with practice.

Other typical obstacles involve logistics and the limits of reality. For example, a child's time is limited, which limits how much can be accomplished within any measure of time. A child can only do so much in a day, a week, a year and even before he or she turns 18 years old. Another logistic obstacle might be the work schedules of the parents or how far apart they live after the separation. If both parents can go to a dental appointment, decision-making about future care might be relatively easy, but if one parent is unavailable, a special procedure might need to be designed.

Some obstacles might be specific to the personalities of the parents. For example, one parent might have a history of making impulsive decisions; the other parent might be overly reliant on advice from others. Here, the DR Skills Model comes into play. If a mother says, "*An obstacle is that you jump to conclusions before having all the information*". The skills of not taking criticisms personally but listening for important information and being vulnerable and admitting to weaknesses, might work. A weakness is not bad thing, but might be an obstacle to making good joint decisions, if not resolved.

Special Problems and Three Examples: Your authors have seen some situations where making a Plan is particularly challenging. In order to illustrate these special problems, even challenging obstacles can be overcome with some creative thinking and a focus on problem-solving, not criticism or blame.

1. Example Problem #1: A mother is more inclined to seek medical help than the father, and he believes that her tendency to do so will adversely affect the child. She sees his failing to get what she believes is needed medical care as neglectful and accuses him of not caring about the children. He sees her 'over-use' of medical care as a reflection of a mental health problem on her part, not as a medical need of the children.

   The parties describe the problem in a way that has no solution. They describe the problem as her having a mental health problem and behaving irrationally and him as not really caring about the well-being of the child, to the point of child neglect.

**To develop a Plan,
the problem has to be described in a way
that can lead to a solution.[68]**

   More Regarding Problem #1: Take the criticisms, blame, name-calling and 'who's right' out of the situation and what do we have left?

---

[68] This is one of the DR Skills in Chapter 6.

All parents have protective instincts, but how and when those kick in, varies with each parent. Think of protective instincts as like a thermostat for a heater. Some protective thermostats kick in at the slightest sign of a medical problem, while others do not kick in right away, thinking that most indications of a medical problem go away by themselves and do not mean anything serious. The mother and father in this situation cannot tell if her thermostat is kicking in too soon or if his is kicking in too late. That is the problem, but it is a problem that has a solution.

The Plan: Either parent can seek a medical assessment, even over the objection of the other parent, but the other parent must have opportunity to be part of the assessment. If the parents disagree regarding treatment, impasse-breaking authority could be delegated to the recommendation of the medical provider. The children can be told that the parents differ on how soon to seek a medical assessment and have decided to seek one if one parent wants one and then make a decision about treatment, depending on the results of the assessment. By doing this, the children are being taught an important lesson about relationships. Think of it this way: If two people want to run together, but one cannot run at the pace of the faster runner, they can only run at the pace of the slower runner. This is a challenge that almost all relationships include.

2. Example Problem #2: The parents have a history of arguing without resolving disagreements; the arguments can get ugly. When the argument is about a child- related issue, they can really get ugly because so much is at stake. However, we also know that arguments get ugly out of frustration, which means that the manner in which they try to solve disagreements is half the problem, and the other half is that they do not have rules about how they treat one another when they disagree.

The Plan: The parents must find a decision-making model that addresses disagreements when both parents believe they are 'right', such as is described in Chapter 6. Rules of conduct will be made so that the disagreements do not get ugly and stay on topic.

3. Example Problem #3: The father is forgetful and might forget the children's appointments or important events at school. When they lived

together, the mother could control her anxiety about the father's forgetfulness because she was there to take care of things. Now that they are separated, she has no way to control her anxiety, and the father remains forgetful. For these reasons, she wants the children with her most of the time and to be in charge of most of the major decisions.

The Plan: The mother agrees to send reminders by text message, and the father agrees to have a calendar on the kitchen counter into which he puts appointments and school events and agrees to check the calendar each morning.

**As you can see in the above three Examples,
the goal is to overcome obstacles, not criticize one another,
or use obstacles to try to prevail on positions.**

Summary: A Sensible Approach- Developing a Custody Plan

1. Sensible Mindset:

The Sensible Mindset is to bargain cooperatively in a goal-based planning process. This recognizes that the divorce is not the day of the final Judgment of Divorce. The divorce is a relationship that lasts for the rest of people's lives. When there are children, the divorce includes interaction on a regular basis. The interaction can be in a messy form, including ex-spouses who avoid each other like the plague, engage in open conflict or complain about one another to anyone who will listen. If messy, it is a miserable relationship for the parents and a miserable experience for the children. If sensible, during the co-parenting relationship, the parents are courteous with one another and proactively plan their lives and those of the children in a sensible manner. To be sensible, the problematic emotions need to be handled in a sensible manner, and the pitfalls need to be avoided.

Decision-making together is the heart of a functional co-parenting relationship. Almost everything else is dependent on this skill. While the law focuses parents on the parenting time schedule, the parents spend not much more than five minutes deciding the legal task, usually choosing 'joint',[69] The reality is that the co-parenting relationship is dominated by the day-to-day decisions necessary for raising children.

The Good news! The approach in this book looks cumbersome and a lot more time working together than most divorcing parents want to spend. While this is true at the beginning of life as divorced parents, two things happen:

- Parents get pretty good at this fairly quickly, and it might take no more than a few minutes in the future to make a major decision.
- This approach prevents so many disagreements, that the co-parenting relationship runs pretty smoothly most of the time.

The Bad News! Parents must have the skills to resolve disagreements in the future. There will be disagreements. The skills needed were presented in Chapter 6, and parents would do well to understand those skills and practice them. A side benefit is that parents who do this can teach and model the skills to their children, preparing them for their adult lives to go well.

2. Take-away Techniques:

The Take-away Techniques are summarized as follows:

1. Never start with a position on an individual issue/task, or worse yet, on a large collection of tasks. Use our Four Step Goal Based Planning Template to reach effective plans.
2. Build the Plan inductively, focusing on and developing a Plan for each individual issue/task, building the whole Plan brick by brick.
3. Always include the goals of both parents; grow the pie first with a cooperative approach.
4. Focus on a Plan for the family; not on the legal task. Prepare the MSA with the legal tasks after the full Plan has been developed.
5. Develop a Plan for making child-related decisions. The Plan should include which decisions will be joint, which can be made by one parent with input from the other and which can be sole decisions but keeping the other parent informed.

---

[69] Many Jurisdictions even make "Joint Custody" a presumption, meaning you need to prove that Joint Custody is not a good arrangement.

6. Most states list between 6 and 11 major decisions. Add decisions that are very likely to be made in the future that should be joint. Keep adding decisions as children get older, preferably before they actually have to be made.
7. Develop rules and procedures for future decision-making
8. Study and practice our Disagreement Resolution Skills in Chapter 6.

Chapter 16
Co-parenting Time Schedule Plan and the Legal and Planning Tasks

The Sensible Approach—
Developing a Co-parenting Time Schedule Plan

WARNING!

Most jurisdictions set the co-parenting time schedule on the basis of overnights, with an assumption that the parent with that overnight will also have one or both of the attached daytime periods. There are two major problems with this:

One, no research has found that where children sleep overnights affects their long-term outcome, with the sole exception of attachment formation for children under three years old. Attachment formation usually includes the child sleeping at least some time at each parent's home. However, even this does not require that it be overnights. The sleeping could be naptimes.

Two, establishing parenting time schedules on the basis of overnights and attached days is an example of one of the 'traps'-previously discussed in Chapter 8: assigning ownership of time with children.

OUR QUESTION: Why does the law do this?

OUR ANSWER: Because overnights can be counted and can establish easy guidelines for child support.

In other words, the law does it in order to serve the interests of the courts, not the interests of the children or the family. Establishing a co-

> *parenting time schedule on the basis of overnights and attached days unfortunately locks parents out of portions of children's lives and traps parents into Zero-sum Games- where each parent (and their children) loses.*

Sensible Mindset for Developing a Co-parenting Time Schedule Plan

As has been true of each section in this book, there is a Sensible Mindset to have in order to be successful, and there are specific techniques to use:

1. Having a Co-parenting Plan for the involvement of both parents in all aspects of the child's life, independent of the parenting time schedule. The goal here is for both parents to be parents 100% of the time, not to have some artificial limitation of a court-ordered schedule. No parent is with their child all of the time, and few parents begrudge the child spending time with others if goals are being achieved. These include time with peers, extended family members, teachers, coaches, music teachers and so on. We wrote earlier about how the legal system traps parents into competing for the limited time of a child, rather than being parents all of the time, even when not with the child.

This is important to parents and crucially important to children. A great deal of research has consistently found that the best outcomes are reached when children have both parents actively involved in their lives. Those children are generally better behaved, do better socially, do better in school, enter adulthood better equipped for relationships and careers and are happier and more satisfied with their childhood.

However, do not be trapped into thinking that this suggests a certain type of co-parenting time schedule. It does not. Children with separated parents can just as easily have the healthy involvement of both parents in their lives, even if they spend most of their time in just one of the two homes. This is especially true when looking only at overnights. Where children sleep should only be a question of logistics, that is, which home is the best choice given where the children are in the evening and what happens in the morning. If there are no logistic obstacles, then it does not matter where they sleep, as long as they have at least some time sleeping in both homes.

The key is having a healthy co-parenting relationship and a parenting time schedule that has at least some of all types of child time with both parents.

This means some school days (not necessarily overnights), when schedules and tasks dominate lives- meaning some weekends and other less structured days; some holiday time; and participation of both parents in child-related activities outside of the homes.

Feelings of loss and sadness (i.e., missing the child or the child missing a parent) is managed with access and flexibility. This is often an emotional hurdle for parents, wanting the most legally designed parenting time to avoid the loss and helplessness of being without children.

Let us give some examples of how access and flexibility overcome this obstacle:

> *"Hi, I am phoning to see if I can pick up the boys and take them out for an ice cream. I am getting off work early."*
> *"Sure, that will actually help because I have to shop for dinner."*

> *"Can I go over to dads? I have math homework and you know how good Dad is with math."*
> *"Give him a call and see if he can come get you."*

> *"My parents are coming this weekend. Could we switch weekends so that the kids can see them?"*
> *"Oh, I bet they would love that. I can switch things around. Say hi to your folks."*

> *"Sorry for the last minute, but I have a meeting I can't miss. Can you pick up Barbara and take her to dance today?"*
> *"Sure. What time is the class?"*

> *"You won't believe it. I caught John with a case of beer in his trunk. Could you come over tonight to talk with him with me? I think having both of us here will be more effective."*
> *"Can we do it after dinner? I could come at 7:30."*

> *"Do you want me to pick you up for the parent-teacher conferences this evening?"*
> *"Yes, that would be perfect."*

2. Developing a parenting time schedule built inductively, not deductively. Each part of the overall schedule is addressed in terms of the long-term goals for that part of the schedule. The suggested order reflects the prioritizing of law. For example, no matter what the weekend schedule is, Holidays take priority.

Use our Four Step template for Goal Based Planning (which you have already learned) to address each part of the overall co-parenting time schedule. Agree on goals for both parents, with a Family Plan aimed at accomplishing as many of those goals as possible.

We will follow the same Goal Based Planning Template
that we introduced in Chapter 15 regarding the Custody Plan
and apply it to the Co-parenting Time Schedule Plan
introduced in this Chapter.

Remember (again), there are Four Steps in our Goal Based Planning Template:

1. Step One: Describe in detail the current situation.
2. Step Two: List each spouse's long-term goals, specific to the decisions being made.
3. Step Three: Plan the steps to reach long-term goals.
4. Step Four: List the obstacles and steps to overcome them and create a Plan.

Step One: Describe in detail the current situation.

1. Make a list of the Parenting Time Schedule Components:
    b. Holidays that are celebrated in the family
    c. Weekends or even individual days on the weekends
    d. Weekends in the summer that might be different from weekends during the winter

    e.   Vacation opportunities that the parents and the children enjoy

    f.   Summer weekdays or even parts of days

    g.   Days during the week that the children are off of school

    h.   School days or even parts of school days

    i.   And so on…

2.   List all of the logistical considerations, such as parent availability, probable distance between homes, [70] support systems (e.g., nearby grandparents), school and daycare hours, locations of the children's activities and friends and so on.

3.   Discuss considerations regarding each of the children, including their ages, temperaments, personalities, interests and activities outside of the family, relationships with siblings and so on. This might include needing additional information about children's needs relative to a co-parenting time schedule and how to get that information.

4.   Discuss relevant considerations in terms of strengths and weaknesses of each of the parents, perhaps including how to improve weaknesses.

Step Two: List each spouse's long-term goals, specific to the decisions being made.

Imagine now that your children are older, say 25 years old.

- What would you like to hear them say about their experience of their childhood from the time of the parental separation until they were 18 years old?

- Looking back over that same time period, when the children are 25 years old, what would you like to be able to say about how you and your ex-spouse handled the rest of their childhood?

- When the children are 25 years old, what would you like their relationships to be like with both parents?

---

[70] If your authors were asked: What two pieces of advice would you give to divorcing parents? Our response would be: (1) Have a sensible co-parenting relationship, and (2) Live near one another if possible. Living near one another makes everything so much easier.

- How would you like to see your adult children handle the normal ups and downs of relationships, and how well would you like to see them handle disagreements with important people in their lives?
- Do you want to look back and view each of you as a parent some percentage of time or view both parents as parents 100% of the time? [Flexibility and involvement independent of the schedule is how the latter is accomplished.]
- Crucial to this Step is to ask probing questions. For example, one parent might say that he or she wants the children to do well academically in school. That is not a goal; it is a means to goals. The probing question is something like, *"In what way will the child's adulthood be better if he/she does well academically in school?"* Likewise, to say that you would like your child to have some input in what activities he participates is not a goal. The goal is for the child to learn how to make good choices.

Participating in those decisions might develop skills that enhance his or her decision-making as an adult, which is a goal, but one might have goals that suggest the parents make those decisions and require the child to participate in certain activities. For example, a parent might want each of the children to have learned to play a musical instrument in their childhood, thinking that this will enhance their adulthoods, if only by learning the skills involved. This discussion is not about philosophy of parenting; it is about outcomes for the child.

There is guidance from the research on outcomes for children.[71]
The most important factor reported by children
is how well their parents got along with one another.
It is certainly separate and distinct
from the parenting time and schedule.

Research informs us that the children got it right. Not only are they most likely to be satisfied if their separated parents got along well with one another, they are most likely to be doing well in their lives.

---

[71] As a reminder, we previously discussed "Factors Predicting Outcomes for Children Following a Divorce" in Chapter 10, Illusion #5 and "Five Parenting Skills Affecting the Outcomes for Children," also in Chapter 10, Illusion #8.

In the words of Robert Emery,
"They were able to be kids—not children of divorce."

Research-based Goals and a Vision of Your Children's Adulthood: Developing a Successful Co-parenting Time Schedule Plan.

We begin with a list of research-based goals and a vision of your children's adulthood:

1. **A courteous co-parenting relationship.** Those courtesies include: keeping each other informed, treating each other with courtesy when in the presence of one another, designing transitions to be smooth and conflict free, making polite requests rather than angry demands, and having rules with regard to behavior that is not permitted. They might include other courtesies specific to the people involved. For example, while the parents should be well informed about the children's experiences, it is not necessary to be informed about each other's personal lives. Some ex-spouses might like to discuss each other's personal life, such as work or extended families, but others might want a rule of privacy and only share information about the children.

2. **Sufficient time spent with both parents.** This is a tricky goal because it has direct implications for the legal outcome of a physical custody schedule (i.e., co-parenting time/schedule). Research informs us that children who spend all types of child time with both parents have the best outcomes. This means some school time, some nights and mornings and some unstructured time like vacations and weekends, and some holiday time. School days are often a source of disagreement, but the social science research is very clear on this.

Children with parental involvement by both parents,
in school-related activities and demands,
are much more likely to do better academically,
socially and behaviorally.

Thus, if for all practical reasons, it makes sense for the children to be in one home during the school week, parents should plan ways for the other parent to be very involved in the school life of the child. If there are no obstacles, then some school days with each parent are likely to be better than no days with one of the parents.

3. **Flexibility in the custody schedule.** We mentioned earlier that children cite flexibility in the schedule as very highly desirable. When children were interviewed after they have grown, research on families supports the advantage of flexibility in co-parenting schedules.

> **Separated parents who have children who turn out well**
> **have a good co-parenting relationship,**
> **and one of the things they allow is**
> **flexibility in the schedule.**

Flexibility can also benefit the parents. Flexibility allows both parents to double the available resources for the children. As another example, one parent might find out about an opportunity, but is not scheduled to have the children in order to take advantage of the opportunity. Having a procedure in place to request the children is important, otherwise both the parent and the children lose out on the opportunity. Another example reflects a goal of having the parents be the caregivers of choice. In such a situation, a parent can call the other parent and say, *"I have to work late today; can you take the children after school to about 8:00 o'clock, including feeding them dinner?"* This flexibility can also be good for the child. In such a family, a child could ask, *"Can I go to Mom's house to work on that school project tonight?"*

4. **Both parents being involved in all aspects of the child's life, independent of the co-parenting time schedule, including involvement in major decisions affecting the child's life.** This goal is essential to the quality of the parent-child relationship for obvious reasons. Attending child-related events, or even being involved in the events (e.g., a coach), demonstrates a higher level of interest in the child. Both the child and the parent get to know each other better, seeing each other in a variety of settings. A mother, who is a 'team mom', for example, will know much more about her child's social skills, friends,

and perhaps even things that the child needs to work on for improvement. The implication for making a co-parenting schedule is to have the schedule facilitate parental involvement when possible. However, parents can be involved independent of the schedule. For example, a mother who is a 'team mom' can request to pick the child up from the dad for soccer practice.

This point makes an enormous psychological difference in a family. Parents are no longer faced with the artificial situation in which they feel like they are only a parent some percentage of time, such as 30%, or 50% or 70%. Although not with the child all of the time, which no parent has even in an intact marriage, both parents can feel like they are parents 100% of the time. The child is also free of the artificial situation of feeling that he or she has each parent for a percentage of time and feels like both parents are his or her parents all of the time.

5. **Children's temperaments and special needs.** Research also helps us with this goal. The more challenging the child's temperament, or if there are special needs, the higher the level of communication and cooperation is required by the parents. Some of these schedules put even more demands on communication and cooperation. The best schedule for a child on the autism spectrum, for example, whose parent works long hours, might be to live nearly full time with the more available parent. This is because many services require parental availability.

6. **Similarity in the two homes: routines, rules, forms of discipline, and expectations (including chores and responsibilities).** The more similarity, the better children turn out. This is another research-based finding. With children under five years old, this is a crucial factor. Older children can tolerate more differences, but the developmental tasks of young children are dependent on both homes being very similar. Some schedules are more helpful with this factor than others.

> **Spoiler Alert:**
> **If parents are highly communicative and cooperative,**
> **almost any schedule can work well for a child.**
> **The less communication and cooperation that parents have,**
> **the more planning has to be done to protect the child.**

Step Three: Plan the steps for reaching long-term goals.

Once you have a good description of the current situation and a clear vision of your long-term goals, the next step is to flesh out the details of how to get to those goals. This involves steps to take and plans for overcoming the obstacles. The Plan must include how the legal tasks, meaning the legal outcomes ordered by a Court at the time of the Judgment of Divorce, fit into the Plan.

Legal outcomes are part of the Plan, but are not the Plan.

A good place to start making the Plan is to ask yourself and your spouse, what types of involvement with the children on the part of both parents will help accomplish the long-term family goals. Some forms of involvement can be accomplished in any schedule, such as both parents attending parent-teacher conferences. Some forms of involvement might by their very nature suggest the involvement of one parent and not the other.

For example, one parent has a very flexible work schedule and works from home, and the other parent has a rigid work schedule that requires a lengthy commute. This might suggest that one parent is much better situated to take the child to doctor, dentist and other appointments. However, the other parent might want to be kept up to date, and for the child to know this, so that the child feels the interest of both parents in his or her well-being. One parent might want to be involved in after-school extracurricular activities and have the flexibility to do so. Another parent might want to continue to do karate classes with the child on Tuesday evenings.

Notice that these are ways that the parents want to be involved with the child, not schedules. Some of these involvements can occur independent of the schedule, while some imply a certain schedule. Rather than arguing about something as inconsequential as overnights, parents should focus on the family plan, one that will help you reach the long-term goals for the child.

The inductive building of a Co-parenting Time Schedule Plan is always the best practice.

Holidays trump other parts of a co-parenting time schedule, so it makes sense to begin with the holidays. This was discussed earlier in the book, and therefore will only be briefly covered here. Start with one holiday and then go through the Four Step Template for Goal Based Planning. For example, if the first holiday tackled is Mother's Day:

Step 1: Describe in detail the current situation. The child is expected to do something to honor mother, such as make a card, help make breakfast or buy a gift. The mother's mother lives in a different state and that usually means a phone call. The father's mother lives in town, and the family usually stops by for a visit. Sometimes, the family goes out with his mother for breakfast.

Step 2: List each spouse's long-term goals, specific to the decisions being made. The parents think it is good for the child to continue to honor his grandmothers and his mother. They want the child to know that his father honors her too, and she honors him on Father's Day. In that way, the child hopefully will continue to appreciate and honor both parents into adulthood.

Step 3: Plan the steps for reaching long-term goals. It will be a tradition for the child to have breakfast with his paternal grandmother on Mother's Day. He will be with his father the morning of Mother's Day to do so. The child will be with his mother from noon through the rest of the day and overnight. The father will help the child do something for the mother, such as make a card, buy a present or bring a treat to her house. The father will speak to his mother to try to undo the estrangement so that the mother can call her on Mother's Day and honour her. The child will be expected to call his maternal grandmother sometime on Mother's Day from the mother's home.

All this can be easily reduced to a Schedule, set forth in the MSA regarding Mother's Day.

"The father shall have co-parenting time with his son from 8:30 a.m. Mother's Day morning until Noon; the mother shall have co-parenting time with her son from Noon on Mother's Day until 9:00 a.m. the immediately following morning." (The additional agreements can be in a co-parenting document, not necessarily submitted to the court).

Step 4: List the obstacles and steps to overcome them and create a Plan.

In our Mother's Day example, the following are examples of obstacles:

a. The child is too young to follow through making/getting a card and present without parental guidance. Plan: the father will help the child make a card, a drawing, get a bakery treat for the mum, etc. for the mother.

b. The child cannot be in two places at once. Plan: there will be a schedule so that the father has time to get the child ready.

c. The father's mother and the mother have become estranged during the divorce. Plan: the father will attempt to reconcile his mother to the spouse so that they can communicate, and in some cases, coordinate the grandmother's involvement with the child.

d. The Mother's Day weekends and Father's Day weekends might interrupt the general schedule, meaning lost weekend time for one of the parents. Plan: If a parent loses a full weekend because of a holiday, that parent will have the immediately preceding or following weekend.

Obviously, obstacles might be specific to family circumstances (e.g., number of children involved). Our point here is to list obstacles to a smoothly flowing schedule and come with a Plan to overcome them.

As can be seen, the parents have created a goal-based Plan, where the legal outcome is just a part of, but supportive of, the overall Family Plan.

The next step is to proceed through the remainder of the holidays, applying the Four Step Goal Based Planning Template to each holiday. Once the holiday schedules have all been planned, it is time to move on to other parts of an overall schedule, applying the GBP Template to each part of the Schedule:

- Vacations
- Summer weekends
- Summer weekdays
- Weekdays off school during the school year
- Weekends during the school year
- School days. Even a day can be subdivided into different times of day.

Our Four Step GBP Template can be applied to planning each sub-schedule. When done, the schedule is put into a form that will work in the MSA.

As you can see in our Mother's Day example, Steps 3 and 4 overlap a bit and can both be worked on at the same time. It can be tempting to accept standard formulas, such as every other weekend. While you might well end up there as the best plan for accomplishing goals, there are many ways to deal with weekends, and some of them might better accomplish your goals.

One parent might have the option of working weekends, for example, as a nurse, make more money and be freer during the week to take care of a child. Weekends can be split, for example, if one parent is particularly interested in supporting religious beliefs. For example, if one of the agreements is that any day the mother can get off early from work and pick the children up from school, she can do that by notifying the father in advance and having the children back to him by a time certain. In a functional co-parenting relationship, this may or may not need to be in the MSA. The parents will know best how to handle this.

The Vision: The vision is for the children to have strong relationships with both parents and to have both parents involved in all aspects of the children's lives where and when possible. They both value education and want the children to be successful in school and to be in a position to choose college if they wish. They also value social development which includes involvement in extra-curricular activities, most of which occur after school in the afternoon.

**A sensible approach to handling the co-parenting time schedule
is for the children to avoid the drama,
which is best accomplished in a goal-based Co-parenting Plan.**

Summary: A Sensible Approach-Developing a Successful

Co-parenting Time Schedule Plan.[72]

In a sensible approach,
the focus is not on the schedule
but rather on how to reach goals.

The co-parenting time schedule has a structure, which is what is set forth in an MSA, so that the parents and the children know what to expect in the future. However, the sensible (i.e., 'real') co-parenting time is accomplished with flexibility and access. This can even include both parents being involved in some way every day.

Let's use the above example. However, we will add an additional part to their Plan- to build in provisions regarding trust issues and unforeseen contingencies, in addition to an actual schedule. What if the Plan further provided what to do if a child wakes up ill on a school day, obviously not known at the time, not known when the MSA was signed, but will be known by one of the parents? They might agree that one parent will take the day off work, if he or she can, but if that is not possible, that parent will call the other parent who will take charge. Such an agreement may not be in an MSA as an enforceable court order, but it could be an important part of a Family Plan.

This Chapter has been complicated, with many details, examples and illustrations. However, just like what we stated when we introduced the Custody Plan in Chapter 15, it boils down to having a Sensible Mindset and learning a few Take-away Techniques.

1. Sensible Mindset:

The Sensible Mindset regarding the Parenting Time Plan is to bargain cooperatively in a Goal Based Planning process, rather than competing for control of and time with children. This recognizes that the divorce is not the day of the final Judgment of Divorce. The divorce is a relationship that lasts for the rest of people's lives. When there are minor children, the divorce includes interaction on a regular basis. The interaction can be in a messy form, including

---

[72] Note that this Summary highlights that goals and procedures regarding the Co-parenting Time Schedule Plan, are basically identical to the Custody Plan presented in this Chapter 15. The Take-away Techniques are also basically indistinguishable. However, repeating them is a good review for the reader.

ex-spouses who avoid each other like the plague, engage in open conflict or complain about one another to anyone who will listen, or worse. If messy, it is a miserable relationship for the parents and a miserable experience for the children.

OR

The interaction of the parents can be in a sensible form. If sensible, the divorce is a relationship in which parents are courteous with one another and proactively plan their lives and those of the children in a sensible manner. They make the decisions together required to provide their children with a good family experience and reach long-term goals.

However, as the song goes, *'It ain't easy'*. To be sensible, Problematic Emotions and Challenging Skills need to be recognized and handled in a sensible manner, and the traps (discussed in Chapter 8) need to be avoided.

2.   Take-away Techniques:

The Take-away Techniques are summarized as follows:

1.   Never start with a position on an individual issue/task, or worse yet, on a large collection of tasks. Use our Four Step Goal Based Planning Template for Making Decisions on the Legal Tasks[73] to make effective Plans.
2.   Build the Plan inductively, focusing on and developing a Plan for each individual issue/task, building the whole Plan brick by brick.
3.   Always include the goals of both parents; grow the pie first with a cooperative approach.
4.   Focus on a Plan for the family; not on the legal tasks. Prepare the MSA with the legal tasks after the full Plan has been developed.
5.   Develop a Plan for making child-related decisions; The Plan should include which decisions will be joint, made by one parent with input from the other parent, made solely by one parent, but informing the other parent, and all other decisions which can be made unilaterally. If later you discover another decision that would be better made jointly, simply

---

[73] Chapter 14.

add it to the list. Include a procedure for each type of joint decision. Include decisions about the co-parenting tasks:

    a. How information will be shared, including rules of conduct (e.g., being courteous, making polite requests rather than demands, etc).

    b. How homes will be organized to be as similar as possible.

    c. How to have child-friendly transitions.

    d. Have rules and procedures for gaining access and flexibility.

    e. Have rules and procedures for making decisions and solving problems.

    f. Establish a schedule for which parent is primarily responsible on what days and at what times. However, the Plan should include procedures for access and flexibility in the schedule and specific ways for both parents to be involved in the child's life, independent of the schedule. Include the legal task of a parenting time schedule, which has been built inductively.

6. If there are any differences and disagreements regarding any of these Take-away Techniques or any other issues, go back to our Ten Disagreement Resolution Skills Model introduced in Chapter 6.

Chapter 17
Financial Plan
and the Legal and Planning Tasks

$

Introduction: In modern times, when people are married, in some manner they share property, debt and income. With these assets and income, they support themselves, and if they have children, they support their children. They have consciously or unconsciously developed a 'Plan' for this life task. The Plan includes how to produce income, how and when and what to purchase, when to take on debt, and how to build savings to absorb the normal ups and downs of their financial lives. If the Plan is a good one, and opportunity allows, how to build wealth for the future.

Although laws apply to this aspect of a marriage, most people are focused on their Plan, not the laws. For example, the laws require that you support the basics of food and shelter for your children, but laws do not dictate that your children be enrolled in activities that cost money. As another example, the law does not require you to have savings or buy a house, but a good financial plan might include those 'requirements'. However, if a house is purchased, in community property states, they consider property purchased during the marriage jointly owned, except in some circumstances.

When divorcing, spouses should develop a Plan for how to dissolve their financial partnership.

This Plan should include the legal requirements with regard to the distribution of property and debt, whether to continue to share income, at least for a while, and when there are children, how to support the children financially. However, as we will show, the very first step is to plan for both spouses to reach long-term goals while financially supporting the children for them to reach goals (i.e., a good education, participation in extra-curricular activities, develop healthy social lives, medical care and have basic needs met).

Our culture gives mixed messages about money. On the one hand, we want to believe that money is not important. We have sayings like, "*You can't take it to the grave*" and "*Money can't buy you happiness (or love)*". Many of us either greatly admire or are prejudiced against 'the wealthy', or both, but most of us would rather be wealthy than not.

Our relationships with money are complex and highly emotional. If we are wise, we try to balance these conflicting emotions and are unashamed about considering the financial implications of our choices. In the end, however, money does matter and it would be foolish to pretend that we should not be serious when making financial choices.

The temptation at the time of divorce is to compete over getting the biggest share of the financial pie in the distribution process. Worse yet, this competition continues with the Co-parenting Time Schedule Plan. Both approaches are BIG mistakes!

Much like a marriage, while there are laws that apply to the distribution of property, debt and income, the focus should be on a Plan that provides for the support of the separated spouses and the children and a property and debt package. Planning will definitely help the spouses reach their long-term financial goals. We call this our 'Financial Plan', which we introduce in this Chapter.

At the same time, money offers some objectivity and predictability, making it easier to deal with at the time of a divorce, when compared to child-related issues, which we presented in detail in Chapters 14-17. A house in a certain area will appreciate, over time, at a probable rate. A savings account at a fixed interest rate, and to which a certain amount is regularly added, has a predictable future value. If more money is made than is spent, wealth will grow. If more money is spent than is made, wealth will diminish, and debt will likely grow.

This makes planning to reach long-term financial goals less complicated and less vulnerable to unknowns, when compared to raising children.

As an example, when people marry, they might not be able to afford to own a house. However, they might have a plan to buy a house at some point in the future and then develop a plan to build enough savings for a down payment and enough income to pay a mortgage. That will likely include making short-term sacrifices to reach a long-term goal. The same type of thinking should dominate the divorce process: identifying the long-term goals of both spouses, developing a Plan to reach those goals and being willing to make short-term sacrifices in order to accomplish those long-term goals.

Selfish short-term thinking can thwart these efforts. In our example of married people saving for a house, if the wife took the savings and bought a boat, she would have a boat, but they would not have a house.

We are well aware that the starting point for many divorcing spouses is a major challenge. Statistics, for example, tell us that about 50% of the people in the United States could not come up with $500 in an emergency. Fortunately, our society has options that cushion the blow, but planning to reach long-term goals at the time of a divorce can feel discouraging. Fortunately, building wealth has been heavily studied and financial advisors can really help. The most inexpensive way to take advantage of this is to learn about reliable financial experts online. Much information is available at no charge or is available in inexpensive books. Our point is that even starting at near zero, you can benefit from a good plan.

The sensible approach to the financial aspects of a divorce follows the same Template as we have discussed earlier regarding the Custody Plan and the Co-parenting Plan introduced in Chapters 15 and 16:

Four Steps of Goal Based Planning:

1. Step One: Describe in detail the current situation.
2. Step Two: List each spouse's long-term goals, specific to the decisions being made.
3. Step Three: Plan the steps for reaching long-term goals.
4. Step Four: List the obstacles and steps to overcome them and create a Plan.

There is an additional obstacle when dealing with money, an issue that was relatively minor when dealing with children. This is the issue: *"What is fair?"*

Fairness. Fairness is extremely important to people. Much of the litigation at the time of divorce, including decisions by appellate courts, has focused on the ambiguous issue and definition of fairness. However, regarding a Sensible Divorce, this is simply the wrong question to ask. The right question is, *"How can we best reach our long-term goals?"* The answer to this question almost always subsumes the issue of fairness. If the focus is on the legal task at the time of a divorce, fairness might dictate that the division be equal or equitable, but not necessarily fair.

If the focus is on both ex-spouses reaching long-term goals, fairness might mean a division that is not equal or equitable but better for reaching the goals of both spouses.

Let us give an example to help illustrate this point. Assume that the wife has built a much larger retirement savings than the husband because she has been much more aggressive in building her career and income. When they were married, there was an assumption[74] that they would share her retirement savings to have a decent retired life. However, when getting a divorce, she might feel that it is not 'fair' to share that account because she earned it by putting in more effort than he had. This could become a bone of contention, and the spouses might have to rely, in the end, on what a stranger (namely a judge), thinks are 'fair' or what is 'legal', whether that be their judge or an appellate court. A lawyer will likely answer the question by referring to the law. Win or lose, at least one of the spouses will feel the decision is unfair.

In a Messy Divorce,
the primary focus will likely be on what is 'fair'
at the time of the Judgment of Divorce.
This is a also a big mistake.

In a Sensible Divorce, the initial focus should be on the long-term goals of both spouses. In the Example above, the focus might be on the retirement goals of both spouses. Sharing the wife's retirement account might be a way for both of them to reach their goals, but if another method is a better way to reach those goals, the retirement account might not have to be shared.

Many lawyers at this point might be thinking in terms of offsetting the value of the retirement account by the value of other property, in order to have an equitable (fair) distribution, but this too misses the point, because it is still primarily focused on what is a 'fair' distribution, not what distribution will help both spouses reach their goals.

To expand on our Example, assume that the wife wants to retire in the marital house, but with the mortgage paid off and an opportunity to travel. Assume that the husband does not want the responsibility of a home and yard maintenance in retirement and wants a simple life with the opportunity to play golf, his main hobby and source of social connection. Calculations might yield the conclusion that the wife is going to need more resources than the husband to reach her goals. Calculating future values, including social security income and the costs of their residences (i.e., house taxes and maintenance versus an apartment in a senior living complex) might yield a conclusion that an unequal division of property at

---

[74] This assumption might have been implicit or explicit, verbal or in writing, at the time of the marriage, but revisionist history almost always reveals a different story at divorce.

the time of the divorce might be the best plan to reach the goals of both parties. In our Example, this means to have both the wife and the husband have happy retirement lives.[75]

Your authors can hear the outcry, 'But that is not fair'. Maybe yes. Maybe no. We also recognize that this Example is a bit simplistic because it is only focused on one long-term goal, retirement. However, our point is that focusing on a vague and ambiguous concept such as 'fairness', can be a mistake. The focus on fairness can thwart the ability of both spouses to reach long-term financial goals. Our point is that wanting more money is human, but might not be the most prudent primary driver and focus at the time of the Judgment of Divorce.

Money is a tool for reaching goals, not a goal in itself. If we simply wanted more money, we would not have children; we would not take vacations; we would not enroll our children in expensive activities or private schools; we would ride a bike to work and not buy cars; and so on. At least we hope we got you thinking!

With this in mind, let us approach financial issues (Property and Support Tasks) using a 'Sensible Mindset' and our Four Step Goad Based Planning Template, identical to the process utilized regarding the child-related Tasks, as set forth in Part IV, Chapters 15 and 16.

Step One: Describe in detail the current situation.

The Sensible Mindset issue here is identical to the mindset when dealing with the child-related tasks previously discussed. First, let's start with complete disclosure. In a competitive approach to bargaining, there is a temptation to hide and mislead (even inadvertently) in order to maximize the financial value of the settlement to oneself. However, not only does this cheat the other spouse, but also it cheats yourself. The Sensible Mindset is to grow the pie, where both parties have all relevant information and a bigger pie to divide.

A clear understanding of the current available resources in the marriage allows the best opportunity for making a goal-based Plan that reaches the long-term goals of both parties. As a reminder, the best form of selfishness is balanced

---

[75] In this Example, it is assumed that this was a long-term marriage, which makes Goal Based Planning for both parties more realistic- and necessary.

with altruism, where the best outcome for oneself is when the process aims at the best outcome for both spouses.[76]

In order to set a foundation for this, both spouses and their attorneys need all of the relevant information. This should include:

- What led up to the current financial situation
- Any information about the current situation that is known by one spouse, but not the other
- Information about future options that have financial implications (e.g., a probable promotion in a couple of years)
- Any other choices the spouses might have (e.g., an ability to increase income by working a weekend day)? Etc.

Lawyers are experts in this process, but a word of caution might be helpful. We discuss in various parts of this book the lawyer inclination to focus on legal outcomes. Pertinent to this Chapter, they focus on what is a 'fair' distribution of assets and income, often relying on law and prior rulings by appellate courts. Not surprising, we submit this is likely another big mistake and certainly inconsistent with Goal Based Planning- the major focus of this book.

A valuation of property, debt and income is necessary, especially if the spouses end up deviating from an equal distribution, but the purpose of this Step is to understand that this is the starting point, without any preconceived notion as to what the ultimate distribution might be.

Values might be an important part of this understanding, but some values might be irrelevant. For example, the values involved in the distribution of household goods might be irrelevant to whether or not the spouses reach long-term financial goals. Assume that they agree on who gets what. It might not matter whether the artwork that the wife received is more valuable than the artwork that the husband received, if one party got the Renoir and the other party got the signed football poster. Compare this to an equal or equitable division in which the artwork must be sold in order to have a 'fair' division. On a subjective level, both parties reached a minor goal, namely the art work that is valuable to each of them.

---

[76] There is reliable scientific support for this conclusion. Game Theory, a branch of mathematics, has shown that this approach 'grows the pie' by focusing on the subjective values involved rather than just the objective amounts involved.

From the planning perspective, it may also be an important part of this Step to calculate future values of certain assets, as well as that can be done. The reason for this is because the focus is on the financial condition of the parties in the future, not necessarily at the time of the Judgment of Divorce.

What might be an unequal division of property at the time of the divorce might actually be much closer to achieving relatively equal long-term goals in the future. For example, assume that the wife has as a goal to continue to live in the family residence until the children are grown, twelve years in the future. Assume that the husband's goal is to live in a rental apartment or house, sufficiently large for the children until they are grown and then have a simple residence from which he would like to travel.

In order to reach these goals, both ex-spouses will require a certain level of income, but the future value of assets might be an important tool for reaching goals. If real estate grows at about a 3% rate per annum in the area, and if historical average for the growth of investments is 4-6%, the division of property might heavily favor the wife in the short term but allow each of the ex-spouses to reach their goals in the long term. The future value of the real estate and investments might be key.

This is a good illustration of how short-term legal outcomes can be tools for reaching long-term goals, not short-term goals based on vague and ambiguous standards like 'equitable' or 'equal'.

**Your authors submit that the standard by which to measure
legal outcomes might be how well they likely help
the parties reach long-term goals.**

The goals that will be made in Step 2 must also include implications for child support and be part of the planning. Most jurisdictions tie child support to calculations based on the relative incomes of the two parents and the co-parenting time schedule. The plus side is that in order to set child support based on just these two factors has been studied. The results of those studies suggest that about 17% of family income is spent on the support of one child, 25% on two children, 31% on three children and so on. The minus side is that this does not holds up at the extremes, meaning at the level of poverty or at the level of serious wealth.. However, when budgeting, it does provide a good estimate of actual child-related costs, which can and perhaps should be modified by child care needs, private education choices, etc.

In brief, this first Step should be a clear and unambiguous picture of the current situation, without any preconceived notions as to how property and future income will be distributed.

This will include valuations, including future values, but the valuations are not for the goal of an equitable or equal distribution or for either spouse to position themselves for selfishly getting 'more'. Subjective values are also important.

In our earlier Example, one spouse's subjective value of the signed football poster might subjectively make it equal to or better than the Renoir.

Step Two: List each spouse's long-term goals, specific to the decisions being made.

This can be a gut-wrenching activity. When people are divorcing, they often believe they are going to lose all they have worked for: retirement money, real estate, savings, income, favorite Christmas tree ornaments, certain heirlooms, tools and likely more.[77] This is, however, an emotional reaction, as well as a factual reaction. Spouses at the point of divorce are at risk of losing something because their financial picture is changing. When things change, choices make a very big difference in long-term outcomes. Being realistic when establishing long-term goals, can be a challenge. This is one of the many reasons why having attorneys involved in the planning can be of great assistance. They are less emotional and have a good deal of experience with financial matters, such as tax planning, determining future values, alternatives available, and so on.

The Sensible Mindset comes into play again and essentially the parties (and the lawyers) need to put on their "thinking caps" and set the panic emotions aside. Imagine, for example, responding to a situation where you are fired from a job. There is panic and a realization that there will be some short-term losses. However, the task at hand is to develop a Plan to get back on your financial feet in order to reach long-term goals.

---

[77] Your authors have known people to spend far more money than the object of the dispute. This is obviously a fantasy to assuage the feelings of loss.

In Step 1, you fleshed out the current situation, that is, what financial resources are and will be available. If what you have is a house, a couple of cars, some retirement money, a little in savings and enough income to cover your expenses, with a little left over for college funds for the children, then making a goal of having a million dollars of net worth in five years is as unrealistic as thinking that you will be bankrupt. The long-term goals might be more modest. (i.e., for both of you to own a residence, which could be a condominium) that will accommodate your children, to continue to provide opportunities for the children to participate in extracurricular activities, to grow the college funds and to own cars without loans).

Many wealthy people who built their own wealth have had episodes when they lost part or all of their wealth and had to rebuild. They did not wallow in their misery or panic. They developed a long-term Plan and took steps to implement the Plan.

A target date for the Plan is often the point at which the children reach adulthood, but circumstances might dictate other target dates. For example, assume a marriage in which the children are already adults. The target date might then be retirement. In another circumstance, decisions at the time of divorce might include an unequal division of property, a certain level of support or perhaps even the continuation of joint ownership of some property, with the long-term goal of the lower earning spouse getting further education and career development in order for both ex-spouses to be financially independent of one another at some point in the future. The target date might be based on the expectation of when that goal is likely to be reached, not a date certain.

The important part of Step 2
is for both spouses to have a clear vision of their futures
based on their financial goals for themselves and for each other.

By having a clear and thorough understanding of the
current financial picture and a clear vision of their
financial futures, the steps to be taken
and the obstacles in the path are easier to
identify and overcome.

Step 3. Plan the steps for reaching long-term goals.

With a good description of the current situation and an understanding of realistic long-term financial goals of both parties, the Sensible Mindset is for both parties to work together to produce a Plan. The importance of working together cannot be overstated. Many attorneys prefer meeting privately with his or her client and then bargaining lawyer to lawyer, without the clients present, instead of Four-way meetings with both attorneys and both clients. This makes for good client control, but ignores perhaps the greatest resource in these situations, namely 'Bounded Rationality'.

DECISION-MAKING:
BOUNDED RATIONALITY VS. SCIENTIFIC METHOD PLUS
A CONVERGENCE OF EXPECTATIONS ON SOLUTIONS

As previously discussed, there are two ways that people make decisions: the Scientific Method and Bounded Rationality. As a reminder,

1. **Bounded Rationality** recognizes that spouses, in their conscious and unconscious minds, have a font of important information that the attorneys do not have, which must be allowed to surface during the negotiations.
2. The **Scientific Method** involves making a list of options available, looking at the pros and cons of each option and then picking the option that has the best balance of pros and cons.

As useful as the Scientific approach can be in some situations, most people do not make life decisions this way. Bounded Rationality involves the way most people make life decisions. This is because people have an enormous amount of information stored in their brains, some of which they might not even be aware of when bargaining.

3. **Convergence of Expectations on Solution.** When people are in a situation where they can share information, and are bargaining, something occurs that is magical. It is called: a Convergence of expectations, in which ideas surface which are creative and can be a complete surprise to everyone involved.

Ideas that seem to come out of nowhere are actually Bounded Rationality at work, and this works best when the spouses are together making the Plan. Four-way meetings[78] with two lawyers and two clients are the best way to do this, because this includes the Bounded Rationality of four people with very different skills and experience.[79]

Taking days by meeting with clients in offices, and then scheduling attorney-attorney meetings, greatly disrupts the process of a Convergence of Expectations, which depends heavily on information and ideas spontaneously popping up.

Assume that in a Four-way Meeting of spouses and attorneys, it becomes apparent that the total income in the family must increase in order to meet the goals of the parties. All four initially sit in silence as the implications of this begins to sink in. Suddenly the father says, "*I have always wanted to work at a store like REI. The employees look like they have fun, and getting employee discounts on outdoor gear is really appealing to me- and the family. Maybe I could get a side job and work on weekends when I do not have the children.*" The mother's eyes get big, and she says, "*If you [the husband] could help more with the children during the Christmas season, I could work at one of the stores at the mall. They are always advertising for seasonal employees.*" The financial obstacle is overcome in a way that no one, not even the spouses (and certainly not the lawyers), might have guessed, had they not been in the same room planning together.

The challenge is setting aside the Problematic Emotions of the divorce,
including the anger, shame, guilt and sadness,
and working together on a long-term Plan for the future.

This Sensible Mindset is a focus on reality: that no matter what the spouses do, time will pass and the children will be older years down the road. They will either reach their goals (if they work together now), or will not reached their goals (because they did not want to work together at the time of divorce to reach long-term goals). Reframing it this way, with two simple choices, hopefully makes the right choice the easy (and really the only) choice.

---

[78]We understand that there are situations where Four-way meetings would be inappropriate and/or ineffective.

[79] Using a skilled mediator is another alternative.

We also note here that this approach (even though we are addressing the Financial Plan and the Legal and Planning Tasks) also addresses another important long-term goal that we pointed out earlier in Chapters 15 and 16, as a consistent, Number One factor affecting outcomes for children: the co-parenting relationship emerging after the divorce.

Having a positive co-parenting relationship is essentially setting aside Problematic Emotions and processing Challenging Feelings and behaving sensibly, by focusing on long-term goals. Engaging in this process when planning sets the stage for and develops the skills involved in a successful co-parenting relationship.

If the parties have a successful co-parenting relationship, this is critically important to reaching financial goals because as objective as money is, unpredicted obstacles sometimes come up later. This might lead to another financial discussion. Having had this earlier experience with making plans can help that later discussion be successful. Parents should think of the obvious benefit to their children to live in a family whose parents model this behavior.

Your authors concede that this Sensible Mindset is challenging.
We all like to prevail and to win, although research tells us
that the bigger issue is that we really hate to lose.

In fact, in gambling research, it turns out that people have much stronger emotional reactions to losing than they do to winning. To lose $100 feels more intense than to win $100. However, sensible decision-making has nothing to do with prevailing or losing. This can be hard to swallow, particularly if both parties believe they are 'right'. The Sensible Mindset that accompanies effective decision-making involves trying to accomplish as much as possible what both people want to accomplish.

Third Party Review?

Depending on the size of the estate involved, both in terms of income and/or property, it might be wise to have the Plan reviewed by a third party. Depending on the Plan, hiring a financial planner, an accountant or a tax attorney might be most appropriate. The purpose would be to see if the Plan could be improved, for at least one party if not for both, without hurting the other party. For example, a different way of structuring the Plan might lead to substantial savings. However, your authors concede that many divorces have a modest estate, and this option might be unaffordable and/or unnecessary.

In some situations, the parties might have little property or income to work with in formulating a Plan. The purpose of the Plan might solely be focused on simply getting by. However, this does not change the overall value of our GBP Model and Template. Taking the time to look at the current situation, setting long-term goals, listing obstacles and creating a Plan might still yield substantial value to one or both the parties. It certainly worthwhile to try.

Building the steps to reach long-term goals will likely already have begun. A Plan starts with understanding a current budget and developing a budget for post-divorce for each spouse. Ideally, the post-divorce budgets should be designed to reach long-term goals, not just to get by. Most financial planners, for example, will place a high premium on paying down debt, with the possible exception of low interest mortgages. Part of the budget or property distribution might be for the purpose of debt paydown. Our point is that the property and income of the spouses are seen as resources for beginning a financial plan to meet the long-term goals listed in Step Two.

**The important part of Step 3
is for both spouses to focus on long-term goals
and planning the steps to get there.**

This includes future income for the goals related to the children. Child support generally fits better with focused financial planning, when compared to applying a simple formula based on incomes and a co-parenting time schedule. Incomes and parenting time are factors to be considered, but considered along with other factors that are related to long-term goals. For example, a higher earner might be very interested in giving the children good educational opportunities with the long-term goal of the children having the option of becoming professionals. Having the money for those opportunities might be part of his or her budget and eventually paying for university attendance might be part of his or her savings plan.

Step Four: List the obstacles and steps to overcome them and create a Plan.

These obstacles are generally very case specific, but usually involve Problematic Emotions. For example, it might be very clear that income-sharing in some form will be necessary to reach long-term goals. This can stir emotions in both spouses. The potential payer might not like the idea of giving the other spouse money, and the potential payee might not like that form of dependence. For example, the emotions of a higher earner spouse about spousal support when it was the other spouse who initiated the divorce might get in the way of developing a good Plan.

**Problematic Emotions and Challenging Feelings
are obstacles to reaching shared goals.[80]**

There are other obstacles too. A more practical example is where it is clear that an increase in total income will be necessary, but current employment will not provide that end result. When you look at your income, a goal might be to increase the income by 7% in order to reach goals. This might mean possible employment changes, such as side jobs, a change in careers and so on. Another obstacle might be that emergency expenditures might arise that thwart long-term objectives. For example, if one of the cars has high mileage, an obstacle might be the need to buy another car at some point.

**At Step Four, one good question to ask
(identical to the one applicable to child-related tasks
discussed earlier in Chapters 15 and 16) is:**
"Why might we fail to reach these goals?"
That question often highlights obstacles to success.

There are two temptations that can get in the way of this Step. One reason is to get through Step Four too quickly because it might seem uncomfortable or

---

[80] See Chapter 2 (Avoiding Four Problematic Emotions: Blaming, Distrusting, Taking Things Personally and Thinking Inferentially) and Chapter 11 (Sensible Solutions for Processing Problematic Emotions and Challenging Feelings and Practicing Kindness).

even distasteful. An unwarranted optimism about the future might be another reason. Planning for children can be challenging, in part because there are so many unknowns about the future at the time of the divorce. (Financial futures, on the other hand, are easier to plan because of the objective nature of money.)

One of your authors knows a man who wanted to own a classic Chevrolet Corvette. He figured out the future price involved and how much money he would need. He then began taking a small sum out of every pay check and putting it in a special savings account. Years later, he bought the car. If you put a dollar a day in a jar, you will have $365.00 at the end of a year. (This is certainly not much money, but you get the idea, and can always put more than $1 per day in the jar.) The objectivity of money is very helpful in this Step, but only if people take the time to focus objectively on the money and make pragmatic decisions.

Another challenge when making financial plans in this Step is the difficulty being honest with yourself and about your spouse. It might be hard to admit that you are not very organized with money or that you have a shopping problem. It might be hard to point out that your spouse wastes a lot of money drinking at bars. However, as important as complete disclosure is when fleshing out the current situation, complete disclosure is crucial to listing the obstacles to success. Otherwise, the Plan will likely fail because you did not disclose the obstacles as part of the planning process.

> **By the completion of this Step, you should have a clear picture**
> **of the starting point, a clear vision of future goals,**
> **the outline of Steps to take to reach goals**
> **and a pragmatic understanding of the obstacles in the path**
> **to reaching those goals.**
> **Adding steps for overcoming obstacles completes the Plan.**

Once the Plan is made, the lawyers will need to construct the legal tasks for the MSA, complete the drafting of the MSA and submit the MSA to the Court for approval.

This approach to the financial legal tasks might sound simplistic and 'pie in the sky'. In Chapter 18, we address this proposition with several examples drawn from real cases and address the Question, "*Are the Financial Tasks Really That Easy*

Chapter 18
Financial Plan: Are the Financial Tasks
Really That Easy?

Many divorcing spouses will read Chapter 17 and exclaim that your authors do not understand how complicated their situation is. Many attorneys might read Chapter 17 and exclaim that those are not the cases they even see.

Our approach to divorce might seem simplistic
and naïve to many people.
Are your authors naïve? NO.
Is the approach we are espousing in this book too simplistic? NO.

Between the two of us, your authors have almost one hundred years of experience working with divorcing or divorced spouses and separated parents. In fact, we are not naïve!

A sensible approach to a divorce is simple.
The challenges and obstacles to a Sensible Divorce
are what complicate the process.

As we have written in detail, those challenges and obstacles include:

1. The pitfalls of marriage, which lead to Problematic Emotions and Challenging Feelings, often culminate in a divorce.
2. Natural human tendencies to perpetuate the same patterns that are the root of the marital problem, especially trying to control the divorce relationship, are the same strategies that failed to control the marriage.

3. Natural human tendencies to cope with sadness and frustration with blame, anger, inferential thinking, living in the past, having trouble letting go, and getting stuck in intractable conflict, continue at divorce, or get even worse.
4. The belief in Illusions continue at divorce.
5. There are traps of the traditional legal system, particularly pitting spouses against one another in a competition for what appear to be limited resources and limited time with children. This establishes artificial disputes, short-term selfish thinking and a desire to prevail or at least not lose at divorce.

In fact, most of this book has been about the challenges and obstacles to a Sensible Divorce and ways to overcome those obstacles.

A Sensible Divorce is somewhat simple. This means recognizing that a divorce is not 'over' on the day of the Judgment of Divorce, but rather is the continuation of life-long relationships, especially if there are children. A Sensible Divorce involves proactively making a good Plan for that relationship.

We have listed (again) our Four Step Goal Based Planning Template, applied to each and every aspect of that Plan:

Step One: Describe in detail the current situation.
Step Two: List each spouse's long-term goals, specific to the decisions being made.
Step Three: Plan the steps for reaching long-term goals.
Step Four: List the obstacles and steps to overcome them and Create a Plan.

**The legal tasks that must be accomplished
as part of the making of a Plan and should be viewed as tools,
subsumed into the Plan,
but not goals in and of themselves.**

Let us take a look at three Scenarios (all of which will sound familiar), based on situations that are 'real' cases and are likely to provoke disputes, difficult negotiations and even litigation.

Scenario One: You brought property to the marriage while your spouse brought mostly debt, associated with student loans and credit card debt. You did not have a Pre-nuptial Agreement. Twelve years later, and now with two children, you are divorcing. You remember the unequal beginning of the marriage and resent that your pre-marital property will not be considered separate. You take the position that you should get the pre-marital property back at the time of the divorce, before the marital property is distributed.

By now, you should be able to spot the mistakes that you are making. The biggest one being that you are focusing on a legal outcome. The second mistake is that you are taking a position, leaping to Step 4 (i.e., creating a Plan), without laying the groundwork with the first three Steps.

Unless your spouse agrees with you (which is highly unlikely), you are provoking an artificial dispute. In this case, your spouse asserts the position that although you brought property to the marriage and she brought debt, there was no agreement to exclude this property at divorce, or any agreement to consider the debt brought to the marriage. Further, she asserts that her education led to her producing significant income, which compensates for any unequal beginning. Not surprisingly, she is making the same mistakes as her spouse. The next danger is that the attorneys might make the same mistakes and focus on the chances of either party prevailing, based on law and the proclivities of the judge.

Adding fuel to the fire, both spouses are being selfish, without the balance of altruistic concern for the other spouse, and are facing in the wrong direction: living in the past instead of the future. The focus is on the vague and ambiguous standard of what is 'fair'. This has become a win-lose situation, fraught with Problematic Emotions and Challenging Feelings, and a thorn in the side of your future divorce relationship. If the issue goes to trial, more damage to the divorce relationship is likely. If other issues in the divorce are handled this way, you are likely off to the races in a messy divorce and a dysfunctional co-parenting relationship.

Sensible Approach: Ask yourself the question, why did you willingly marry your spouse, knowing that the decision included starting the marriage with an unequal financial contribution- without taking any legal protection? There might be many answers to this question, but our bet is that all of those answers reflect a balance of selfish and altruistic motives, reflecting your positive feelings towards your spouse at the time, kindness, and a focus on the long-term goals of a happy marriage.

What is the primary Problematic Emotion at play? Sadness at how everything is turning out. So, ask yourself; Is a life-long problematic relationship likely to harm your children worth attempting to exclude the property you brought to the marriage? Are you angry at yourself for having been kind and hopeful? Do you think that prevailing on the legal issue will be a salve for the hurt and sadness of the divorce? What will you feel like if you do prevail? Or don't prevail? In the latter instance, will you be on your way to 'falling in hate'?

A Sensible Approach recognizes that you are both 'right', but what is fair or what a judge will decide is irrelevant to your futures. The sensible approach is to withdraw your position and start over with Step 1. When fleshing out the current situation, some of the property that you brought to the marriage might have meaning to you (financial or otherwise), and that subjective value can be put on the table. When listing obstacles in Step 4, you can include your sense of fairness as a potential obstacle to be overcome.

In Step 4, that might or might not include your claim to the pre-marital property, but that decision will be based whether that property will or will not aid in reaching long-term goals, not what seems fair. Now you are off to the races in a Sensible Divorce relationship and the potential of a functional co-parenting relationship.

You just need to manage your Challenging Emotions: LET IT GO!

Scenario Two: When you married, you and your spouse were making sufficient income to pay a mortgage. However, saving enough money for a down payment at the rate that housing in your area was appreciating looked impossible. Recognizing this, your parents gave as a wedding present enough money for a down payment on a house. You bought a house, but nine years later and with one child, you are divorcing. You take the position that the down payment gift was to you, not both of you, and your parents state that they are willing to sign a document to that effect. You assert that the down payment should be excluded from the distribution of marital property because it was a personal gift. Your spouse takes the position that the gift was a wedding present, and by definition, a gift to both of you.

Sensible Approach: At this point, we doubt that we have to repeat what we stated above in Scenario One above. You likely see the mistakes being made and the long-term self-defeating outcomes lying in wait for you. You also likely see that the Sensible Approach is to back up to Step 1. If in Step 2, part of your vision is owning the family residence and providing that stability to your child, you can take that vision to Step 4 and see if it is possible.

Assume that your spouse also wants to be in a property that he owns for some of the same reasons that you want to keep the house. If you can do it and preserve the amount of the down payment, then both of you reach your goals of owning residences and providing geographic stability for your child. If some or all of the down payment is needed to reach those goals, then that should be the Plan. If the only way to reach the goals of both parties is to sell the house and both buy more modest homes, then that should be the Plan. The focus is on what will happen in the future, not what happened nine years ago.

Scenario Three: The wife worked hard to earn her advance degree, worked full-time while in school and did her share of taking care of the children. The husband was a lineman for the telephone service when first married and is a lineman now, at about the same income level. He is a hard worker, but has little ambition. Now the wife is asking for a divorce because she met someone who was more ambitions and with whom she has much more in common. She takes the position that she has already contributed much more than he has to their financial lives and lifestyle and that he should be solely responsible for the financial support of the children when they are with him.

The wife refuses to pay child support, and even more vigorously refuses to pay spousal support. She says that any financial struggling that he endures in the future is his own fault. On top of that, he incurred debt on his '*toys, like a fancy boat*', and she takes the position that those are his separate debts, not marital debt. He takes the position that he should get one-half of everything, including her income and that she should share the debt. In his mind, the wife is the selfish one going out and having an affair.

It does not take a genius to see where this is going. There is even a very real danger that the children will be caught up in the blame and criticisms. They might choose sides and become aligned with one of the parents. That could be their mother, who has met this wonderful, very successful man who has a great lifestyle, or it could be their father, because they like his activities, his steadiness in life, or even be angry with their mother for hurting him by having an affair. The nightmare is beginning.

Sensible Approach: This situation is more complex because the marriage had so many elements of the pitfalls and now so many of the Problematic Emotions and Challenging Feelings. The differences in their expectations, what they had in common and even the structure of their personalities likely made the control phase of the marriage particularly challenging, if not impossible. The wife 'decided' to divorce, although she might not have been aware of it, long before having an affair.

That made her vulnerable to being drawn into a relationship with someone who at least seemed more like the kind of person with whom she wanted to make a life. She probably has shame and guilt, unless she is a complete sociopath. Yet, she blames her spouse for not being the type of person she wanted him to be in the marriage, at least when it came to financial matters. For his part, he might have been indifferent to her criticisms, but he might also have taken those criticisms personally and felt like a failure in her eyes. His wife running off with an ambitious successful man might prove it in his mind. His self-hatred is confounded by the real anger at her for having the affair. The biggest mistake that they are both making is taking positions based on the past, rather than making plans based on future goals.

Sensible Approach: Because this situation is dominated by Problematic Emotions, and some Challenging Feelings, resolving them will take some planning. Assume that the wife recognizes the self-defeating direction the family is taking and decides to be sensible. Perhaps she read this book, and if she did, this is what she would learn:

- The wife should begin to process the Problematic Emotions of shame and guilt.
- Presumably she will become more objective about herself, and realize that falling for someone else and leaving her spouse to pursue that new relationship is a hurtful thing to do.
- She will need some clarity and might benefit from meeting with a counselor to try to get an objective understanding of what happened.
- Effectively processing the guilt will likely include apologizing to her husband and perhaps making amends.
- Rather than being critical of and blaming him, presumably she will come to terms with the obstacles in the marriage, which might be

that her husband's choice of lifestyle is a legitimate one, but one which did not fit with her personality and goals in life.

- Her husband could be a perfectly good man and did not deserve her having an affair, but she needs to come to terms with having made the emotional decision to divorce (perhaps unconsciously) and put herself and her family at risk by doing so.

- Her husband needs to come to terms with his self-hatred and taking her judgments of him personally. If he did not share those same judgments of himself, he would not have taken her criticisms personally. The sadness to be resolved is the sadness that a person can fall in love with someone, but have a hard time staying married to that same person. Living with someone is completely different from loving someone. Some problems have no solutions. This is likely one of those cases in that the spouses appear to seek very different lifestyles.

When the Problematic Emotions are being resolved, or at least contained, then they can take Step 1 with their financial decisions, which now will include total family income as an 'asset', to be used to reach long-term financial goals for both of them. Their goals for supporting their children will dictate support issues, not judgments or criticisms of one another.

For example, he might be expected to pay for the daily needs of the children and she might be expected to do the same in her home. In addition, she might be expected to pay for all of the other child-related expenses, such as medical, extracurricular activities, mutually decided upon educational expenses, expensive items like bicycles and so on.[81] The focus will be on their goals for themselves, for each other and for the children. If, for example, they want the children to have choices of extracurricular activities, the task is to determine how to pay for those out of total family income. The legal task is how to word the support order in order to accomplish this goal.

Bottom Line: In this Chapter, we tried to apply our Goal Based Planning approach to common but challenging financial situations. Our sole purpose is to

---

[81] Your authors understand the daunting leap for this husband, and likely his attorney, to achieve the "required" new Sensible Mindset. On the other hand, the messy divorce is a worse alternative for him and the family.

demonstrate the application of the approach of our GBP Model to challenging financial situations.

Take-aways Techniques:

The key take-aways of this Chapter are:

1. One person can be sensible, whether or not the other person is sensible. Regardless, the result is some improvement in the process of the divorce.
2. Avoid being trapped by the traditional family law system; stay in your world of reaching life goals and do not move into the world of lawyers, judges and other professionals in the system where the focus is on the legal outcomes.
3. Bargain for the future, don't fight over the past. Face the right direction.
4. Plan for your life and not for legal outcomes. Parts of that Plan will include the legal tasks, but parts of the Plan will not.
5. A balance of selfishness and altruism leads to the best outcomes for both people. The most selfish approach is to have that balance.
6. Always apply the Four Step GBP Template, but at times, you have to clear the way by addressing obstacles first- especially Problematic Emotions and Challenging Feelings.
7. While this approach might seem complicated, idealistic and perhaps unrealistic, this is essentially what spouses do who have a Sensible Divorce.

Chapter 19
In a Nutshell-Summary and Documents
Putting it All Together

Documents Summary

1. No. 1: Problematic Emotions Can Lead to Unnecessary Conflict.
2. No. 2: Challenging Feelings Must be Overcome to Develop a Sensible Divorce.
3. No. 3: Illusions are Important to Understand, and Be Realistic About Divorce.
4. No. 4: Ten Traps Inadvertently Are Embedded in the Traditional Family Law System and Should Be Avoided.
5. No. 5: There are Two Critical Characteristics of Goal Based Planning; Four Steps in Goal Based Planning and Long Term Goals.
6. No. 6: To Complete a Sensible Divorce, Spouses (And Attorneys) Must be Skilled in Multitasking.
7. No. 7: Stating a Clear Parenting Vision of How the Parents Want Their Children to Turn Out When They Will Be Raised with Separated Parents (For At Least Part of Their Childhood) is Part of the Process of Agreeing to Long Term Goals.
8. No. 8: The Most Important Tasks and Rules for Successful Co-Parenting are to Provide High Quality Parenting in Both Homes When There are Minor Children Involved.
9. No. 9: Having Effective Parenting Skills and a Successful Co-Parenting Relationship Are the Two Most Important Factors to Ensure High Quality Outcomes for Children.
10. No. 10: Disagreement Resolution Skills are Needed for a Sensible Divorce.

You have covered a lot of territory having read our book to this point. While there is no substitute for the details presented in the previous eighteen chapters, a Summary might be helpful.

HOW CAN YOU PLAN FOR A SENSIBLE DIVORCE
AND
HOW CAN YOU AVOID THE TOXIC DANCE OF A MESSY DIVORCE?

Our book specifically addresses the issues raised in the questions above. The Summary and ten Documents below are organized into two groups:

I. Headwinds and Challenges
II. Skill Building

We offer this Summary as brief reminders and Checklists regarding the important information and skills necessary for planning a Sensible Divorce.

While this book is primarily designed for those going through a divorce, or for those already divorced but having post-divorce issues, it is also a great read for divorce attorneys who want to learn more about how to guide parties to optimal outcomes: i.e., a Sensible Divorce. We hope these documents will assist you on your journey.

I. HEADWINDS AND CHALLENGES

In a divorce or a post-divorce, there are many potential obstacles to having a Sensible Divorce. The following are examples of headwinds and challenges presented in detail in the book:

NO. 1: PROBLEMATIC EMOTIONS CAN LEAD TO UNNECESSARY CONFLICT.

1. Blaming
By blaming others for problems, people make themselves helpless. Unfortunately, they must wait for the others to change, something which might never happen.

2. Distrusting

It is wise to distrust people who are dishonest, even when the dishonesty is subtle, like giving incomplete information or giving situations a self-serving 'spin'. The solution in a co-parenting relationship is for both parents to commit to complete honesty.

3. Taking Criticisms Personally

Criticisms tell us more about the person doing the criticism than they do about us. However, sometimes there can be very useful information in a criticism. Therefore, it is important to listen carefully for useful information. Do not take the criticism personally. Consider taking action based on any useful information. Reacting with guilt, shame or anger is a waste of psychological energy.

4. Thinking Inferentially

Making guesses is human and often useful. However, guesses can be wrong. Many guesses without much real information can lead to prejudice, paranoid ideas and unsupported negative beliefs. The antidote is to check thoughts out by asking questions and getting information.

NO. 2: CHALLENGING FEELINGS MUST BE OVERCOME TO DEVELOP A SENSIBLE DIVORCE.

Challenging feelings are inevitable in a divorce, but taking a healthy approach to resolving those feelings and practicing kindness minimizes the damage.

Resolving Challenging Feelings[82]

It is a well-known fact in scientific circles that approximately 50% of the population in the United States makes most of their decisions based on feelings. That might be fine when choosing a movie, but can be problematic when making

---

[82] In Chapter 2, we introduced four 'Problematic Emotions': blaming, distrusting, taking things personally and thinking inferentially. In Chapter 11, we added additional emotions, named 'Challenging Feelings', which are additional obstacles to having a Sensible Divorce. **Bottom line:** All emotions need to be addressed in order to plan for a Sensible Divorce.

choices in a divorce. This is particularly true because a divorce is not only frontloaded with Problematic Emotions (No. 1), which are likely to lead to really poor choices, but also because one or both of the spouses may be suffering from one or more of the following six Challenging Feelings:

1. Guilt
2. Shame
3. Anger
4. Trauma Triggers
5. Distorted Perceptions
6. Sadness of Loss

Practicing Kindness

In Chapter 11 (Sensible Solutions for Processing Challenging Feelings and Practicing Kindness), we provided guidance on how to process these feelings in order to prevent their interference in making a good Plan for the future.

We also posited that the 'realistic' application of kindness to a changing spousal relationship can lead to optimal solutions for both spouses' futures. When there are no minor children, this can 'clear the air' of a problematic or messy divorce and allow the spouses to move forward untainted by leftover problems from the marriage. When there are minor children, starting the co-parenting relationship in a sensible manner is critical to a positive experience for the parents and successful outcomes for the children.

To have a Sensible Divorce requires not only resolving these challenging feelings but also practicing kindness to yourself and to your spouse.

NO. 3: ILLUSIONS ARE IMPORTANT TO UNDERSTAND AND BE REALISTIC ABOUT DIVORCE.

DISPELLING TEN ILLUSIONS AS OBSTACLES TO PLANNING A SENSIBLE DIVORCE

When focusing on our Ten Illusions as obstacles to a Sensible Divorce, hopefully the following Illusions Table will assist your understanding of the Solutions and their corresponding Reality.

Table: Summary of Ten Illusions: Obstacles to a Sensible Divorce

ILLUSION #	ILLUSION	REALITY
1	*"My spouse is so controlling, and that is the marital problem."*	Both spouses are trying to change each other to fit his/her Template of what a good spouse does. The problem is not that they were controlling. The problem is that they were unsuccessful in their positions because their strategies clashed. **Let the blame go**.
2	*"We live in the same world."*	We do not. We share much of what we think of as reality, but we also have realities that are different from one another. **Communication is how we bridge the gap.**
3	*"When is he/she going to change?"*	In a messy divorce, we are tempted to continue to try to make the ex-spouse fit our Template of what a good ex-spouse should be. This is a waste of psychological energy. **Our focus should be on what type of ex-spouse we are.**
4	*"Time heals all wounds."*	Time does not do it. **A Plan plus action heals wounds.**

ILLUSION #	ILLUSION	REALITY
5	*"Trusting lawyers as guides will always lead to success. Lawyers know what is best for us."*	Lawyers are indispensable to achieving legal outcomes that help divorcing spouses begin their Plan to reach long-term life goals. However, only the spouses can determine what those goals are, and only the spouses can keep the focus on legal outcomes as tools for reaching goals, not as goals in themselves. **The parties, not the lawyers, should lead and set goals.**
6	*"The divorce is final."*	The Judgment of Divorce finalizes the end of the legal status as marriage, but the divorce is everything that happens after that Judgment. Realizing this sets the stage for the spouses to decide every day what type of divorce to have. **The divorce is never really final.**
7	*"People don't change."*	To act as if the ex-spouse has not changed (when true or not) is a self-defeating strategy. Communication bridges the gap between who our ex-spouse has become and what we believe is true. **People do change.**
8	*"The children are not watching."*	Children are sensitive to the goings-on between their parents and are heavily affected by the quality of the parental relationship. **In a Sensible Divorce, ex-spouses imagine (correctly) that the children are watching and learning from everything they do.**

ILLUSION #	ILLUSION	REALITY
9	*"I just want my child to be happy."*	Focusing on whether or not a child is happy is unrealistic, misleading and misguided, and doing more harm than good. **The focus should be on promoting confidence, competence and independence, not happiness.**
10	*"Vengeance is sweet."*	Forgiveness is sweet. **Vengeance is sour and creates a perpetual cycle of suffering.**

NO. 4: TEN TRAPS ARE INADVERTENTLY EMBEDDED IN THE TRADITIONAL FAMILY LAW SYSTEM AND SHOULD BE AVOIDED.

It is important to resist the temptation and become focused on disputes over distribution (likely required by law), instead of staying focused on planning to reach agreed-upon goals for an important and successful life transition. It is also important for the spouses to refocus on the future and not the past.

1. **Trap #1:** In the traditional family law system, the parties are (inadvertently) directed to and often pressured to focus on legal outcomes (e.g., dividing the children's time and dividing property, debt and income) and not on planning to reach life goals.
2. **Trap #2:** The traditional family law system turns Non-zero Sum games (e.g., raising children and financial planning) into Zero Sum Games (e.g., dividing the children's time and dividing property, debt and income).
3. **Trap #3:** The traditional family law system assumes that disputes exist and that the interests of the parties are in conflict and often foist these assumptions onto their clients.
4. **Trap #4:** Children are treated as property in the traditional family law system. In general, the term 'custody' is defined as someone having immediate charge and control over something. In modern times, parents

are not 'awarded' ownership of the children, but are 'awarded' ownership of certain times with the children.

5. **Trap #5:** Selfish strategies permeate the traditional family law system. Optimal solutions occur when the emphasis is on both spouses doing well.

6. **Trap #6:** Winning on legal outcomes is most important. This supports the selfish goal of winning, or at least not losing.

7. **Trap #7:** Escalating anger and blame, rather than resolving sadness, permeates the traditional family law system.

8. **Trap #8:** Deductive decision-making and bargaining is encouraged from the beginning of a divorce in the traditional family law system. Inductive bargaining achieves better results.

9. **Trap #9:** The day of the final Judgment of Divorce is the end of the case for the spouses, as well as for the attorneys, mediators, judges and other professionals involved. The opposite is true: the final Judgment of Divorce is the beginning of the divorced lives of the spouses.

10. **Trap #10:** The attribution of fault and blame has a long history in the traditional family law system. Sadly, the focus on fault and blame with a focus on the unchangeable past is a waste of psychological energy. A divorce is a major life transition, and the focus should be on planning for the future.

**You might ask, quite reasonably,
what does all this have to do with planning a Sensible Divorce?
The answer is EVERYTHING!**

**Spouses cannot change the past, BUT
they have a great deal of control over the future.**

**Spouses can also affect their happiness in a positive way IF
they control the headwinds and challenges
(summarized above and presented in more detail in the book).**

**Control over the future comes from planning for the future.
Planning comes from skill building!**

The antidote to having a messy (and toxic) divorce is
GOAL BASED PLANNING and SKILL BUILDING.

ROADMAP TO A SENSIBLE DIVORCE
(The Goal Based Planning Way)

We introduce three types of Plans to achieve a Sensible Divorce under the umbrella term 'Family Plan':

1. Children Plan
2. Co-parenting Time Schedule Plan
3. Financial Plan

The Children Plan is further broken down:

1. Custody Plan (decision-making)
2. Co-parenting Plan (schedule when the minor children are with each parent)

We also introduce and implement the Tasks and Rules relevant to each of the two applicable Plans:

1. Legal Tasks and Rules
2. Planning Tasks and Rules

NO. 5: THERE ARE TWO CRITICAL CHARACTERISTICS OF GOAL BASED PLANNING; FOUR STEPS IN GOAL BASED PLANNING AND LONG-TERM GOALS.

GOAL BASED PLANNING- FOUR STEP TEMPLATE FOR MAKING COLLABORATIVE DECISIONS

1. Step One: Describe in detail the current situation.

2. Step Two: List each spouse's long-term goals, specific to the decisions being made.
3. Step Three: Plan the steps for reaching long-term goals.
4. Step Four: List the obstacles and steps to overcome them and create a Plan.

**There is one additional and important issue here,
which should be framed as a question:**

**The question SHOULD NOT be: '*What is fair?*'
The question SHOULD BE:**

*'How can we best reach the individual
long-term goals* **for both parties?'**

Fairness is extremely important to people. The answer to the above question almost always subsumes the issue of fairness. However, if the focus is on the legal tasks at the time of a divorce, fairness might dictate that the division be equal or equitable.

If the focus is on long-term goals, fairness generally dictates that the goals of both spouses are given equal attention and weight. In other words, the Plan is fair if it provides both spouses as good a chance of reaching long-term goals as possible, even when at the time of the divorce, distribution is unequal.

NO. 6: TO FINALIZE A SENSIBLE DIVORCE, SPOUSES (AND ATTORNEYS) MUST BE SKILLED IN MULTITASKING.

Multitasking means focusing on the legal tasks required by law **and** the planning tasks to reach long-term goals. This is especially true when dealing with children. Because our focus is on planning, not litigating, we break down the legal and planning Tasks differently: Legal Tasks (Children and Financial Plans) and Planning Tasks (Children Planning Tasks and Financial Planning Tasks) are differentiated. We can understand why you might find this confusing. Hopefully what follows will simplify and clarify this critically important matter.

I.   LEGAL TASKS

1. **Children Plans:**
    a. **Custody Plan:** This Plan determines the type of legal custody that will be in effect, specifically, whether major decisions will be made jointly by both parents, solely by one parent or some hybrid version. This is a subject of Chapter 15 (Custody Plan and Legal and Planning Tasks). The list of major decisions about the minor children are usually enumerated in the applicable State statutes and various appellate court decisions.

    However, these lists are inadequate in two respects: First, they do not cover all of the important decision-making that parents will do. Second, they do not provide a plan on how to make those decisions, especially when parents disagree. These inadequacies are addressed in the Planning Tasks.

    b. **Co-parenting Time Schedule Plan:** This Plan determines what type of parenting time schedule will be in effect for the minor children, specifically which parent will be principally responsible for the children at various times of the day and night. This is the subject of Chapter 16 (Co-parenting Time Schedule Plan and the Legal and Planning Tasks).

2. **Financial Plan:** This Plan has two component parts which distributes assets and debts and allocates income between the parties.
    a. Distributing marital and non-marital property and allocating debt
    b. Sharing future income
        i.   Spousal Support
        ii. Child Support

Note: The Legal Tasks presented above are separate and distinct from the Planning Tasks below.

Therefore: Get Ready to Multitask!

The only way to accomplish a sensible and effective Marital Settlement Agreement ("MSA") is to multitask. This means you must work within the law and simultaneously accomplish a goal-based Family Plan that addresses all custody, co-parenting time schedule and financial issues. While the legal tasks are not particularly important in the long run, agreements on the legal tasks are legally required.

**Our point is that you must multitask-
addressing the Custody Plan, the Co-parenting Time Schedule Plan,
as well as the Financial Plan. It's that simple!**

Caveat: Linking child support to a parenting time schedule is one of the traps of the family law system. Do not fall into that trap. See Chapter 8 (Ten Traps of the Traditional Family Law System: Additional Challenges), where the ten Traps are presented in detail.

II.   PLANNING TASKS

Note: The Planning Tasks enumerated below form the foundation for the Legal Tasks presented above.

1. **Children Planning Tasks.**
    a. Setting forth the actual parenting time schedule
    b. Having information-sharing procedures
    c. Establishing rules and procedures for flexibility in the parenting time schedule and access of parents to children and children to parents
    d. Designing child-focused transitions
    e. Coordinating parenting across homes
    f. Having a more extensive list, with rules and procedures, for making parenting decisions about the children

Reminder: The above child-related goal-based **planning tasks** focus on PLANNING Tasks and not on DISTRIBUTION Tasks (meaning the legal tasks). This focus will likely optimize outcomes for the children!

2. **Financial Planning Tasks.**
   a. Planning a budget, including child-related expenses
   b. Planning for paying down debt, using income and property
   c. Planning saving for future retirement of both spouses
   d. Planning for owning/renting homes that accommodate the children
   e. Planning the distribution of property to facilitate these plans
   f. Planning the distribution of future income to facilitate these plans, including, if needed, increasing total family income

Note: Income-sharing is often required but should not be seen as a burden to the payer and a boon the receiver. In our GBP Model, income-sharing is seen as a tool for reaching the goals of both spouses!

Reminder: Like child-related goal-based **planning tasks**, financial-related goal based planning does not focus on distribution, The questions are not about who gets the house and how much support a judge is likely to order. The questions are about the long-term financial goals of each of the parties and how their current property and future income can be used to reach those goals. This approach is also likely to optimize outcomes for both spouses!

NO. 7: STATING A CLEAR PARENTING VISION OF HOW THE PARENTS WANT THEIR CHILDREN TO TURN OUT WHEN THEY WILL BE RAISED WITH SEPARATED PARENTS IS PART OF THE PROCESS OF AGREEING TO LONG-TERM GOALS.

Parents usually want their divorce to have the least negative impact on their children and perhaps even the most positive impact in the long run. Researchers have examined the impact of divorce on children and have determined the factors that are most important.

Interestingly, they found that parents who handle their divorce and co-parenting relationship sensibly have children who turn out, on average, as well as children growing up in families with intact marriage between their parents.

They even tend to do better on two measures when they have sensible co-parenting relationships: (1) successful marriages when they are grown and (2) successful careers.

For example, children who grow up with divorced parents who have sensible co-parenting relationships have about a 35% divorce rate themselves, whereas children who grew up with parents in messy co-parenting relationships have about a 65% divorce rate.

What follows is an ideal **Parenting Vision** of a child's adulthood, to be considered when the parents develop a Co-parenting Plan:

1. **A courteous and effective co-parenting relationship**
   See Chapter 7 (Five Tasks and Rules for Successful Co-parenting).
2. **Sufficient time spent with both parents**
   Children do best if they have all different types of time with each parent.
3. **Flexibility in the custody schedule**
   See Chapter 7 (Five Tasks and Rules for Successful Co-parenting) regarding access and flexibility.
4. **Both parents being involved in all aspects of the child's life, independent of the custody schedule, including involvement in major decisions affecting the child's life.** (Text is **bolded** because of its importance)
   Children need the involvement of both parents in all parts of their lives, independent of the co-parenting time schedule.

   For example, in a major national study, children who had both parents actively involved with their schools (e.g., parent-teacher conferences) did better academically, socially and behaviorally when compared to children who just had one parent involved.
5. **Children's temperaments and special needs**
   Some children were struggling before their parents' divorce, and some struggle with the divorce, whereas some children are resilient before the

divorce and handle the divorce fairly well. In a good Plan, steps to bolster the coping ability of a challenged child should be included.

6. **Similarity in the two homes**

Making the two homes as close to similar as possible is a laudable goal because it teaches children important lessons on how to be successful in life. If the homes are too different, the child wastes energy on adapting to the differences rather than learning those important life lessons. For example, if both parents insist that the child do chores or homework before play, the child learns to take care of business and then enjoy free time. If the parents differ on this, the child makes the permissive parent the favorite and struggles with getting work done.

NO. 8: THE MOST IMPORTANT TASKS AND RULES FOR SUCCESSFUL CO-PARENTING ARE DESIGNED TO PROVIDE HIGH QUALITY PARENTING IN BOTH HOMES WHEN THERE ARE MINOR CHILDREN INVOLVED.

[Note: Nos. 8 and 9 present research-based skills that can be learned and put into action!]

FIVE TASKS OF SUCCESSFUL CO-PARENTING

1. **Sharing information. Goal: both parents have the same body of information about the children's lives, independent of the Co-parenting Time Schedule.**
   a. General information, usually in a weekly, or more frequent, meeting (e.g., telephone call). It is often useful to have a specific list of the information to be covered
   b. Emergency information. A list of emergencies should include immediate contact with one another. Rules should be made for how and when to make that contact
   c. Transition information. Information that the parent with the children has will be helpful to the parent to whom they are going
   d. Rules and procedures for sharing paperwork (e.g., school bulletin)

2. **Having access and flexibility in the co-parenting time schedule. Goal: for both parents to be parents all of the time (i.e., not locked out by a co-parenting time schedule).**
   a. Rules and procedures for telephone contact between the children and the parents
   b. Rules and procedures for when a parent wants access to the children, including a temporary change in the parenting time schedule
   c. Rules and procedures for when a child wants access to a parent off schedule
   d. Rules and procedures for extended family access to the children, independent of the parenting time schedule

3. **Planning child-focused transitions. Goal: keeping the stress of spending time in separate homes to a minimum.**
   a. Times and locations of transitions
   b. Rules and procedures (e.g., courteous interaction between parents; clothing exchanges; entering each other's homes; etc.)
   c. Taking input and ideas from children on how to make transitions easier and simpler
   d. Ongoing discussions of rules, consequences, chores and responsibilities, routines, expectations and so on

4. **Coordinating homes to be similar. Goal: teaching children good skills and habits for successful living.**
   a. Ongoing discussion of rules, consequences, chores and responsibilities, routines, expectations, and so on
   b. Privileges and rewards, expectations for school and extracurricular activities

5. **Making decisions, solving problems and taking action. Goal: Having child-related decisions include the values and goals of both parents.**
   a. A clear list of what decisions must be joint.
   b. Rules and procedures for making those decisions.
   c. Rules and procedures for identifying and solving problems that require the involvement of both parents.

GENERAL RULES FOR SUCCESSFUL CO-PARENTING

To perform our Five Tasks of Successful Co-parenting, CPP's [83] must establish Rules. Those can be General Rules that apply to all five Tasks, such as:

1. Be pleasantly respectful at all times.
2. Never make demands; always make polite requests.
3. Be completely honest at all times.
4. Never blame; always identify problems or decisions to address.
5. Always check first if it is a good time to talk before launching into a discussion.
6. Only ask personal questions if you have already received permission to do so.
7. Always apologize for missteps.

SPECIFIC RULES FOR SUCCESSFUL CO-PARENTING

There are also specific Rules for Successful Co-parenting, which can be specific to a task, such as:

1. When sharing information, cover everything on the list.
2. When sharing information, if a problem or a decision comes up, make a separate appointment to address it.
3. If a CPP gets too upset to talk reasonably, end the discussion, but the upset CPP must make an appointment to get back to the discussion first.
4. Always take turns talking and listening. Never interrupt or escalate before the other CPP is finished.
5. When access or flexibility is requested, always try to grant it, and if impossible, look for alternatives.
6. Never bring up a problem or a decision at a transition. Stay focused on a smooth transition for the child.
7. Before initiating a new routine, rule or expectation with the children, make an appointment with the other parent to discuss it. Make both homes as close to similar as possible. with regard to routines, rules and expectations.

---

[83] CPP is an abbreviation for Co-Parenting Partner.

8. If a CPP defines a problem in a way that has no solution, coach the other parent on coming up with a different definition of the problem that does have a solution.

9. All problem-solving and decision-making should include attempting to accomplish the goals of both CPP's.

NO. 9: HAVING EFFECTIVE PARENTING SKILLS AND A SUCCESSFUL CO-PARENTING RELATIONSHIP ARE THE TWO MOST IMPORTANT FACTORS TO ENSURE HIGH QUALITY OUTCOMES FOR CHILDREN.

[Note: Nos. 8 and 9 present research-based skills that can be learned and put into action!]

EFFECTIVE PARENTING SKILLS REGARDING SUCCESSFUL OUTCOMES FOR CHILDREN

1. **Authoritative parenting, including protection and limit setting (juxtaposed with permissive or authoritarian parenting)**

   Authoritative parenting does not imply being bossy or even bullying children to get compliance. Authoritative parenting simply means having verbal control of children. Verbal control is accomplished by pairing predictable incentives for compliance and predictable consequences for non-compliance.

   For example, a parent establishes a limit on screen time, and as an incentive says that extra screen time will be allowed on Saturdays if the child follows the weekday rule. If the child goes over the agreed-upon screen time, no screen time is allowed on Saturday. If the child 'sneaks' screen time, no screen time is allowed for the following week. In neither case does the parent need to escalate. In fact, the parent can be sympathetic—"*I am so sorry that you won't have any screen time this weekend. We will work on that next week*".

2. **Nurturance, warmth, pride and affection**

   This is the other side of the coin regarding authoritative parenting. Life is so much easier for a child who meets certain standards and understands how expectations work.

For example, always making the bed before getting breakfast leads to a child living an orderly life. If the bed is not made, breakfast is not served. If the bed is made, the child has a nice time at breakfast.

3. **High standards and clear expectations**

Setting high standards with clear expectations will enhance the likelihood of having healthy and successful children.

4. **Good instruction, teaching negotiation of control issues in relationships (e.g., effective bargaining), and modelling social maturity**

The challenge of all relationships is dealing with differences and disagreements. People are naturally prone to wanting to control their experiences, and when in a disagreement, two people want to control what happens. This can escalate into conflict, or people can resolve the differences and disagreements successfully.

Children learn how to do this, by being instructed by their parents and by watching how their parents resolve disagreements, both with them and with others.[84]

5. **Intellectual stimulation and exposure to diverse activities, including monitoring those activities**

The happiest and most successful children are exposed to many situations, develop many abilities, and are involved in many activities. Parental involvement and direction help maximize the rewards of that involvement.

In an ideal co-parenting relationship, parents work as a team to improve the parenting of both parents. This includes identifying parenting weaknesses in each other and making decisions together about improvements in those skills.

NO. 10: DISAGREEMENT RESOLUTION SKILLS ARE NEEDED FOR A SENSIBLE DIVORCE.

Inevitably, parents will disagree about parenting decisions and will have differences in parenting approaches that need to be managed after a separation.

---

[84] See Chapter 6 (Disagreement Resolution Skills Needed for a Sensible Divorce and our Four Step Goal Based Planning Template Needed for Making Collaborative Decisions).

In order to accomplish this important task, our research-based **Disagreement Resolution Skills** are summarized in this Chapter and presented in detail throughout our book.

TEN DISAGREEMENT RESOLUTION SKILLS NEEDED FOR A SENSIBLE DIVORCE

There are ten Disagreement Resolution Skills needed for a Sensible Divorce, especially applicable when the spouses have minor children. All problem-solving and decision-making should include attempting to accomplish the goals of both CPP's. These Skills fall into four categories.

1. **Having the Right Mindset**
    SKILL #1: Overcoming personal bias
        a.   Overconfidence Bias
        b.   Us-Them Tribal Warfare Bias
        c.   Judgment Bias
    SKILL #2: Bridging the gap between realities, with communication
    SKILL #3: Getting perspective, with imagination and questions

2. **Managing Feelings and Emotions**
    SKILL #4: Identifying and processing core feelings, including the ability to have mixed feelings and ambivalence
    SKILL #5: Developing the ability to be vulnerable in relationships
    SKILL #6: Hearing criticism in a healthy way

3. **Implementing Effective Problem-solving and Decision-making Techniques**
    SKILL #7: Identifying a problem in a way that leads to a solution
    SKILL #8: Resolving a disagreement when both people are 'right'
    SKILL #9: Making decisions that accomplish both people's goals

4. **Recovering from Destructive Conflict Quickly;**
    SKILL. #10: Keeping it short and clean, resolving the disagreement and repairing the relationship damage quickly

Research Conclusions:

1. The highest level of co-parenting conflict is found in co-parenting relationships in which one, but often both parents, are lacking or lagging in some or all of the skills presented in this Chapter and throughout our book.
2. The most sensible and amicable co-parenting relationships are those with parents who have strong skills presented in this Chapter and throughout our book.
3. This is not a moral judgment. It simply means that parents do the best, as do their children, where all of them have the best life experiences, after the parents learn these skills.

We hope this Chapter and our Summaries are helpful. However, if you are confused or simply forget, please refer back to this Chapter or the previous chapters of our book.

Chapter 20
Our Elevator Speech and Goodbyes

1. Why is it important to have a Sensible Divorce?
2. Does it make sense to have a Sensible Divorce when there are no minor children or only adult children?

We end our book with our response to these two core questions.

In this book, we described the headwinds, challenges and traps[85] that tend to channel people into a messy (even toxic) divorce . We also pointed out the mindset[86] and skills[87] needed to overcome these obstacles plus how to have a sensible divorce. The key is understanding that divorce is a major life transition

---

[85] Chapters 4, 8, 9.
[86] Chapters 1 and 2.
[87] Chapter 6.

that is much more likely to turn out well by planning how to meet new long-term goals. We recommend you use our Four Step Goal Based Planning Template .[88]

For divorcing spouses without children, the Sensible Divorce approach might or might not be applicable. However, the approach might be a healthy way to say goodbye, though it might be more emotionally challenging than wanted by certain spouses.

For spouses with adult children, the approach is potentially very helpful. Although the need for interaction might be substantially less, the quality of the co-parenting relationship still has an enormous effect on children and the divorced spouses. The parents are still linked to one another for life.

For some spouses, they might have accepted the loss of the relationship and be relatively independent of one another financially and emotionally. In addition, they might prefer a simple divorce, perhaps not amicable but at least peaceful. Or, the marriage might have been very short, and while disappointing, might not have many implications to either of the spouses' futures. Nevertheless, we hope that some of the information in this book will be helpful, even if spouses choose not to engage in any or all of the steps involved in having a Sensible Divorce.

What about a Sensible Divorce when there are minor children?
By now, after reading this book,
you should know the answer to this rhetorical question!

Divorce presents unfamiliar terrain. Navigating this terrain requires great strength of purpose, especially if your spouse keeps sending you invitations to do the toxic dance. Emotionally, you might be seduced to accept the invitation, but like the Songs of Sirens in Greek Mythology, this will turn out badly for you.

We understand it is difficult to avoid Problematic Emotions,[89] Challenging Feelings[90] taking things personally,[91] avoiding the Ten Traps of the traditional Family Law System, [92] or dispelling Illusions [93] - all obstacles to having a Sensible Divorce.

---

[88] Part IV.
[89] Chapter 2.
[90] Chapter 11.
[91] Chapter 2.
[92] Chapter 8.
[93] Chapter 10.

With emotions running high during a divorce, it can be very tempting to take things personally and fight back. Just don't do it! It might also be tempting to prove you are 'right' or to prevail, or at least not to lose.

Resist the temptation of the toxic dance!

Having a clear vision of what type of person that you want to be during and after the divorce (i.e., a proud person who models social maturity to children), he or she can help overcome these temptations and obstacles. Life inevitably includes periods of unavoidable reduced happiness and suffering The saddest of all situations is when people make conscious choices that reduce their happiness and increase their suffering. This will likely occur in a Messy/Toxic Divorce, unless at least one spouse remains sensible.

The navigational path we have offered in this book may not be perfect. We do not expect you to follow it perfectly. However, when you stray, try to get back on the path as quickly as you can.

With that, your authors say goodbye and best wishes.

PLEASE REMEMBER...

A messy divorce is a toxic dance of two paranoid co-conspirators,
and when one stops doing the dance, the dynamic changes for both.

HAPPY DANCING!

Word Index

Notes:

1. The page numbers designate the most relevant page(s) in the Book.
2. Abbreviations:

    a. CPP→ Co-parent Partner
    b. GBP→ Goal Based Planning
    c. DR→ Disagreement Resolution (DR) Skills
    d. MSA→ Marital Settlement Agreement

3. We hope you find this Word Index helpful.